| | | | |
|---|---|---|---|
| | | | |
| | | | |
| | | | |
| | | | |
| | | | |
| | | | |
| | | | |
| | | | |
| | | | |
| | | | |
| | | | |
| | | | |
| | | | |

# TROTSKY
## FATE OF A REVOLUTIONARY

Also by Robert Wistrich:
*Revolutionary Jews from Marx to Trotsky*
*The Left Against Zion*

# TROTSKY
## FATE OF A REVOLUTIONARY

### ROBERT WISTRICH

STEIN AND DAY/*Publishers*/New York

*In memory of my father, Jacob*

Published in the United States of America in 1982 .

Copyright © 1979 by Robert Solomon Wistrich

Printed in the United States of America
Stein and Day/*Publishers*
Scarborough House, Briarcliff Manor, N.Y. 10510

*Library of Congress Cataloging in Publication Data*

# CONTENTS

# PREFACE

In spite of the attention which he has attracted in recent years, Leon Trotsky, both on the psychological and political level, remains an enigmatic figure. Few revolutionaries in modern history have been the object of such partisan commentary and aroused such intense feelings among detractors and admirers alike. For decades, Trotsky's name has been shrouded in mythology; for some, the epitomy of perfidious betrayal, the arch-heretic of international communism; for others, the symbol of unsullied revolutionary purity. The man and his legacy continues to haunt both East and West alike even though so many of his predictions concerning Russia and Europe have failed to materialize. The 'charisma' of a revolutionary intellectual who for a time successfully fused the pen and the sword, theory and practice, the word and the deed, continues to fascinate even those who feel little affinity for Trotsky's ideas or his Marxist commitment.

In this study I have tried to do justice to the heroic dimension of Trotsky's life and thought without concealing the serious flaws that vitiated his personality and politics. Ideas were the very marrow of Trotsky's being and since his idiom was turn-of-the-century Russian Marxism, one cannot avoid theoretical discussion without stripping his personality of its life-substance. On the other hand, too many historians and scholars ranging from Isaac Deutscher to Irving Howe and more recently, Baruch Knei-Paz have allowed themselves to be taken in by Trotsky's flamboyant rhetoric and grandiose theories. To be sure, they have exposed particular failings in the classical Marxist schema as it was applied by Trotsky, but ultimately they have remained sophisticated apologists unable to free themselves from the strait-jacket of ideology. Only Joel Carmichael, among recent bio-

graphers, has avoided this pitfall while straying perhaps too far
in the direction of reductionist common-sense.

This book does not claim to be a comprehensive biography
nor is it a textual analysis of Trotsky's writings, though I have
quoted these extensively where it seemed appropriate. It should
rather be seen as an attempt to capture and evoke the singularity
of Trotsky's fate, of his experience and ideas within the context
of the Marxist tradition to which he owed allegiance. Trotsky's
successes and failures, his triumphs and his ultimate tragedy are
inextricably bound up with the Russian revolution which he
inaugurated together with Lenin, and the mythology which has
surrounded it. He was carried to greatness by an enterprise whose
catastrophic consequences he helped to set in motion and whose
most illustrious victim he eventually became. But though his
destiny was to fight against the Stalinist tidal-wave, he could never
bring himself to acknowledge the deeper roots of this phenomenon and his own complicity in it. To the end of his life he clung
to the fiction that there was a *socialist* content in the Russian
Revolution which had been perverted and betrayed by Stalin.

In this study I have emphasized the ambiguities in Trotsky's
theory and practice; the tension between libertarian and totalitarian tendencies in his politics, between his individualism and
an almost desperate need to root himself in the Communist
movement; the conflict between his intellectual independence
and the tyrannical zeal with which he exercised authority. The
problem of Trotsky's attitude to Bolshevism, his complex and
ambivalent relationship to Lenin and the antagonism which he
inspired among the Bolshevik Old Guard are inextricably linked
to his character, temperament and sense of personal identity. In
disentangling these connections one can better understand
Trotsky's strengths and weaknesses as a Marxist theoretician as
well as his relative ineptitude as a statesman and politician.

Beyond the purely political dimension there is another aspect
of Trotsky which deserves more attention than it has customarily
been given, namely the imaginative power of his literary work.
Trotsky was not only an actor and participant in events which have
transformed the twentieth century; as an historian and writer,
he also helped to shape our perceptions of modern revolution.

Gifted with an unusual dramatic flair, his contribution to the socialist literary tradition may well prove to be his most enduring legacy. Much of his literary output was, to be sure, concerned with questions of revolutionary strategy and tactics, with self-justification or polemics against his adversaries. Nevertheless the quality of his writing, its ability to convey the sense of great historical movements, the interaction between individuals and the masses, the dialectic of concrete image and abstract idea, often gives a depth and insight to his political analysis rare in socialist literature. This aesthetic quality shines through his best work wherever it is not straitjacketed by his Marxism and explains, perhaps, his enduring magnetism for the literary intelligentsia. After Trotsky's flawed prophecies and tactical blunders have long been forgotten, it is the style of the man and the intense drama of his personal fate that will be remembered. In this book I have tried to show how this singularity of style was related both to his character and to the content of his political discourse. It is here, at the crossroads of politics and life, literature and revolution, abstract theory and human experience, historical dialectics and personal fate, that Trotsky's enduring significance resides.

ROBERT WISTRICH

London, January 1979

CHAPTER ONE

# IN SEARCH OF AN IDENTITY

'Only that is lasting which is gained through combat'
Leon Trotsky, *My Life*

Lev Davidovich Bronstein was born on October 26, 1879 (or November 7 according to the 'New Style' calendar) in Yanovka, a small isolated village on the steppes of the Southern Ukraine. By a strange twist of fate, the boy's birthday coincided precisely with the date, thirty-eight years later, when under his pen-name of Leon Trotsky, he established the Bolshevik power in Petrograd. 'Mystics and Pythagoreans may draw from this whatever conclusion they like', Trotsky remarks in his autobiography, he himself had noticed 'this odd coincidence only three years after the October uprising'. Perhaps even more fateful was the birth only two months later of his deadly adversary, Joseph Djugashvili (Stalin), in the squalor and poverty of a small Georgian county town.

The boy Bronstein was named Lev (the Russian word for 'lion') after his grandfather who, some twenty-five years earlier, had left a small Jewish town in the province of Poltava for the free and open steppes of the Province of Kherson. David Leontievich Bronstein, the boy's father, was a tough, hardworking ploughman who had become prosperous enough to detach himself from the Jewish colony and set up as an agricultural entrepreneur in Yanovka. It was here that Lev Bronstein spent the first nine years of his life in a rural Russified environment far removed from the traditional *mores* of the *shtetl*. It was a corner of the world 'where nature is wide, and manners, views and interests are pinched and narrow' – life was entirely regulated by the rhythm of toil on the farm – looking back it appeared to

Trotsky as 'the grayish childhood of a lower middle-class family'.[1]
Though Lev Bronstein did not suffer the miseries of hunger,
cold and poverty his recollections of life at Yanovka are tinged
with a sense of emotional deprivation.

'Of the eight children born of this marriage, four survived.
I was the fifth in order of birth. Four died in infancy ...
deaths almost as unnoticed as was the life of those who
survived. The land, the cattle, the poultry, the mill, took all
my parents' time; there was none left for us. The seasons
succeeded one another, and waves of farm work swept over
domestic affection. There was no display of tenderness in
our family, especially during the early years, but there was
a strong comradeship of labour between my mother and
father.'[2]

The domestic routine was centred around work and thrift –
'nothing else mattered, nothing but the price of grain in the world
market.'[3] The main influence on the boy in his early childhood
was not so much his parents as the chief mechanic on the farm,
Ivan Vassilyevich Grebien, who first taught him how to use tools
and materials. This untutored country life was briefly interrupted
when at the age of seven his parents sent him to a Yiddish-
speaking *Kheder* in the nearby colony of Gromokley. Trotsky later
recalled that he had no intimate friends among his schoolmates
'as I did not speak Yiddish.'[4] This assertion appears strange at
first sight as Yiddish was the language of the overwhelming mass
of Russian Jews.[5] In the teeming ghettoes of the Pale of Settlement where the bulk of the Jewish masses were still concentrated,
and later politically organized in movements like the Bund, it
provided the basis for an independent culture. Bronstein's grand-
parents had come from the urban, Yiddish-speaking heartland
of the Pale, yet according to his own account 'the language in my
family and household was Russian-Ukrainian.'[6] His father
apparently spoke a broken mixture of the two tongues, 'with a
preponderance of Ukrainian'.

Later, in Odessa, the son would become thoroughly Russified
and dismissive of both the Ukrainian and Yiddish languages as
mere 'dialects' or 'jargon'. In any event his first encounter with
traditional Jewish culture and the Hebrew scripture, at his

school in Gromokley, made little impact. What did unfavourably impress him was the contrast between the German and Jewish settlements in the colony. 'In the German section the houses were neat, partly roofed with tile and partly with reeds, the horses large, the cows sleek. In the Jewish section the cabins were dilapidated, the roofs scattered, the cattle scrawny.'[7] He also recalled with distaste the Jews of Gromokley dragging a young woman of dubious morals through the village streets, screaming, spitting and shouting angry abuse at her. 'This biblical scene', he wrote, 'was engraved on my memory forever.'[8]

In his autobiography, which is not free from attempts to re-touch his childhood, Trotsky appears to play down the signifi-cance of his Jewish background.[9]

'In my father's family there was no strict observance of religion. At first appearances were kept up through sheer inertia: on holy days my parents journeyed to the synagogue in the colony; Mother abstained from sewing on Saturdays at least within the sight of others. But all this ceremonial observance of religion lessened as years went on – as the children grew up and the prosperity of the family increased.'[10]

It is, however, clear that his mother (who had not been brought up in the country) had absorbed something of the Jewish orthodoxy and observed conventions more attentively than her husband who 'did not believe in God from his youth'.[11] But even David Bronstein, illiterate as he was and outwardly resembling a *muzhik* (peasant) more than a descendent of the ghetto, was not so assimilated as might appear at first glance. His occupational links, to be sure, were mainly with Gentiles – whether peasant labourers, local merchants or members of the declining Polish and Russian gentry in the vicinity – but he still insisted on Hebrew lessons in Odessa for his son. Trotsky put this down merely to 'parental vanity' and it is not clear from his own account, whether or not, the lessons were in preparation for his Bar-mitzvah. In any event they lasted only a few months and did little to confirm him in the 'ancestral faith'.[12]

In 1888 the young Bronstein had been sent to Odessa to stay with his mother's nephew, a translator and journalist, Moissey Filippovich Schpentzer, who had recently married the head-

mistress of the State School for Jewish Girls. It was here in
Odessa that Bronstein was first faced with the new law on
*numerus clausus* which restricted the admission of Jews to secondary
schools to ten per cent of all pupils.[13] Having failed the entrance
examination, he lost a year in the preparatory class at St
Paul's *Realschule*, originally a German institution, which was
becoming progressively Russified. But no single nationality or
religion predominated at his school – there were Germans,
Russians, Poles and Swiss as well as Jews – among the teachers
and pupils. The heterogeneous'racial'composition of the *Realschule*,
which reflected the colourful, multi-national atmosphere of the
Black Sea port, no doubt diluted any sense of discrimination
which Bronstein may have felt as a pupil. He recalled that before
the religious lessons

> 'boys of different persuasions would divide into separate
> groups, and those not of the orthodox Russian faith would
> leave the classroom, sometimes under the very nose of the
> Russian priest. On such occasions, he put on a special -ex
> pression, in which contempt was only slightly softened by
> Christian forbearance. ... "Where are you going?" he
> would ask some boy. "We are Catholics,' came the answer.
> ... "And you?" "We are Jews." "Oh Jews, I see, Jews!
> Just so, just so!" '[14]

But Bronstein did not appear unduly perturbed by such isolated
examples of religious prejudice. In contrast to the leader of
Russian Menshevism, Julius Martov, who had been traumatized
as a child by the 1881 pogroms in Odessa, 'nationality' played no
significant role in his own radicalization.[15] For all the suppressed
chauvinism of some of his teachers, the St Paul's *Realschule*
appeared as a model of tolerance and liberal enlightenment. The
growing tendencies towards Russification did not as yet lead to
an 'open baiting of nationalities' and the victims were as much
German Protestants and Roman Catholic Poles as the Jewish
boys. In his autobiography Trotsky insisted that 'national inequality' (he preferred this diluted expression to the more specific
term 'anti-semitism') never played a leading part in his grievances
against the existing order – 'it was lost among all the other phases
of social injustice'.[16] Outwardly, then, it was not'racial' per-

secution or a sense of inferiority which drove the young Bronstein to rebel against his environment. Indeed, it was precisely at school in Odessa that the diligent, methodical pupil acquired the ambition, the competitive drive to excel, the self-assertiveness and *superiority complex* which characterized him throughout adulthood.Signficantly, in the preface to *My Life* he observed:

'I am rather pedantic and conservative in my habits. I like and appreciate discipline and system. . . . I cannot endure disorder or destruction. I was always an accurate and diligent schoolboy, and I have preserved these two qualities all my life.'[17]

What then drove this model schoolboy (always at the top of the grade) to cut himself adrift from his own childhood and adolescence? What motivated this son of a prosperous landowner, who by his own admission 'belonged to the privileged class rather than the oppressed' to take the revolutionary road? Nothing in his early experiences or schooling in Odessa suggests a convincing explanation. By all accounts, he was handsome, a fastidious dresser, buoyant and well-mannered. He was almost compulsively driven by the thought that 'he must become better and more intelligent than the rest' – not a frame of mind normally associated with sympathy for the downtrodden and oppressed. Personal cleanliness, self-esteem bordering on vanity and a preoccupation with 'cultured speech' were among the traits that already distinguished his adolescent personality. At the Schpentzer home he also came to appreciate the Russian classics and to learn about type, layout, printing and binding – his passion for the fresh smell of the printed word never left him. He was entranced by the theatre, the Italian opera in Odessa and the world of literature. 'Authors, journalists and artists', he later recalled, 'always stood for a world which was more attractive than any other, one open only to the elect.'[18]

But neither at school nor in the Schpentzers' home was there anything approaching a revolutionary mood. Odessa lagged far behind St Petersburg, Moscow or Kiev where numerous socialist circles already existed. In this relatively stagnant atmosphere even a liberal-humanitarian like Bronstein's guardian, Moissey Schpentzer, who had vague Populist and Tolstoyan sympathies, never openly discussed politics. Yet the subconscious strivings of the adolescent Bronstein were already tinged by a spirit of opposition. His summer homecomings to Yanovka alienated him from the coarse manners, the provincialism, the preoccupation with 'primary accumulation' of his hard-working parents. He was struck by the brutality and narrowness of rural life, by occasional instances of ruthless treatment of the *muzhiks* and labourers on the farm, though his father on the whole enjoyed good relations with the peasants who worked for him. No doubt Lev Bronstein felt some vague feelings of guilt at his own privileged position but this was overshadowed by his indignation at the superstitions, the narrow horizons and obtuseness of the life which reigned at Yanovka. It drove him to despair that the peasants refused to accept the superiority of science and wasted many hours trying to measure out the area of a field when he had already calculated the answer in a few minutes.

Looking back in 1929, Trotsky was convinced that his aggressive rationalism played a major role in converting him to revolution. 'The feeling of the supremacy of the general over the particular, of law over fact, of theory over personal experience, took root in my mind at an early age and gained increasing strength as the years advanced.'[19] He was infuriated by 'dull empiricism', by the unashamed, cringing worship of facts. 'The social-revolutionary radicalism which has become the permanent pivot for my whole inner life grew out of this intellectual enmity towards the striving for petty ends, towards out-and-out pragmatism, and towards all that is ideologically without form and theoretically ungeneralized.'[20] Undoubtedly this inexorable rationalism, which led him to scorn all half-measures and vacillation, subsequently influenced his revolutionary style and political positions. His intolerance of inconsistency, his love of abstract generalizations (verging at times on doctrinaire pedantry) and the broadness of his intellectual sweep reflected an absolute faith in the omnipotence of reason. It influenced the intransigence with which he later stuck to his theory of 'permanent revolution', his single-minded concentration on the unchanging goal of world socialism and his commitment to transforming the whole of life according to rational principles.

But this intellectual rationalism did not of itself produce an oppositional mood. At most it fostered a diffuse hostility towards the social conditions existing during the reign of Alexander III: the high-handedness of the police and officialdom; the exploitation practised by the landlords; the nationalistic restrictions. Bronstein sought to escape from this constricting atmosphere by constructing an idealized picture of the Western world 'imperceptibly absorbed from my environment of liberal smug citizenship' – the vision of an ideal democracy, literate, cultured, tolerant and free.[21] Unconsciously he was becoming a 'Westernizer' but he was not yet a radical, let alone a Marxist.

In *My Life* Trotsky conceeds that he was 'poorly equipped politically even for a seventeen-year-boy of that period'. He felt a general indignation at injustice and an awakening sense of revolt at human indignity but he had as yet crystallized no theory which could give shape to his scattered impressions. He would in the coming year frequently catch himself 'taking a bookish, abstract and therefore sceptical view of the revolution' which he had to fight constantly before he could overcome 'the elements of psychic inertia'.[22] In conversations he would stubbornly oppose the advocates of 'socialist utopias' – his reaction to political questions remained one of ironic superiority. In 1896, the year in which he had left Odessa for the smaller, provincial seaport of Nikolayev, his passion was still for pure mathematics rather than left-wing politics.

Bronstein had gone to Nikolayev to finish his secondary education but it proved to be the turning-point of his youth, 'for it raised within me the question of my place in human society'.[23] Within a few months he began to neglect his studies and to swing leftwards with bewildering speed. What caused this dramatic overcoming of his inner resistance and his sudden, enthusiastic advocacy of socialist ideas? Partly, it would appear, he simply succumbed to the mood of the new environment, the current of opposition which was overtaking the student youth in Nikolayev. Through the intermediary of a Czech gardener, Franz Shvigovsky, whose orchard was a meeting-place for the town's radical intelligentsia, he came into contact for the first time with the old Populist exiles. He adopted the *Narodnik* doctrines impulsively, without systematic study, more as a debating weapon than a coherent theory. He read nervously, without plan – Bentham, Mill and Chernyshevsky.[24] He soon attracted attention as a youthful dragon-slayer of Karl Marx's theories, eagerly crossing swords with the circle's only Marxist, a young woman, Alexandra Sokolovskaya, who was to become his first wife. The truth was that he had as yet no real conception of Marxism beyond an emotional repugnance to a theory that appeared to make man the prisoner of social and economic circumstances. This seemed a dry, unappealing doctrine, fit only 'for shopkeepers and traders', one that allowed no room for heroism, self-sacrifice and the voluntarism which attacted Bronstein in the Populist outlook.

Bronstein's cohabitation in the Nikolayev Populist commune was the first stage in his search for a new identity. It was an act of defiance against his father, a rupture with his old image of the dutiful bourgeois son and star pupil, an assertion of independence. There were stormy scenes with the elder Bronstein but the young man, after a brief stay at Odessa University in deference to his father's wishes, returned to Shvigovsky's radical garden and refused to accept any more money from home.

It was the turbulent student protests and demonstrations in St Petersburg and Kiev in 1897 which first led Bronstein and his friends to take the decisive step of establishing the South Russian Workers' Union, to organize the factory and dockworkers in Nikolayev and other nearby towns. This dramatic leap from endless tea-table discussions to forging social ties with the local working class is depicted with starting terseness in *My Life*. Bronstein was walking along the street with Alexandra Sokolovskaya's younger brother, Grigory, a member of the Nikolayev student commune. The following dialogue developed. 'It's about time we started,' I said. 'Yes, it is about time,' he answered. 'But how?' 'That's it, how?' 'We must find workers, not wait for anybody or ask anybody, but just find workers, and set to it.'[25]

In the working-class quarters their first contacts were with Baptist sectarians, part of the rich evangelical Christian subculture that flourished in the port. By the end of the year, the South Russian Workers' Union had two hundred members and Bronstein was its moving spirit – throwing himself with fervour into the illegal propaganda and agitational work. Only eighteen years old, he displayed remarkable energy and inventiveness, writing numerous proclamations and articles, printing them all out in longhand for the hectograph. The Union's agitation was mainly centred around bread and butter issues and its leaflets were eagerly digested in the factories and mills. But in January 1898 the police closed in and there were mass arrests. Bronstein found himself in solitary confinement in an unheated winter cell in Kherson prison, with no change of linen, no soap, starved, dirty, 'eaten alive' by the lice. 'The solitude was unbroken, worse than any I ever experienced afterwards, although I served time in nearly twenty prisons.'[26]

Instead of breaking the prisoner's spirit, this harsh regime, which lasted three months, hardened him into a fearless revolutionary. It had established a point of no return. Conditions in the Odessa prison to which he was transferred were much better and here, for the first time, after some initial resistance Bronstein announced his conversion to Marxism. His friend Ziv found this metamorphosis somewhat astonishing in retrospect[27] though it was typical enough of the pattern of Trotsky's enthusiasms: first attraction, then stubborn resistance, a period of doubt and finally a passionate embrace of the new cause.

Bronstein had pursued an independent route to Marxism in prison and exile arriving at his conclusion by somewhat unorthodox and autodidactic methods. His earlier adherence to Socialism had been improvised rather impulsively; it was superficial and smacked of dilettantism. Not surprisingly, perhaps, his idol was the temperamental, romantic figure of Ferdinand Lassalle, the founder in the 1860s of the German Social Democratic Party.[28] Bronstein came from a similar background to Lassalle, himself the son of prosperous middle-class Jewish parents. He was no doubt struck by certain psychological affinities, by Lassalle's *sacro egoismo*, his flaming oratory, his cult of aristocratic elegance and passion for liberty, his energy and devotion to the victims of social injustice. Lassalle, too, had been estranged from his Jewish origins and had abandoned his class for the cause of the proletariat. In later years Trotsky would indeed emulate or even surpass his hero as a crowd orator, as an organizer, and a charismatic personality capable of galvanizing dormant energies in the masses. Trotsky certainly had Lassalle's sense of rhetorical effects, his flamboyant style, his messianic faith in the working class and his dictorial temperament. Though he lacked Lassalle's shrewd eye for *Machtfragen* he proved far more principled and committed to a consistent theoretical line.

Marxism tempered his youthful dreams of becoming the Russian Lassalle by providing him with a coherent philosophy of history derived from materialist dialectics. It was not from Marx or Engels but from the Italian neo-Hegelian philosopher Antonio Labriola, whom he read in the Odessa prison in French translation, that Bronstein learned his first important Marxist theoretical lesson – 'Ideas do not drop from the sky.'[29] Immediately he sought to test out this materialist hypothesis by writing a history of freemasonry. It was a strange choice, unless perhaps Bronstein felt inwardly attracted to this international secret brotherhood, revolutionary in its origins and conspiratorial in spirit. In any event, though he discovered nothing new in the field of Marxist methodology, Bronstein displayed a characteristic independence of mind in his manner of approaching historical materialism. It did not interest him as a dogma but as a 'living spring' with which to grasp the totality of the historical process.

In November 1899 Bronstein was sentenced to exile in eastern Siberia for four years where he was to complete the first phase of his education as a professional revolutionary. In the Moscow transfer prison he had heard for the first time of Vladimir Ilyich Lenin, the rising leader of Russian Marxism, and began to read intently his book on the development of capitalism in Russia.[30] In Siberia itself he also studied Marx, 'brushing cockroaches off the page', but did not get past the first volume of *Capital*. His conditions of exile were almost idyllic compared to those prevailing today under the Soviet regime. He had been banished to the village of Ust-Kut with his first wife, Alexandra Lvovna Sokolovskaya whom he had married in the Moscow transfer-prison (the ceremony was carried out by a rabbi, and in the face of his father's opposition). The village was very quiet and utterly remote from the rest of the world but communication among the exiles along the river Lena route was free and continuous. 'The

exiles exchanged letters with each other, some of them so long
they were really theoretical treatises. It was comparatively easy
to get a transfer from one place to another from the governor of
Irkutsk. Alexandra Lvovna and I moved to a place 250 versts
east ... where we had friends. I found a job there for a while as
a clerk to a millionaire merchant.'[31] Later, Bronstein and his wife
moved south to Verkholensk, where he recalled, 'the young
Marxists formed a district section by themselves. ... For them
exile proved an invaluable school for politics and general culture.'
It was on the great Lena route in Siberia that he first met such
future comrades as Uritsky and Dzerzhinsky, the founder of the
Soviet secret police. In 1929, he vividly evoked the scene:
> 'On a dark spring night, as we sat around a bonfire on the
> banks of the Lena, Dzerzhinsky read one of his poems, in
> Polish. His face and voice were beautiful, but the poem was
> a slight thing. The life of the man was to prove to be the
> sternest of poems.'[32]

Bronstein's own literary career also began in Siberia where
under the pseudonym 'Antid Oto' he contributed articles to an
Irkutsk newspaper *Vostochnoye Obozreniye* (Eastern Review). His
first essay on Friedrich Nietzsche already displays a remarkable
gift for intuitively adapting Marxist analysis to the field of
literature as well as to the relations between the individual and
society.[33] Nietzsche's cult of the Superman was of course anathema
to any orthodox Socialist but the young critic nevertheless paid
tribute to the 'cynical sincerity' and 'great talent' with which the
German philosopher had unveiled the hypocrisies of bourgeois
society. Attracted by Nietzsche's originality and iconoclasm he
was nonetheless scathing in exposing the corrupt and pernicious
*social* basis of this philosophy. The contempt for the masses,
already implied in the writings of such classical Victorian ideol-
ogists as Herbert Spencer, had found its extreme expression and
dialectical conclusion in Nietzsche's 'master' morality designed
for a 'superior' caste of unscrupulous adventurers and rapacious
plunderers. The 'Superman' ideology was nothing but an
aristrocratic revolt against middle-class moral norms and legal
codes in the name of a new *Parasitenproletariat* which lived at the
expense of capitalist society and hitherto lacked a higher justifica-

tion for its greed. Further essays followed on Ibsen, Zola, D'Ann-
unzio, Maupassant, Gogol, Herzen, Belinsky, Gorky and others.
They were generally free from any narrow sectarian attitude or
vulgar reduction of artistic creation to the play of economic
interests. They already presaged the mature Trotsky's sympathy
for the artist's opposition to bourgeois society, while recognizing
that it sprang from assumptions different from those of the
political revolutionary.

His own radicalism nevertheless contained a strikingly lyrical,
almost Faustian quality of striving to reach out to the infinite
possibilities of human nature. Impatient with all bourgeois
platitudes, with mocking philistinism and petty-mindedness, he
identified himself with the great Russian writers who had risen
above the prejudices of their time and asserted their faith in
reason, truth and human solidarity. From his Siberian exile, at
the age of twenty-one, the young Bronstein defiantly flung his
own credo of indestructible optimism at the new century. 'As
long as I breathe, I shall fight for the future, that radiant future
in which man, strong and beautiful, will become master of the
drifting stream of his history and will direct it towards the
boundless horizon of beauty, joy and happiness.'[34] This messianic
faith 'in the clear, bright future of mankind' was to echo as a
leitmotif through the next forty years of Trotsky's revolutionary
struggles. Even in the darkest hours of exile, his credo remained
*Dum spiro spero*! (While there's life, there's hope) – a passionate
and militant denial of the established order in the name of the
'radiant future'. Marxism helped to focus and sharpen his
emotional opposition to the status quo and provided the 'scientific'
instrument by which he could finally cut himself adrift from the
petty-bourgeois environment of his youth. 'The instinct of
acquisition, the petty-bourgeois outlook and habits of life', he
wrote in *My Life*, 'from these I sailed away with a mighty push,
and I did so never to return.'[35]

By the time he arrived at Lenin's lodgings in London, in 1902,
Bronstein had become Trotsky, the name by which he was to be
known for the rest of his life. He had scribbled the name, which
belonged to one of his jailors in Odessa, into his false passport
before he made his escape from Siberia. It was a curious choice

yet one which almost perfectly mirrored the ambiguities in his search for a new identity. The heavy-set chief guard of the Odessa jail (the original Trotsky) was a majestic, dominating figure symbolizing the arrogance of power against which Bronstein was now in revolt. At the same time the name which he had chosen was also synonymous in German with boldness, defiance and disdain – fighting qualities which the young Marxist revolutionary was consummately to display in the future. It was almost as if Trotsky had unconsciously taken into himself a part of that power he was fighting against. The ambivalent attitudes to authority which had played a significant role in his revolutionary 'pre-history' were to be even more important in the struggles that lay ahead.

## CHAPTER TWO

# THE BREAK WITH LENIN

'... the process of self-devourment has begun ...
All that has stood in the way has had to be swept
away so that comrade Lenin ... could become,
through the medium of the Council, the man who
unhampered plants a "republic of virtue and terror." '
Leon Trotsky, *Our Political Tasks*

It was in Verkholensk, during the summer of 1902, that Bronstein had first read *Iskra* and received a copy of Lenin's new
work, *What is to be Done?* He did not as yet fully grasp the
significance of Lenin's ideas on the character of the revolutionary
party but they appeared to correspond to his recent advocacy of
a centralized organization with strong leadership. Following his
escape from Siberia, Trotsky reached Samara where he made
contact with the *Iskra* organization. Shortly he was summoned
by Lenin to report as soon as possible to foreign headquarters
in London. The literary reputation of *The Pen* (Pero) – this was
his nickname in Samara – had preceded him and Lenin was eager
to meet and win over the new recruit. Their first encounters in
London were warm and friendly, and within four months of his
arrival, Lenin was recommending that 'Pero' be co-opted to the
Editorial Board of *Iskra*. He emphasized that in spite of his youth
and an excessively florid *feuilleton* style, Trotsky was 'a man of
rare abilities' who must not be allowed to slip away.[1] The other
members of the Board, including Martov, Axelrod and Vera
Zasulich agreed with this assessment but it was opposed by the
veteran founder of Russian Marxism, Georgi Plekhanov. Plekhanov intensely disliked the young man's intellectual flourish
and sharp-witted arrogance, as well as suspecting that Lenin

was trying to build a majority against him.

Trotsky was at first blithely unaware of these conflicts on the editorial board. He had fallen in love with *Iskra* (to which he began to contribute regularly), displaying a respectful reverence for the Party veterans which they reciprocated – his ties of friendship to Vera Zasulich and Paul Axelrod were particularly close. He made public appearances in Whitechapel, Brussels, Liège and Paris, where he met Natalia Sedova, his second wife. He passionately believed in *Iskra's* mission. It seemed to him an idyllic revolutionary family in whose bosom he could finally resolve his adolescent crisis of identity. But the rifts opening up in the organization even before the Second Congress of the Russian Social Democratic Party were becoming more evident. Trotsky sensed the new coldness that was developing in relations between its two leaders, Lenin and Martov. Even before the split, as Trotsky later observed, it was apparent that Lenin was 'hard' and Martov was 'soft'.

> 'Lenin would glance at Martov, whom he estimated highly, with a critical and somewhat suspicious look, and Martov, feeling his glance, would look down and move his thin shoulders nervously. When they met or conversed afterwards, at least when I was present, one missed the friendly inflection and the jests. Lenin would look beyond Martov as he talked, while Martov's eyes would grow glassy under his drooping and never quite clear pince-nez.'[2]

The clash came into the open in July 1903 at the Second Congress in Brussels. Until that point there had been general agreement between Lenin and Trotsky on political questions. The younger man still considered himself a pupil – Lenin was his senior by nine years, and Martov six years older. He still had much to learn from the 'veterans' of the Party. Indeed Trotsky's vehement assault on the Jewish Bund and the Economists (who emphasized trade-unionism and the struggle for reforms) earned him the epithet of 'Lenin's big stick'. At the Congress the twenty-three year old Trotsky specifically referred to himself as a Jew (this was a rare event in itself) in order to repudiate more effectively the Bund's advocacy of Jewish 'cultural autonomy' and a decentralized, federal Party organization. He lashed out at

the Bund's claim to be the *sole* representative of the Jewish proletariat, calling this a demonstration of distrust towards non-
Jewish members in the Party and a denial of Socialist internationalism. He denounced the demand for 'cultural autonomy'
as a form of separatism which created barriers between the
nationalities instead of sweeping them away.[3]

Trotsky's attack on the 'Economists' was no less zealous and
very much in line with Lenin's emphasis on centralism, strict
party statutes and vigilant control from above over the organization. It was the last gesture of solidarity among the Iskraites, for
with Lenin's proposal to reorganize the editorial board (effectively
excluding Zasulich and Axelrod) the debate over party statutes
now became envenomed. Martov submitted an alternative draft
to Lenin's definition of party membership along the lines
practised by the German Social Democratic Party. Supported by
the former 'Economist' Martynov, Martov wished to extend
membership to include all those who supported the party by
'regular *personal assistance* under the direction of one of the party
organizations'.[4] He opposed Lenin's concept of an organization
of professional revolutionaries which would exercise tight control
over its regular membership. Lenin's insistence on a conspiratorial
network capable of functioning effectively under Russian conditions of police terror, struck Martov as a denial of the mass
party and its role as the conscious expression of proletarian
class interests.[5] Plekhanov, who had previously stood on the
sidelines, supported Lenin's project as a necessary safeguard
against intellectual opportunism. Trotsky unexpectedly rose to
challenge this assertion and declared his opposition to Lenin's
formula.

> 'I do not give the statutes any sort of mystical interpretation
> ... Lenin's formula should be rejected ... It defeats its own
> purpose; it will make it far more difficult for workers to
> join the party than for the intelligentsia, since organizations
> of workers are subjected to more pressures and break down
> more easily – for instance, through strikes.'[6]

Lenin was evidently surprised at this volte-face by his former
protégé and again pointed out why he sought to 'narrow' the
concept of party membership. Martov's formula had ignored the

fact that under Russian conditions 'it is difficult if not impossible to distinguish in the party between babblers and actual workers.' Trotsky's objections were irrelevant – he had forgotten that 'the party must constitute only the *leading ranks* of the vast masses of the working class. Wholly or almost wholly, these masses, in turn, work under the leadership and control of party organizations, but generally they do not and should not come into the party . . .'[7] Lenin was determined that real control should remain in the hands of the Central Committee 'in order to preserve the firmness and maintain the purity of our party'. Although Lenin lost this particular debate, he won a small majority which to all appearances was decisive over every other issue at the Second Congress.

The recriminations following this victory which split the Russian Social Democracy into Bolshevik ('majority') and Menshevik ('minority') factions were to assume an importance that none of the participants could foresee at the time. Trotsky found himself ranged with his Menshevik friends Axelrod, Zasulich and Martov, who now refused to serve on *Iskra's* new editorial board. All Lenin's repeated efforts to detach him from Martov had failed: he even found himself accused by his young disciple of trying to build up a closed organization of conspirators instead of a party of the working class. Trotsky evidently misunderstood Lenin's motives, which he saw as a ruthless attempt to achieve personal domination over the party. His closest connections were still with Martov, Zasulich and Axelrod while he stood furthest from Plekhanov, whose hostility understandably grated on him. Lenin's personal attitude to Trotsky had been benevolent but 'now it was he, who in my eyes, was attacking the editorial board, a body which was, in my opinion, a single unit, and which bore the exciting name of *Iskra*. The idea of a split within the board seemed nothing short of sacrilegious to me.'[8] He could not yet grasp the revolutionary objectives behind Lenin's 'irreconcilable' and 'relentless' insistence on removing the party veterans (for whom he felt respect and 'personal affection') from leadership positions.

'My whole being seemed to protest against this merciless cutting off of the older ones when they were at last on the

threshold of an organized party. It was my indignation at
this [Lenin's] attitude that really led to my parting with him
at the Second Congress. His behaviour seemed unpardonable
to me, both horrible and outrageous.'[9]
   In addition to these personal and moral objections, Trotsky
felt repelled by Lenin's intense and ruthless centralism on
organizational issues, which he refused to accept as 'the logical
conclusion of a clear revolutionary concept'. In his *Report of the
Siberian Delegation*, written shortly after the Congress, Trotsky
echoed Martov's critique of Lenin's power-drive and his imposition on the party of a 'state of siege', which he put down to
'self-centredness' rather than to the imperatives of Russian
revolutionary centralism. Lenin had assumed in his eyes 'the
role of the party's disorganizer', whose wrecking tactics had
destroyed the Congress'[10] and split the Social Democrats into
warring factions. In the *Report* Trotsky made it clear that he
regarded Social Democracy as a broad mass movement in which
local organizations closely attached to their grass-roots origin
must have as much freedom as was compatible with party unity.
Centralism should be freely accepted, not imposed from above
in a legalistic and 'purely formal' manner. He claimed that
Lenin's centralism offered a straitjacket instead of an organic
framework for the growth of working-class consciousness. It
would result in an organization without a movement or at any
rate one that was out of touch with the rank-and-file. According
to Trotsky, Lenin's real objective was simply to gain control of
the party apparatus for personal ends in order to establish his
own hegemony.
   'The practice of organized mistrust demands an iron fist. A
   system of terror is crowned by the emergence of a Robespierre. Comrade Lenin made a mental roll-call of the party
   personnel and arrived at the conclusion that he himself was
   to be the iron fist – and he alone. . . . The hegemony of Social
   Democracy has led, in accordance with the logic of the state
   of siege, to the hegemony of Lenin over Social Democracy.'[11]
For the first time Trotsky pointed out the dangers of a 'Thermidorean' reaction implied in Lenin's attempt to transform 'the
modest party Council into an omnipotent Committee of Public

Safety so that he may play the role of an "incorrupt" Robespierre.'[12] The Bolshevik leader was however a mere caricature of Robespierre – he differed from the original 'as a vulgar farce differs from a historic tragedy'. Trotsky did not believe that Lenin's administrative methods would succeed, but the danger remained that by discrediting the idea of centralism in general they would open the doors to the 'Thermidoreans of Socialist opportunism'.[13]

Trotsky's strident tone came out even more sharply in *Our Political Tasks* (1904), one of the most vehement denunciations of Leninism ever written. Once again he inveighed against the exclusion of the mass of workers from the tightly-knit Bolshevik organization of professional revolutionists. The chief task of a Social Democratic party was, in his view, to create a mass movement within its own walls, to achieve direct contact with the workers and to involve them in day-to-day work. The goal of Marxism must be to *educate* a politicaly developed proletariat, to imbue it with confidence in its own capacities. Trotsky was at this stage completely committed to the principle of rank-and-file consent, to the 'self-activity' (*samodiatelnost*) of the proletariat, its mass participation in the collective struggle.[14] The democratization of party life entailed rejection of all the mechanical forms of discipline associated with the capitalist production system and the 'barracks regime'. Leninism had merely perpetuated these evils. Trotsky equated it with an automatic 'Asiatic' type of centralism which aimed to create authority and power instead of producing a framework for the collective co-ordination of the revolutionary struggle.

In Trotsky's opinion, the tactics of Bolshevism submerged the very essence of the Socialist revolution – that it must be the work of the proletariat itself. Leninism viewed the workers as an unreliable mass with only a limited ideological consciousness; hence they were to be neutralised by an élite leadership, so that they would not hinder the revolution. Lenin's emphasis on professionally trained revolutionists, disciplined, obedient and subject to no rank-and-file control, would 'substitute' for the proletariat, an autonomous organization of the Party speaking in the name of Marxism. This *substitutionism* which claimed to preserve the 'purity' of the movement was in reality a negation of Marxist teaching which would make redundant the role of the working-class as a conscious social force. The Bolsheviks, by *thinking for* the proletariat and claiming to speak in its name, condemned the workers to passivity.[15] This was an attempted short-cut to success which reflected despair at the backwardness of the Russian proletariat and the colossal task of educating it to consciousness of its historical mission. The Bolsheviks were erecting revolutionary politics into an autonomous conspiratorial activity divorced from society, a policy that would cut the Party off from its grassroots and undermine the goals of Socialism. Lenin's hierarchical, non-democratic pattern of organization would transform the party into a bureaucratic structure and its members into a narrow clique of functionaries. These methods, Trotsky declared, in a famous prophecy, contained the seeds of authoritarian dictatorship: '. . . the party organization substitutes itself for the party, the Central Committee substitutes itself for the organization and, finally, a "dictator" substitutes himself for the Central Committee'.[16]

At the heart of Leninist ideology, Trotsky diagnosed a *Jacobin* deviation which was absolutely incompatible with his vision of Social Democracy. In his opinion there was a clear choice to be made between 'two worlds, two doctrines, two tactics, two mentalities, separated by an abyss'. Jacobins were utopians, idealists, rationalists – Marxist Social Democrats were realists, materialists and dialecticians.[17] The French Jacobins represented the highest point achieved by radicalism within bourgeois society but they had proved unable to reconcile the contradictions produced by their abstract theories except through recourse to the guillotine. Social Democrats, on the other hand, favoured the free struggle of different tendencies, not the guillotining of dissidents. French Jacobinism had been based on an 'absolute belief in a metaphysical idea' and an 'absolute disbelief in living people': Social democracy drew its support from a living class, it expressed the realities of social development and acknowledged the existence of concrete antagonisms.

Trotsky denounced Lenin's 'malicious and morally repulsive suspiciousness' as nothing but a caricature of the 'tragic intolerance of Jacobinism'.[18] This was allegedly the source of Lenin's 'paranoic' excommunication of dissent and his doctrinaire attempt to ensure the purity of the movement. Bolshevism saw enemies everywhere and sought to proclaim its own orthodoxy as the fountain of all truth. This self-righteousness, 'engraved on the heart of Maximilien Lenin' could only lead to a regime of terror headed by a dictator. In place of Marx's 'dictatorship of the proletariat', Lenin and his followers intended to substitute a 'dictatorship *over* the proletariat' through the medium of a powerful commanding Party organization. Such a Jacobin-Blanquist conspiracy reflected the opportunism and impatience of the Russian intelligentsia which had lost faith in the workers and sought to bypass rather than educate them for revolutionary struggle.[19]

*Our Political Tasks* outlined a concept of the Party, a theory of revolution and a road to Socialism that sharply diverged from the Leninist model. It rejected as absurd Lenin's proposition that revolutionary consciousness could only be introduced from *outside* into the ranks of the working class. It subordinated the role of the Marxist intelligentsia to that of the spontaneous labour movement and denounced Bolshevism as a 'reactionary' attempt to fetter the self-determination of the proletarian masses. The task of the Social Democratic Party was to lead without becoming the *guardian* of the working class. Trotsky in 1904 envisaged the Party not as an organization of professionals or even as a *political vanguard* but as the Marxist kernel of the workers' movement whose goal was to heighten the self-consciousness and self-activity of the proletariat. Lenin emphasised the leadership role of the professionals and saw the Party, not the class, as the decisive lever of revolution. Trotsky rejected such élitism as excessively *dirigiste*. It was social classes not political parties which moved history forward in accordance with the elemental laws of the class-struggle.

Trotsky's attack on Leninism was part of a wider theoretical onslaught on the organizational concepts of Bolshevism undertaken by Martov, Zasulich, Axelrod and Plekhanov, who had meanwhile fallen out with Lenin. Axelrod, in particular, (to whom Trotsky dedicated his pamphlet) had originated many of the themes which became the stock-in-trade of the Menshevik counter-offensive. Without mentioning Lenin by name, he had warned against excessive centralism, the curbing of proletarian self-activity, the dangers of ideological tutelage and the stifling of creative initiative by the masses.[20] Rosa Luxemburg, the leading figure in the German left, also stepped into the fray with two articles for *Iskra* which elaborated on Axelrod's critique, though temperamentally she stood closer to Lenin. Her boundless faith in the creative power of the masses, her romantic optimism about the spontaneity of the workers' movement led her to formulate an attack on Bolshevism remarkably close to that of Trotsky. 'The ultra-centralism advocated by Lenin is not something born of a positive creative spirit but of the negative sterile spirit of the night-watchman. His line of thought is cut to the control of party activity, not to its fructifying; to its narrowing, not to its unleashing; to the role of taskmaster, not of gatherer and unifier.'[21]

This offensive did nòt in the least shake Lenin's belief in his own organizational creed which drew its strength from the Russian conspiratorial heritage and its populist traditions of revolutionary centralism. In *One Step Forward, Two Steps Backward*, Lenin answered his critics by reaffirming his faith in hierarchy and the need for a strong organization of revolutionaries. 'Bureaucratism versus democratism, i.e. precisely centralism versus autonomy, such is the organization principle of revolutionary social democracy as against that of the opportunists ... [it] strives to go from the top downward, and defends the enlargement of the rights and plenary powers of the central body against the parts.'[22] Though Lenin would later modify this authoritarian doctrine to the more diluted and ambiguous concept of 'democratic centralism' he never altogether abandoned his distrust of the spontaneous class struggle of the proletariat.

This more than anything divided him from Trotsky, who until 1917 clung to the notion of a broadly-based party (derived from Martov and Axelrod) even though he had become disillusioned with Menshevism by the end of 1904. The political differences between Lenin and Trotsky through this period, especially on the issue of party organization, were deep enough to preclude any real collaboration. But they do not adequately explain the extra-ordinary personal venom with which the young Trotsky turned on his former mentor. The epithets he hurled at Lenin, which almost amounted to character-assassination, were extreme even by the standards of Russian Marxist polemics, and far outdid other Menshevik leaders in their vituperation.[23] Yet however far-sighted his criticisms (and many of them were uncannily prophetic), they anticipated future possibilities rather than any immediate dangers. Lenin was as yet far from conceiving any-thing approaching a design for totalitarian dictatorship. Trotsky could have no inkling of how one day he himself would rally unconditionally to the Leninist theory of the Party which he execrated in 1904. The young Trotsky's flaming imagination intuited the risks inherent in a Bolshevik 'substitutionism' ex-ercising an absolute dictatorship over society but he could scarcely foresee under what vastly different conditions the emergence of a monolithic state would actually occur.

Behind his assault on the Bolshevik doctrine of organization stood more complex emotions connected with his own self-image as a revolutionary and his individualistic rebellion against authority. Lenin's realism and practicality, his hard-headed in-sistence on discipline and his preoccupation with organizational controls were alien to Trotsky's romantic, impulsive tempera-ment – they also offended his vision of a spontaneous mass movement creating its own organs of power. Trotsky's revolt against parental, social and institutional authority was still too fresh to allow him to submit readily to Lenin's leadership. More-over, his obsession with the *unity* of the Party was based on a failure to perceive the depths of the rift which had now opened up between Bolsheviks and Mensheviks. He still envisaged the Party in terms of the old *Iskra* organization as a peer-group in which all factions could freely express their differences. His feel-ings of self-esteem were bound up with the existence of this harmonious 'family' where he had been the favourite son and star pupil. His attachment to the Party veterans expressed a sense of *personal* involvement which he could not easily shake off. Lenin was responsible in his eyes for wrecking this idyllic harmony and establishing an impersonal, ruthless discipline over the Party which Trotsky mistakenly attributed to morbid egocentrism. He did not yet share Lenin's mistrust of the world, his single-minded concentration on the long-term goal, his refusal to tolerate any conciliation or compromise. Lenin's splitting tactics by threatening the cohesion of the group with which he had identified himself, constituted a direct assault on Trotsky's most compulsive need – to assert his independence *and* to find his place in society.

Trotsky's attack on *substitutionism* did not deny the necessity for proletarian dictatorship (or for political direction as such) but it did assert that an independent working class 'will not tolerate any dictatorship over itself'.[24] On a psychological level his relations to Lenin were for the moment unconsciously governed by a similar principle. His own independence and amour propre, his aesthetic tastes and impetuous temperament precluded him from submitting to a man of Lenin's iron will and unbending authority. His fertile imagination and personal ambition could not be easily satisfied by the dry, prosaic, routine work which Lenin required from his lieutenants.

Trotsky was to pay a heavy price for his break with Lenin which ultimately left him isolated in the party as a man without a faction of his own or a secure political base. His flirtation with the Mensheviks could not last long for his activist temperament baulked at the relegation of socialist revolution to the distant future. By adopting a stance 'above' the party, which viewed both the Bolshevik and Menshevik factions as an obstacle to unity, Trotsky attracted fire from all sides. His 'conciliationist' approach which argued for the unification of all tendencies in Russian Social Democracy in a broad front, ignored the fundamental principles which irreconcilably divided Bolsheviks and Mensheviks alike. Many years later Trotsky himself would repudiate this 'conciliationism' as profoundly erroneous,[25] just as he would minimize into insignificance his differences with Lenin.[26] In retrospect he claimed that his attitude stemmed from a 'fatalistic optimism' that the course of events would automatically bring the divided factions to an identical revolutionary position.[27] He willingly conceded that he had underestimated Lenin's capacities for leadership and misjudged his underlying motives, but avoided any analysis of the inner-party struggle as it had unfolded before 1917.

Trotsky's later silence on the underlying causes of the historic split with the Mensheviks was no accident. After the October Revolution he had little to gain from any raking up of earlier differences with Lenin and reminders of his own non-Bolshevik past. Yet the rift was undoubtedly more important than he suggested and partly explains the suspicion with which he was later regarded by the Bolshevik Old Guard. Before 1917 the differences were centred less around Trotsky's theory of permanent revolution than over his efforts to realize the mirage of Party unity on his own terms.

For Lenin these attempts at conciliation were a direct challenge to the theory and practice of the vanguard party. Trotsky seemed to him little more than a poseur and 'phrasemaker', a general without troops who clung to a sentimental fiction of unity that stood in the way of his own uncompromising principles of organization. He never quite rid himself of the distrust he felt for Trotsky's magniloquence, so alien to his own economy of phrase and austere habits. Trotsky was behaving like a political chameleon – '. . . he comes and goes between the liberals and the Marxists, with shreds of sonorous phrases stolen right and left. Not all is gold that glitters.'[29] At the time of the 'August bloc' in 1912 when Trotsky tried to organize under his own leadership the Bolshevik conciliators, the Bolshevik *Vperyodists* (Duma boycotters), the 'Liquidators', the Martovites, the Bundists, the Plekhanovists and the non-factionalists, Lenin was predictably enraged. This 'diplomat of the basest metal' who had no definite conceptions of his own, was trying to supplant the close-knit, militant organization that Lenin had spent years in building up. Trotsky was contemptuously dismissed as a professional non-factionalist who 'today plagiarises the ideology of one faction, tomorrow of another, and then declares himself above all the factions'.[30]

Trotsky's own language was even more acrimonious. He called Lenin 'a professional exploiter of all the backward elements in the Russian workers' movement', claiming that his doctrines were 'founded on lies and falsifications' and carried in themselves 'the poison germ of their decomposition'.[31] It was not until the First World War when Trotsky was 'finally convinced of the utter hopelessness of the Mensheviks' that a rapprochement between the two men became possible. Even then it took the imminence of an insurrection to rally Trotsky to the Bolshevik banner and erase past differences. Yet, looking back on his earlier break with Lenin, Trotsky expressed no regrets. In 1903, he conceded, 'revolution was still largely a theoretical abstraction to me'.[32] He could not at the time regard Lenin's centralism as the harsh, imperative necessity which in his eyes it later turned out to be. He needed to see a problem independently. This temperamental trait 'has always been my most imperious intellectual necessity'.[33] He was to return to Lenin a second time: 'later than many others, but I came in my own way, after I had gone through and had weighed the experience of the revolution, the counter-revolution and the Imperialist war.'[34] The unyielding pride, self-assured individualism and independent judgement so deeply rooted in Trotsky's character was to be the source of both his political weakness and his intellectual strength.

## CHAPTER THREE

# BAPTISM OF FIRE

'No great work is possible without intuition – that is,
without that subconscious sense which, although it
may be developed and enriched by theoretical and
practical work, must be ingrained in the very nature
of the individual. . . . this gift takes on decisive
importance at a time of abrupt changes and breaks –
the conditions of revolution. The events of 1905
revealed in me, I believe, this revolutionary intuition,
and enabled me to rely on its assured support during
my later life.'

Leon Trotsky, *My Life*

Trotsky's connections with the Bolsheviks had ended with the
Second Congress. By the end of 1904 he had also broken away
from the Mensheviks and was obliged to strike out on his own.
The shining white knight of 'conciliation' was now a man without a following, an outsider in the very party he sought vainly to
unite. At this critical moment he found a formidable new colla-
borator in the Gargantuan shape of Alexander Israel Helphand
(Parvus).[1] This brilliant, exuberant and unorthodox Russian
Jewish émigré had played a considerable role in the revisionist
controversy that shook the German Social Democratic Party at
the turn of the century. Together with Rosa Luxemburg he had
led the assault on Eduard Bernstein's revision of Marxism and
earned both respect and enmity for his penetrating scholarship,
his massive knowledge of economics and slashing polemics
against reformist 'opportunism'. Parvus was a man of international horizons who effortlessly straddled the German and
Russian Socialist movements – contributing to both *Iskra* and
Karl Kautsky's *Neue Zeit* – the leading Marxist periodical in

Europe. Trotsky (who was Parvus's junior by twelve years) was deeply impressed by his 'extraordinarily creative personality' and warmly acknowledged his intellectual debt to the older man. In his autobiography, Trotsky wrote:

> 'Parvus was unquestionably one of the most important of the Marxists at the turn of the century. He used the Marxist methods skilfully, was possessed of wide vision, and kept a keen eye on everything of importance in world events. This, coupled with his fearless thinking and his virile, muscular style, made him a remarkable writer. His early studies brought me closer to the problems of the Social Revolution, and, for me, definitely transformed the conquest of power by the proletariat from an astronomical "final" goal to a practical task for our own day.'[2]

It was Parvus who first gave Trotsky the broad internationalist perspective from which he henceforth viewed Russian social and political conditions. In that sense Parvus was the midwife of the theory of 'permanent revolution' though not its originator. His central idea that the nation-state had become obsolescent as a result of the development of the world market, profoundly shaped Trotsky's future outlook. No less important were Parvus's ideas on Russian history and his predictions of a coming political upheaval in Russia as a result of the war with Japan. Tsardom, he argued, was being driven to expand eastwards as a result of domestic and external pressures caused by 'the world-wide process of capitalist development'.[3] In the coming upheaval the Russian proletariat might well play the role of 'the vanguard of social revolution' which would in turn herald the world revolution. Parvus's vision of a cataclysmic era of imperialist wars in which the capitalist nation-states fought for their economic survival fascinated the young Trotsky. From Parvus he also learned to see how the industrial backwardness of Tsarism and the instability of the Russian social structure made it peculiarily vulnerable to revolution.

His conversations with Parvus in Munich culminated in a preface which the older man wrote at the beginning of 1905 for Trotsky's pamphlet 'Until the Ninth of January'. In his introduction Parvus outlined the social peculiarities of backward Russia and drew some bold and original inferences. He demonstrated that the weak development of petty-bourgeois democracy in Russia was due to the absence of a significant artisanal production and to the bureaucratic-administrative character of Russia's cities in the pre-capitalist period.[4] The capitalist process had however begun to establish large industrial cities and accelerated proletarian class consciousness by the rapidity with which it concentrated workers in the factories. Hence, Parvus envisaged an exceptional role for the Russian proletariat in the coming revolution on account of its growing political awareness and energy. The Social-Democrats would soon be confronted with the dilemma of assuming responsibility for the provisional government or standing aside and losing all influence in the labour movement. Parvus had concluded that in Russia '. . . only workers can accomplish a revolutionary insurrection. In Russia the revolutionary provisional government will be a government of the *workers' democracy*.'[5] But this government could not accomplish 'a socialist insurrection in Russia', it would have to remain content 'with liquidating the autocracy and establishing a democratic republic . . .'[6] Parvus's strategic prognosis remained within the Marxist framework of a 'bourgeois revolution' yet deviated from orthodoxy by suggesting that Russia was on the eve of a workers' seizure of power. It was not Parvus but Trotsky who was destined to break through the framework itself and construct a fully-fledged theory of permanent revolution which fleshed out the ideas of his senior partner.

Parvus's scenario of a workers' provisional government being established in a backward, pre-democratic society predictably struck the Mensheviks as an absurdity. But Lenin in 1905 also dismissed out of hand 'those half-baked, semi-anarchist ideas which envisage the speedy implementation of the maximal programme and the seizure of power in order to carry through the socialist revolution'.[7] In his view such a project ignored the low level of Russian economic development and lack of socialist consciousness and organization among the working class. The coming revolution would be bourgeois and democratic – to aim at an immediate socialist overturn without the support of the 'colossal majority of the people' still struck Lenin as unrealistic and futile. Alone among the Russian Marxists, Trotsky took Parvus's preface seriously and organically absorbed its line of thought into his own perspective.

Trotsky's brochure had been completed just as the Imperial troops massacred in cold blood a peaceful demonstration of Petersburg workers which assembled on January 9 before the Tsar's Winter Palace. In his pamphlet Trotsky outlined with remarkable prescience the future course of events, and in particular, the crucial role which the general political strike was to play later in the year. He sketched a 'plan of action' strikingly close to the way in which the revolution was actually to unfold in October 1905 and again in February 1917.

> 'To make the workers quit their machines and stands; to make them walk out of the factory premises into the streets; to lead them to the neighbouring plant; to proclaim there a cessation of work; to make new masses walk out into the street; to go thus from factory to factory, from plant to plant, incessantly growing in numbers, sweeping aside police barriers, absorbing new masses . . ., crowding the streets, taking possession of buildings suitable for popular meetings, fortifying the buildings, holding continuous revolutionary meetings with audiences coming and going, bringing order into the movements of the masses, arousing their spirit, explaining to them the aim and meaning of what is going on; to turn finally, the entire city into one revolutionary camp, this is, broadly speaking, the plan of action.'[8]

The factories and plants in the city would be the main arena of the popular revolution but Trotsky did not overlook the vast potential reservoir of support in the Russian peasantry. Nor did he forget the decisive importance of morale in the army, which had been disintegrating under the pressure of military defeats and inadequate supplies. The fiasco of the Russo-Japanese war had stunned the Russian masses. Slowly, imperceptibly yet irresistibly it was doing the work of 'accumulating indignation, bitterness, revolutionary energy'. The same soldiers who yesterday fired shots in the air might tomorrow hand over their weapons to the workers. The task of revolutionary propaganda was to mobilize this mass discontent 'to make the idea of a National

Constituent Assembly popular among the people'. Intense agitation among the troops was necessary 'so that at the moment of the general strike every soldier sent to suppress the "rebels" should know that in front of him is the people demanding the convocation of the Constituent Assembly'.[9]

Trotsky's brochure breathed a spirit of revolutionary romanticism tempered by a realistic assessment of the social forces at work. His vehement attack on Russian liberalism (which had alienated him from the Mensheviks) ruthlessly exposed the half-hearted, compromising and timid attitude of the *zemstvo* opposition to the Monarchy. *Zemstvo* liberalism was pleading with the Tsar to bring about reforms but appeared organically incapable of challenging the status quo, or even imagining a social order without the autocracy. Its aim was not to defeat the government 'but to lure it to its side, to be worthy of its gratitude and trust'.[10] The liberal intelligentsia was as vacillating in its attitude to revolution as the gentry – its democratic illusions lacked credibility and deprived of any mass base of its own it would recoil from change at the crucial moment. Thus already before the 1905 revolution, Trotsky together with Parvus had anticipated the endemic weakness of the Russian bourgeoisie, its inability to lead a revolution and the disproportionate role which the workers at the head of the peasantry would play in the coming upheavals.

Armed with this broad view of the situation, Trotsky was impatient to abandon the endless debates of the émigré movement and he returned to Russia in February 1905 under an assumed name. During the first few months he could not appear openly but turned out a flood of pamphlets, essays and other writings on the strategy of the coming insurrection. More than ever he was convinced that the proletariat under Social Democratic leadership and not the peasantry, middle class or intelligentsia was alone capable of exercising an independent revolutionary role.[11] His diatribes against Russian liberalism became more virulent, the tone of his journalistic articles more ecstatic and militant, rousing each class of the Russian population in turn against the iniquities of Tsardom. To escape the attentions of the police and *agents provocateurs* he had to leave suddenly for Finland. The lakes, pine-trees and tranquillity of the Finnish countryside, where he took up residence in an isolated pension called 'Rauha' (peace), were 'scarcely a reminder of a permanent revolution'.[12] The pension was almost empty, 'like death' – there was a heavy snow and 'the pine-trees were wrapped in a white shroud'. Here Trotsky meditated in solitude until news of the October general strike in Petersburg roused him from his writing. 'In the evening', he recalled, 'the postman brought a bunch of St. Petersburg papers. I opened them, one after another. It was like a raging storm coming in through an open window. The strike was growing, and spreading from town to town. In the silence of the hotel, the rustling of the papers echoed in one's ears like the rumble of an avalanche. The revolution was in full swing.'[13] That same evening, Trotsky was already in the great hall of the St Petersburg Polytechnic Institute making a speech. It was mid-October and the general strike was at its peak.

On October 17 the Tsar, bowing to the mass agitation, issued his manifesto, promising a constitution based on universal suffrage. Trotsky found himself caught up in the excitement of the festive crowds in the streets. He soon became a member of the first Soviet (Council) of Workers' Deputies which had sprung up spontaneously as the strike movement developed. In this capacity he harangued the crowds from the balcony of the Technological Institute, warning them not to trust the illusory promises of freedom extracted from the 'hangman on the throne'. For the first time he discovered in himself that theatrical panache and power of oratory which enabled him to galvanize the Petrograd masses in two revolutions. '. . . Citizens! Our strength is in ourselves. With sword in hand we must defend freedom. The Tsar's Manifesto, however . . . see! it is only a scrap of paper. Today it has been given us and tomorrow it will be taken away and torn into pieces as I am now tearing it into pieces, this paper-liberty before your very eyes.'[14]

For the next two months Trotsky was to stand at the very centre of the revolution, as the moving spirit of the Petersburg Soviet. He became its most effective leader, speaking and propagandizing tirelessly on its behalf. The Soviet of Workers' Deputies was the axis of all events, 'every thread ran towards it, every call to action, emanated from it'.[15] It had arisen spontaneously in the course of events in response to an objective need to unite the diverse currents within the Russian proletariat. It was 'the greatest workers' organization to be seen in Russia until that time', providing a living bond with the masses based on a fairly broad representation. During the fifty-two days of its existence, Trotsky found himself sucked into a whirlpool of activity on the Executive Committee, involved in endless meetings and writing editorials, appeals, manifestos and resolutions for the official Soviet organ, the *Izvestïa* (The News). In addition to this he had taken over with Parvus the tiny *Russian Gazette* and raised its circulation in a few days from thirty thousand to one hundred thousand. On November 13, Trotsky and Parvus, in alliance with the Mensheviks, had started another political newspaper, *Nachalo* (The Beginning) which was an even greater success, soon outstripping the rival Bolshevik organ.[16]

The Bolshevik Central Committee, deprived of their leader's presence (Lenin did not arrive in Petrograd until November), adopted a sectarian attitude to the Soviet which deprived them of any decisive role. Nevertheless the Bolsheviks had three representatives on the Executive of the Soviet, the same number as the Mensheviks and the Social Revolutionary Party. The activities of the Bolshevik and Menshevik Committees in Petersburg were co-ordinated in a Federal Council set up on Trotsky's initiative. On major issues he spoke for both factions before the Executive Committee as well as the whole Soviet. The revolution had temporarily 'deprived the factional struggle of any reasonable grounds' and both factions, as well as their newspapers, sought to restore party unity.[17] Lenin himself took no active part in the work of the Soviet and never spoke there, though he watched its steps closely and helped influence its policies through his representatives. According to Lunacharsky he not only agreed with its general line but was impressed by the 'tireless' and 'striking work' of its Chairman and leading figure.[18]

But for all their unexpected cooperation, the Socialist parties, hampered by the 'occupational disease of clandestinity' were outstripped by events and too weak to effectively channel the fervour and impulsiveness of the masses. Trotsky himself emphasized that the history of internal friction between the three major Socialist groupings 'rendered the creation of a *non-party* organization absolutely essential'.[19] The Soviet was well adapted to represent the Petersburg factories and plants: it was not a league of like-minded revolutionaries but on the other hand it was also free of the tactical sophistries to which 'we Russians are almost pathologically prone'.[20] Trotsky saw the Soviet as 'the organized expression of the class will of the proletariat' whereas the aim of the revolutionary and Social Democratic organizations had always been to achieve influence *over* the masses.[21] The Soviet had developed organically 'as the natural organ of the proletariat in its immediate struggle for power as determined by the actual course of events': according to Trotsky, it came under the influence of the Social Democrats because the Marxist training of the Party enabled it to offer political clarity in the midst of chaos.[22] In that sense the party had a role to play in educating, guiding and providing theoretical inspiration for the proletariat but it could not hope to match the influence of the Soviet.

'The social-democratic organization, which welded together a few hundred Petersburg workers, and which several thousand more were ideologically attached, was able to speak for the masses by illuminating their experience with the lightning of political thought; but it was not able to create a *living* organizational link with the masses, if only because it had always done the principal part of its work in clandestinity, concealed from the eyes of the masses.'[23]

The experience of the 1905 revolution reinforced Trotsky's faith in the spontaneous movement of the working classes and their capacity for institutional innovation. It confirmed to him the priority of mass action over organizational forms and his distrust of the party as a vehicle for revolutionary leadership. In the heat of battle the Soviet had provided a broader front of activity than any political party. It had waged a campaign for freedom of the press, organized armed detachments for self-defence and introduced an eight-hour working day in several major metal-working plants in Petersburg. Even though these campaigns ultimately failed when faced with employers' lock-outs and the intervention of state power, they 'left an indelible mark on the consciousness of the masses'.[24] The political general strike had demonstrated its ability to disorganize the state power by paralysing the whole apparatus of production.[25] The workers had proved their 'anarchic' power to momentarily render the state organization obsolete, though as yet they were unable to assume state functions. Through the pressure of strikes, the Soviet had taken the postal and telegraph services and the railways into its hand. 'It intervened authoritatively in economic disputes between workers and capitalists . . . Paralysing the activity of the autocratic state by means of the insurrectionary strike, it introduced its own free democratic order into the life of the labouring urban population.'[26]

The Soviet was not merely the organizer of the proletarian struggle against absolutism. It also constituted 'the first appearance of democratic power in modern Russian history', it had created an 'embryonic organ of revolutionary power' through deputies directly elected by the workers.[27] Trotsky tended to exaggerate this broad representative mandate of the Soviet which 'organizationally speaking . . . represented approximately 200,000 persons, principally factory and plant workers . . .', though its political influence was admittedly wider. It had attracted support from the professional intelligentsia, the students and the lower strata of the civil service – indeed all who were 'oppressed, dispossessed, honest, life-affirming in the city were consciously or instinctively drawn towards the Soviet'. According to Trotsky it was opposed by 'all that was coarse, dissolute, and doomed to death'. By this, he meant the representatives of predatory capitalism, the householders' syndicate, the higher bureaucracy, 'the *poules de luxe* whose keep formed part of the state budget, highly paid, highly decorated public men, the secret police. . .'[28] But without the support of absolutism, whose strength lay in its *muzhik* (peasant) army, these enemies would allegedly have been impotent against the organ which represented the overwhelming mass of the Petersburg population. The Soviet crumbled because it could not seize state power. The Monarchy still controlled the material organization of the State – the police, the army, the bureaucracy and the machinery of justice. 'The Soviet's weakness', Trotsky concluded, 'was not its own weakness but that of any purely urban revolution.'[29]

In his striking defence of the Soviet's actions before a Tsarist court (on October 4, 1907) Trotsky vehemently denied the charge that it had 'prepared' a popular rising. 'An insurrection of the masses', he said, 'is not made; it accomplishes itself. It is the result of social relations, not the product of a plan. It cannot be created; it can be foreseen.'[30] He did not deny that the goal of the political strike was 'insurrectionary', that it aimed to paralyse the economic apparatus of the State (railways, telegraph, postal services etc.) and create a new popular power based directly on the masses. But these aims were perfectly legitimate once the old apparatus had broken down and was incapable of maintaining public order. '. . . the strike had thrown hundreds of thousands of workers from the factories into the streets, and had freed these workers for public and political life. Who could direct them, who could bring discipline into their ranks? . . . The police? The gendarmerie? The secret police? I ask myself: who? and I can find no answer. No one, except the Soviet of Workers' Deputies.'[31]

The Soviet had become nothing other than 'the organ of self-government of the revolutionary masses.' It claimed to represent 'the organized will of the majority calling the minority to order'.[32] According to Trotsky the insurrection was rendered inevitable by the character of the Tsarist military-police state. If it had not intervened and 'introduced real anarchy into national life . . . the result would have been a new, reborn Russia, without the use of force and without bloodshed'.[33] With an eloquence reminiscent of his boyhood hero, Ferdinand Lassalle, Trotsky skilfully turned the indictment *against* the autocracy, whose power, based only on bayonets, had sowed nothing but confusion, chaos and disintegration. The Soviet, on the other hand, embodied discipline, order and consensus as well as the defence of popular freedom and civil rights. Far from initiating a military conspiracy according to a preconceived plan, it relied on enlightening the people and winning over the army to the side of the revolution. The working masses possessed no machine guns, rifles or other arms in significant quantities. Their strength lay not in weapons but in their *moral* force and determination.

'Not the capacity of the masses to kill, but their great

readiness to die, that, gentlemen of the court, is what we believe ensures, in the last count, the success of a people's rising. When the soldiers, sent out into the streets to repress the masses, find themselves face to face with the masses and discover that this crowd, the *people*, will not leave the streets . . . that it is prepared to pile corpses upon corpses . . . then the soldiers' hearts will falter, as they have always done in all revolutions, for they will be forced to doubt the stability of the order which they serve, they will be forced to believe in the triumph of the people.'[34]

Trotsky's speech from the dock closed with a searing indictment of the criminal bankruptcy of the Tsarist regime. A government which had sent the Black Hundred gangs (anti-Semitic hoodlums paid out of state funds) into action 'to cover the streets in blood, to loot, rape, burn, create panic, cheat and slander . . .' was not worthy of the name. It was nothing but 'an automaton for mass murder' against which the Soviet had no recourse but to arm itself.

'If you tell me that the pogroms, the murders, the burnings, the rapes . . . if you tell me that Kishinev, Odessa, Bialystok are the form of government of the Russian Empire – then I will agree with the prosecution that in October and November last we were arming ourselves . . . against (this) form of government . . ..'[35]

Both before and during his public trial, Trotsky had established himself, at the age of only twenty-six, as a popular tribune and a revolutionary Marxist of exceptional abilities. The other émigré leaders had not arrived in Russia until October or November 1905 and none was to make such an impact on events. The Bolshevik writer, Lunacharsky, pointed out that of all the social Democratic leaders of 1905–6,

'Trotsky undoubtedly showed himself, in spite of his youth, the best prepared, and he was the least stamped by the narrow émigré outlook which, as I said before, handicapped even Lenin. He realized better than the others what a state struggle is. He came out of the revolution, too, with the greatest gains in popularity; neither Lenin nor Martov gained much. Plekhanov lost a great deal because of the

semi-liberal tendencies which he revealed. But Trotsky
from then on was in the front rank.'[36]
Even outside the Soviet and the socialist parties, the impact of
Trotsky's personality and political drive was considerable, and
the Kadet leader Miliukov felt compelled to acknowledge that
'the revolutionary illusions of Trotskyism' were a force to be
reckoned with.

Trotsky himself remarked that 1905 was a watershed 'in the
life of the country, in the life of the party, and in my own life'.[37]
He had completed the apprenticeship which had gropingly begun
in Nikolayev as 'a provincial experiment' and had now catapulted
him into the centre of Russian and international events. In his
opinion there was no longer anyone from whom he could learn,
he himself had assumed the position of 'teacher' and made rapid
decisions under fire. He had come through the dress-rehearsal of
1905 with flying colours and that gave him the 'absolute resolution
and confidence' with which he took part in the events of 1917.

Beyond this significant personal gain, 1905 strengthened Trotsky's faith in the *spontaneous* revolution of the masses but also
reinforced his tendency to underestimate the importance of
organization. He angrily rejected any suggestion that the cal-
culation of forces could determine the outcome of revolutionary
conflicts in advance. To those Social Democrats who argued
that the proletariat should not have accepted battle in December
1905 because it lacked sufficient strength, he replied: 'It is not
only the party that leads the masses: the masses, in turn, sweep
the party forward. And this will happen in any revolution, however powerful its organization.'[38]

In justification of his viewpoint that no retreat was possible,
Trotsky quoted a text from Engels's *Revolution and Counter-
Revolution in Germany*: 'In revolution as in war it is absolutely
necessary at the decisive moment to stake everything, whatever
the chances of the struggle. . . . Defeat after persistent struggle
is a fact of no less revolutionary significance than an easily
snatched victory . . .'[39] On the other hand, Trotsky sharply
disagreed with Engels's 'very one-sided assessment of the significance of modern techniques in revolutionary risings'. The experience of 1905 had convinced Trotsky that the rapid

development of technology made the Tsarist State even more vulnerable, in certain circumstances, to an insurrectionary general strike.

'The telegraph and the railways are, without any question, powerful weapons in the hands of the modern centralized state. But they are double-edged weapons. And while the existence of society and the state as a whole depend on the continuance of proletarian labour, this dependence is most obvious in the case of the railways and the postal and telegraph service. As soon as the rails and wires refuse to serve, the government apparatus is fragmented into separate parts without any means of transport or communication (not even the most primitive ones) between them.'[40]

But the impact of technology and communications was by no means the only, or even the most important imponderable in the strategy and tactics of modern revolution. The experience of 1905 convinced Trotsky that the political mood of the army – the great unknown of every revolution – 'can be determined only in the process of a clash between the soldiers and the people'.[41] This was not only a moral process and a question of political agitation but involved complex and unpredictable psychological factors. Urban guerilla fighting, such as occurred in Moscow in December 1905, could not lead to military success but when it was transformed into a mass struggle it could help to sap the morale of the troops. Once the soldiers became convinced that 'the people have come out into the streets for a life-and-death struggle', only then was it possible for them to cross over to the revolutionary camp. The essence of insurrection was 'not so much a struggle against the army as a struggle *for* the army'.[42] Where, as in the Black Sea Fleet, in Kronstadt, in Siberia, in the Kuban region and many other places, 'the class, moral and political heterogeneity of the army causes troops to cross over to the side of the people', the most modern weapons of militarism could be turned against the government. Hence, the crucial role of agitation in the barracks.

But the behaviour and mood of the army depended also on its class composition. Trotsky recognized that in the struggle for state power the decisive factor would be the attitude of the armed *muzhiks*. The colossal numerical preponderance of the peasantry, which formed the nucleus of the Russian infantry, had defeated the proletariat in 1905. The peasantry lacked the technical expertise, the intelligence and capacity for concerted action of the working-class gunners, sappers, and engine-crews who were always in the forefront of the military and naval risings in 1905. The future prospects of the Russian revolution would in large part depend on whether the proletariat could place the peasant masses under its leadership and 'carry the revolution to the end'. Between 1905 and 1917 all the Russian Marxists would wrestle in different ways with this dilemma. The agrarian question was after all the axis of Russian political life, a potential aid but also the greatest challenge to the revolutionary parties. Trotsky by no means underestimated this challenge in spite of his harsh assessment of the 'local cretinism' which afflicted all peasant movements and sapped their independent initiative. It was one of the inescapable knots of Russia's 'social and political barbarism' which his theory of permanent revolution was designed to cut. His analysis of this problem provided an incisive and prophetic conclusion to the experiences of 1905.

'The first wave of the Russian revolution was smashed by the dull-wittedness of the muzhik, who, at home in his village, hoping to seize a bit of land, fought the squire, but who, having donned a soldier's uniform, fired upon the worker. All the events of the revolution of 1905 can be viewed as a series of ruthless object lessons by means of which history drums into the peasant's skull a consciousness of his local land hunger and the central problem of state power. The preconditions for revolutionary victory are forged in the historic school of harsh conflicts and cruel defeats.'[43]

## CHAPTER FOUR

# PERMANENT REVOLUTION

'The permanent revolution, in the sense which Marx attached to this concept, means a revolution which makes no compromise with any single form of class rule, which does not stop at the democratic stage, which goes over to socialist measures and to war against reaction from without; that is, a revolution whose every successive stage is rooted in the preceding one and which can end only in complete liquidation of class society.'

Leon Trotsky, *The Permanent Revolution*

Trotsky's theory of the 'permanent revolution' was originally formulated in the aftermath of 1905 as an attempt to define the place of the Russian revolution in the context of modern European history. It has been fairly described as 'the most radical restatement, if not revision, of the prognosis of Socialist revolution undertaken since Marx's *Communist Manifesto*' and to this day it remains the theoretical touchstone of 'Trotskyism'.[1] The conceptual framework which Trotsky outlined in his cell in the Peter-Paul fortress, while awaiting trial for his participation in the Petersburg Soviet of 1905, provided the basis for his revolutionary activity through the rest of his life. Expounded for the first time with an abstract, almost mathematical precision in his eighty-page brochure *Itogi i Perspektivy* (Balance and Prospects) it contained the distilled essence of the man and his ideas.

Trotsky's formula of the 'permanent revolution' had been anticipated by Karl Marx in his 'Address of the Central Committee to the Communist League' written in 1850. Marx had argued that while

'the democratic petty bourgeois wish to bring the revolution

to a conclusion as quickly as possible . . . it is our interest
and our task to make the revolution permanent, until all
more or less possessing classes have been forced out of their
position of dominance, until the proletariat has conquered
state power, and the association of proletarians, not only
in one country but in all dominant countries of the world,
has advanced so far that competition among the proletarians
of these countries has ceased and that at least the decisive
productive forces are concentrated in the hands of the
proletarians.'[2]
Marx had concluded his address with a warning to the workers
not to be seduced by 'the hypocritical phrases of the democratic
petty bourgeois'. The party of the proletariat should create an
independent organization whose battle cry must be: 'The Revolution in Permanence'.[3] In November 1905 the German left-wing
historian Franz Mehring had revived Marx's old formula in an
article written for the *Neue Zeit* and immediately translated for
the Russian journal *Nachalo*.[4] In the same issue, Trotsky for the
first time spoke of the permanence (*nepreryvnost*) of the revolution.[5]
Lenin also, had used the term 'uninterrupted' (*nepreryvnaja*)
revolution at this time, though within the different context of
helping the Russian peasantry to carry through to the end a
bourgeois-democratic revolution.[6]

In Russian Marxist terminology, 'permanent' revolution was
really an attempt to theorise the continuous or 'uninterrupted'
movement from one historical conjuncture to another – it had no
mystical or metaphysical implications. Marx's own use of the
term was significant in so far as it had suggested that there was
an inner momentum within revolutions that might carry them
beyond their initial goals. This was allegedly true of Germany
in 1848 where the proletariat had already emerged as a significant
force before the *bourgeois* revolution had occurred. In these conditions of belated social and political development, Marx could
anticipate that the proletarian revolution might follow *immediately*
on the heels of the bourgeois revolution. Nevertheless Marx saw
the two revolutions as distinct events and certainly did not
anticipate a workers' government as being on the agenda in the
'backward' Germany of 1850. The notion that a proletarian

revolution might triumph first in an underdeveloped society was a dramatic novelty that went against the unilinear pattern of historical evolution envisaged by Marx. The 'heresy' arose directly out of the dilemmas inherent in transplanting Marxism into a semi-feudal backward society such as Tsarist Russia.[7] It had been hinted at by Parvus in 1904 who argued that the workers could seize power in Russia precisely because it was the weakest link in the world capitalist chain. But even Parvus had insisted that a workers' government could do no more than carry out the *democratic* tasks of the bourgeois revolution. Russian backwardness would prevent it from moving in a socialist direction.

Alone among the Russian Marxists, it was left to Trotsky to demonstrate that the revolution could not stop at the bourgeois stage (or at Russia's borders) but would have to combine the liquidation of absolutism and feudalism with an *immediate* socialist transformation. Russia's social and economic problems could not be solved by democratic reforms. It was 'vulgar Marxism' to believe that 'every bourgeois society sooner or later secures a democratic regime, after which the proletariat . . . is gradually organized and educated for socialism.'[8] Democracy and socialism were not two distinct stages in social development 'separated by great distances of time from each other' as Plekhanov, the Mensheviks and even the overwhelming majority of leading Bolsheviks believed, until the eve of 1917. Trotsky insisted that to view the revolution in terms of such 'separate' stages was a schematic abstraction – the process had to be seen as an *organic whole* defined by its *telos* or ultimate end. The theory of permanent revolution pointed out that for the backward bourgeois nations 'the road to democracy passed through the dictatorship of the proletariat'.[9] Democracy was not a self-sufficient regime that would last for decades but a prelude to socialist revolution, bound to it by an unbroken chain of development.

Trotsky derived this conviction from a remarkable analysis of the 'peculiar character' of the Russian revolution which had been determined by a social and historical development sharply diverging from the Western model. The events of 1905 could not be understood unless certain unique features of Russian history – its slow rate of economic development and social crystallization,

the peculiar structure of the autocratic Tsarist State and its
vulnerability to foreign military and financial pressures – were
taken into account. Because of its backwardness and isolation the
pendulum had swung much further in the direction of state power
in Russia than in the West.

'In its endeavour to create a centralized state apparatus,
Tsarism was obliged not so much to oppose the claims of
the privileged estates as to fight the barbarity, poverty, and
general disjointedness of a country whose separate parts led
wholly independent economic lives. It was not the equilibrium of the economically dominant classes, as in the West,
but their weakness which made Russian bureaucratic
autocracy a self-contained organization. In this respect
Tsarism represents an intermediate form between European
absolutism and Asian despotism, being, possibly, closer to
the latter of these two.'[10]

Under the impact of European technology and capital, the
Tsarist State had continued to play a decisive role in the economic
sphere, becoming 'the largest capitalist entrepeneur, the largest
banker, the monopoly owner of railways, and of liquor retail
shops'.[11] The financial and military power of the autocracy was
strengthened at the expense of Russian society, depriving the
liberal middle-classes of any faith in an open trial of force. On
· the other hand, the growing gulf between absolutism and the
popular masses drawn into the new economic development,
ensured the inevitability of an extremely radical revolution.
European capital, by setting up major industries and proletarianiz-
ing the backward peasants was 'automatically undermining the
deepest foundations of Asian-Muscovite "uniqueness" '. Russian
industry already had a large-scale and highly concentrated
character precisely because it had not grown in an organic
manner out of artisanal trade and manufacture but incorporated
the most modern technology transplanted from Western Europe.
In an overwhelmingly agricultural country where the pauperized
peasant masses bore almost the entire weight of taxation and
remained in a state of semi-starvation, industrial progress was
creating explosive social contradictions.

Trotsky's analysis emphasized the lack of indigenous roots

which prevented big capital from placing itself at the head of the
national struggle with Tsarism. He considered the Russian
bourgeoisie to be an impotent, artificial growth, an alien tissue
grafted onto a hostile body, dependent on the State and antog-
onistic to the popular masses.[12] European finance-capital and not
the native bourgeoisie had played the decisive role in Russian
industrialization. Instead of an entrepreneurial bourgeois class of
self-made men schooled by centuries of self-government and
conscious struggle to storm 'the Bastilles of feudalism', Russia
had been provided with a privileged professional intelligentsia,
small in numbers, economically dependent and politically powerless. This diploma-carrying intelligentsia of journalists, doctors,
lawyers, professors and schoolteachers were allied with the
liberal gentry in the Constitutional-Democratic (Kadet) party,
which at the first sign of rural disorders in 1905 had swung over
to support the ancien régime. Trotsky's verdict on this 'hopelessly
retarded bourgeois intelligentsia' was scathing but eloquent:
'. . . suspended over an abyss of class contradictions, weighed
down with feudal traditions, and caught in a web of academic
prejudices, lacking all influence over the masses, and devoid of
all confidence in the future.'[13]

    If Russian bourgeois democracy was 'a head without a body',
its proletariat, concentrated in large masses in the factories and
industrial centres, had an economic and political importance out
of all proportion to its numbers. 'Scarcely emerged from the
cradle, the Russian proletariat found itself faced with the most
concentrated state power and the equally concentrated power of
capital. Craft prejudices and guild traditions had no power whatsoever over its consciousness.'[14] As a consequence it had taken
over the historical role of the petty bourgeois in previous European revolutions. It was imbued with a revolutionary energy and
freshness that directly derived from 'the absolutely specific
character' of the capitalist baptism which the new Russia had
received at the end of the nineteenth century. Hence the 1905
Russian revolution had not followed the West European models
of 1789 and 1848. The great French Revolution had been a truly
*national* revolution but also one in which the bourgeoisie had
become conscious of its messianic role on the world stage. By

1848, however, it used the old order as a defence against the masses who were trying to batter it down. No other social class, neither the petty bourgeoisie nor the peasantry, nor the democratic intelligentsia had been willing or able 'to kick the political corpse of the bourgeoisie out of its way'.[15] In Germany, and especially Austria in 1848, the students and workers had fought bravely on the barricades but they were unable to impel the democratic bourgeoisie to assume the national leadership.

Trotsky took his cue from Lassalle's observation that henceforth 'no struggle which is outwardly waged under the banner of national resurgence or bourgeois republicanism, can ever again be successful.'[16] The role of representing the nation as a whole and the universal goals of the class struggle would devolve on the new messianic class – the proletariat. The 1905 events in Russia pointed to a novel pattern adapted to the structural peculiarities of a backward society. 'In this bourgeois revolution without a revolutionary bourgeoisie, the proletariat is driven, by the internal progress of events, towards hegemony over the peasantry and to the struggle for state power.'[17]

Trotsky clearly recognized that the attitude of the peasantry would be crucial if the workers were to succeed in overthrowing the autocracy. A strategic alliance with the peasants was necessary, if only to win over the army and prevent the isolation of urban Russia as had happened in 1905. At the same time Trotsky also insisted that the hegemony of the towns over the countryside was a necessary feature of the history of modern capitalism and inevitably made the proletariat the principal revolutionary force. The peasantry was unorganized, scattered, removed from the nerve centres of politics and culture; it lacked any traditions of unified struggle, it was politically inexperienced and socially immature. But if the peasants were utterly incapable of any *independent* role (this was one of Trotsky's main objections to the Bolshevik formula of a dictatorship of the proletariat *and* the peasantry), they were equally sure to be a source of resistance to proletarian rule. In Trotsky's actual scenario of the permanent revolution, peasant opposition would inevitably arise as soon as a workers' government began to carry out socialist measures. The peasantry would reject any nationalization and collectivization of the land, it would even oppose legislation to protect the agricultural proletariat, indeed any reforms that threatened private property. In order to break down this resistance and win broader support

'the proletariat will be compelled to carry the class struggle into the villages and thus to destroy the slight community of interests undoubtedly to be found among the peasants. In its further advance the proletariat will have to find support by setting the poor villagers against the rich, the rural proletariat against the agrarian bourgeoisie. This will alienate the majority of the peasants from the workers' democracy ... The strong adherence of the peasants to private ownership, the primitiveness of their political conceptions, the limitations of the village horizon, their isolation from world-wide political ties and allegiances, are terrible obstacles in the way of revolutionary proletarian rule.'[18]

Faced with such resistance and with the inevitable opposition of capitalist employers to measures such as the eight-hour day the workers' government would be obliged to pursue a resolute *class* policy. In the case of industry, this would mean the 'expropriation of closed factories and the reorganization of production along socialized lines. There could be no question, Trotsky insisted, of a workers' democracy confining itself to making a 'bourgeois revolution' and then going into opposition once the democratic programme had been carried out.[19] On the contrary, it was precisely at this point that its historical task would begin – to break through the barriers of the bourgeois revolution and place the principle of collectivism on the agenda. But in laying this groundwork for socialist policies the *internal* momentum of the Russian proletariat to carry through the revolution would reach its limits. The workers' regime in a backward country like Russia would inevitably be crushed by counter-revolution 'the moment the peasantry turns its back on it. It will have no alternative but to link the fate of its political rule, and hence the fate of the whole Russian revolution with the fate of the socialist revolution in Europe.'[20]

Thus in order to convert its temporary dominance into 'a lasting socialist dictatorship' the Russian working class would depend on the 'direct state support of the European proletariat'. It could not maintain the *socialist* revolution on national foundations alone because it would be confronted with the hostility of all those bourgeois groups and the overwhelming mass of the peasantry who had supported it at an earlier stage. The only way out of this impasse lay in the victory of the European proletariat and the development of international revolution as a permanent process. World revolution as the consummation of this chain of events was therefore a necessity if the Russian proletariat was to remain in power. Trotsky clearly believed that it was also a realistic possibility and in the case of a general European war, absolutely inevitable.

It was on this general perspective that he staked his whole career and in the long run he was to be bitterly disappointed in his expectations. His exaggerated optimism stemmed from the belief that a successful Russian uprising would necessarily ignite the Western proletariat, infecting it with 'revolutionary idealism' and destroying the conservative inertia of the European Social Democratic parties.[21] Driven by its backwardness, the Russian working class would then be forced to carry through the struggle for political emancipation to new heights and would thereby initiate the process of liquidating capitalism on a world scale. The permanent revolution would become the signal for a single, continuous process of uprisings in Europe which alone could ensure the establishment of socialism.

Trotsky's work was a stirring call to action but it was seized and confiscated by the authorities almost as soon as it appeared. It reached few readers (even Lenin had not read it before 1917) and exercised no great influence on the inner-party debates in the pre-October period. Nevertheless, it retains its seminal importance not only because Stalin later made 'permanent revolution' the central plank in his indictment of 'Trotskyism', but because of its intrinsic merits as a remarkable, if flawed political prophecy. Through his bold application of the dialectical method Trotsky had turned Marx on his head. He had demonstrated that the proletariat could come to power in economically backward Russia more easily than in the advanced capitalist countries. He had shown that the economic and political prerequisites for a 'workers democracy' were not identical in all circumstances. In Russia the revolutionary consciousness of the working class had outstripped the material development of the country and made imminent a proletarian seizure of power. These arguments were regarded by Mensheviks and Bolsheviks alike as a denial of Marxism. The proletariat, according to the orthodox view, could not jump over the stage of the bourgeois-democratic Republic – its *political* hegemony could not precede that of the bourgeoisie. The semi-feudal heritage of Tsarism must first be overthrown so that a modern capitalist society could arise in Russia, creating the framework for a proletarian revolution in the fairly remote future.

Even Lenin accepted that historical development must proceed through an orderly progression of clearly defined stages adapted to the socio-economic environment. The original *Iskra* programme had envisaged the overthrow of the Tsarist autocracy and its replacement by a republic with a democratic constitution based on popular self-rule and universal suffrage. Admittedly, Lenin insisted that the peasantry was a revolutionary force and the natural ally of the proletariat. This divided him from the Mensheviks who looked to the liberal bourgeoisie as the spearhead of the coming democratic revolution. In April 1905 Lenin had indeed drawn up a new Bolshevik formula 'the revolutionary democratic dictatorship of the proletariat and peasantry' which emphasized that there would be no smooth, peaceful transition to a parliamentary system. In 1905 he envisaged a revolutionary coalition government, in which the proletariat was the *leader*, leaving open the possibility of a full-scale land distribution and pledging himself to extend the revolution to Europe. But he had not yet destroyed the framework of classical Russian Marxism which regarded the introduction of socialism as dependent on a high level of economic development, political freedom and mass organization.

From this perspective, Trotsky's theory of permanent revolution could only appear as an inadmissible attempt to leap over the orderly stages of development imposed by Russian economic backwardness. If the coming revolution was indeed 'bourgeois' in its objectives, as Lenin assumed, why should the alliance with the peasantry not maintain itself? Why should it not succeed

in a purely national context? Victory in the *bourgeois* as opposed
to the socialist revolution did not seem to depend on extending
it to the European or the world-wide arena.

Trotsky, on the other hand, rejected the orthodox Marxist
interpretation of historical epochs as a logical succession of inflexible social categories (feudalism, capitalism, socialism) or
forms of government (autocracy, bourgeois republic, proletarian
dictatorship). He was particularly severe on the Menshevist
theory of the Russian revolution in a speech made at the London
congress of the Russian Social Democractic Party in May 1907.
The Mensheviks, he argued, had invented a Russian bourgeois
democracy 'out of the rich fund of their own imagination'.[22]
There was no such urban bourgeoisie in Russia as had once
supported the Jacobins during the great French Revolution of
1789.

> 'Comrade Martynov [a leading Menshevik theoretician] has
> searched for it many a time, magnifying glass in hand. He
> has found schoolteachers in Saratov, lawyers in Petersburg,
> and statisticians in Moscow. He and all those who think
> like him, refuse to admit that in the Russian revolution it is
> the industrial proletariat which occupies the position once
> occupied by the artisanal semi-proletarian bourgeoisie of the
> sansculottes at the end of the eighteenth century.'[23]

The Menshevik analysis which regarded the bourgeois democracy, represented in the Kadet Party, as the natural claimant to
revolutionary power was based on a chimera. The first sign of
revolution would drive the Kadets with their 'most vulgar
bourgeois fear of street terror' into the camp of reaction.[24] The
Mensheviks had dressed up the Kadets for a historical role which
'they cannot, will not, do not want to play'.[25] This Menshevik
attitude completely overlooked the fact that Russian liberalism,
lacking any democratic backbone, was 'unparalleled in the
history of the bourgeois countries for its intrinsic shoddiness
and concentrated imbecility'.[26]

The Mensheviks had allegedly failed to grasp the inner logic
of the revolutionary development of the masses, the class dynamics
which made the *political* role of the workers infinitely greater
than their number; they were scholastics who looked at the

world through Marx's texts and produced endless quotations to prove the 'untimeliness' of proletarian hegemony. Against such 'barren reasoners' Trotsky answered with his own text from Lassalle.

'The instinct of the masses in revolution is generally much surer than the good sense of the intellectuals . . It is precisely the masses' lack of education that protects them from the underwater reefs of "sensible" behaviour . . . In the last analysis, revolution can only be made with the help of the masses and their passionate self-sacrifice.'[27]

Trotsky thoroughly approved Lassalle's contrast between the revolutionary instinct of the uneducated masses and the 'sensible' tactics of the 'bookkeepers of revolution'. A Marxist politician like Trotsky felt that revolution was his natural element, because it bore 'the veil of mystery from the true face of the social structure': the 'sensible' Menshevik such as Plekhanov, waited impatiently for the revolutionary 'fever' of the masses to be exhausted before proferring his pedagogical moralism. The Mensheviks were really *pessimists* at heart, whose 'absurd conclusions' derived from their equation of Russian economic and political development with that of Western Europe.[28] Failing to recognize Russia's 'special nature', they were unable to see that the weaknesses of its bourgeois democracy were the very source of proletarian strength and influence.

Trotsky's critique of the Bolshevik position was more restrained since he fundamentally shared Lenin's hostility to Russian liberalism. But he sharply disagreed with the Bolshevik formula of the 'revolutionary-democratic dictatorship of the proletariat and the peasantry'. This was a purely formalist attempt to resolve the contradiction between the low level of productive forces and the hegemony of the proletariat by imposing a 'self-limitation' on the working class. Trotsky predicted that this 'idyll of quasi-Marxist asceticism' would collapse utterly as soon as the prolaterariat seized power. There was no logical boundary-line which could keep the working class in the confines of a 'democratic dictatorship' if it shared power with the *muzhiks*. Conflicts would arise immediately which could only result 'either in the repression of the workers by the peasant party, or in the removal

of that party from power'.[29] The class-struggle could not be
dissolved in the form of a 'democratic' coalition in order to
establish a republican system. The Bolshevik concept of 'self-
limitation' (which Lenin finally abandoned in 1917) overlooked
the permanent character of the revolutionary process which
would not allow Russian society to achieve any equilibrium.
There could be no escape from the contradictions of backwardness
within the framework of a national revolution.

'The workers' government will from the start be faced with
the task of uniting its forces with those of the socialist
proletariat of Western Europe. Only in this way will its
temporary revolutionary hegemony become the prologue to
socialist dictatorship. This permanent revolution will become, for the Russian proletariat, a matter of class self-
preservation'.[30]

Following the October Revolution, Trotsky maintained that
despite an interruption of twelve years, his analysis had been
fully confirmed. This claim was justified in so far as it postulated
that the 'bourgeois' revolution would have to be made in Russia
*against* the resistance of the bourgeoisie itself. Moreover, the
theory of an unbroken chain between the bourgeois-democratic
and socialist tasks of the revolution which have to be fused in one
continuous process was in practice adopted by Lenin in April
1917. Here again Trotsky's leaping over the classic Marxist
schema of distinct and separate stages (to which Lenin was much
more attached) would appear to have been vindicated. Trotsky's
revolutionary strategy, because it recognized the *peculiarities* of
Russian historical development, did prove to have greater
predictive power than any other Marxist theory formulated
before 1917. On the other hand, because of Trotsky's failure to
grasp the organizational problem and the need to build a political
instrument capable of implementing such a strategy, his disembodied theories appeared irrelevant to contemporaries. His
isolation in the party prevented his grandiose perspective of the
permanent revolution from being taken seriously. Yet in 1917
his theory was to provide not only a link between Western
Marxism and backward, semi-Asiatic Russia but also a sophisticated justification for the Bolshevik coup.

CHAPTER FIVE

# INTERLUDE IN VIENNA

'In the old imperial, hierarchic, vain and futile
Vienna, the academic Marxists would refer to each
other with a sort of sensuous delight as "Herr
Doktor". Workers often called the academicians,
"Genosse Herr Doktor". During all the seven years
that I lived in Vienna, I never had a heart-to-heart
talk with any one of this upper group, although I was
a member of the Austrian Social Democracy,
attended their meetings, took part in their demonstrations, contributed to their publications, and sometimes made short speeches in German.'

Leon Trotsky, *My Life*


From 1907 to 1914, Trotsky lived in Vienna, following a dramatic
escape from Siberia and brief stays in London and Berlin. He
took up residence in a working-class suburb of the city with his
wife and two young sons. Politically, these were seven lean years
for Trotsky in which he occupied himself mainly with radical
journalism, editing a Russian socialist bi-monthly called *Pravda*
(The Truth), committed to the idea that 'the unity of the class
struggle must stand above all differences of opinion and factions'.
The paper was smuggled into Russia either across the Galician
border or by way of the Black Sea. Its chief contributor was Adolf
Joffe (later a leading Bolshevik diplomat) with whom Trotsky
struck up one of his few close and enduring personal friendships.
It was through Joffe (who suffered from frequent nervous break-
downs and was a patient of the Viennese psychologist Alfred
Adler) that Trotsky first became acquainted with psychoanalysis.[1]
It was this early contact with the new science that was being
pioneered in Vienna that was at the origin of Trotsky's later

fascination with Freud and his attempts to reconcile psychoanalysis with Marxism.

Apart from Joffe, *Pravda*'s contributors included a number of
other intellectuals such as Uritsky and David Ryazanov (the
founder of the Marx-Engels Institute in Moscow) who subsequently became prominent in the Bolshevik Party. But the
paper was singularly unsuccessful in its main objective to unite
the divided factions of Russian Social Democracy and restore
harmony to the ranks. All Trotsky's efforts to rally an anti-
Bolshevik coalition around his own person were crowned with
failure. In the twisting maze of pre-war Russian émigré squabbles
and internal party politics he demonstrated an incapacity for
manoeuvre which already foreshadowed his fall from power
many years later. His feud with Lenin continued and was
aggravated by the fact that Trotsky carried his campaign into
the German socialist press, presenting the Bolshevik émigré
clique as conspiratorial intriguers who were sabotaging the unity
of the Russian party.[2] Though he approved of Bolshevik hosility
to the 'liquidators' (those who had turned their back on the
underground struggle in Russia) Trotsky allied himself with the
Mensheviks when Lenin demanded the expulsion of these
dissenters from the party. His enmity towards liberalism and his
activist temperament made him a potential Bolshevik, but his
personal resentment towards Lenin and long association with
Martov and Axelrod kept him in the Menshevik camp on most
issues. In seeking to establish a 'synthesis' between Bolsheviks
and Mensheviks, Trotsky merely fuelled the antagonism of the
former and aroused the distrust of his new allies.[3]

But if the Vienna years deepened Trotsky's political isolation
they found him receptive to a host of new intellectual and
artistic influences which profoundly shaped his personal development. In particular they exposed him to the world of European
Social Democracy, opened up contacts with many of its leaders
and greatly extended his knowledge of their social and cultural
milieu. In this period of relative calm and sterility on the political
front, which appeared to negate all Trotsky's visionary perspectives of 'permanent revolution', his lifestyle became that of
a bohemian *littérateur*. He frequented literary gatherings, went to

museums, indulged in endless conversations in the cafés of
Vienna, travelled around Europe and even became a Balkans
war-correspondent for the Russian liberal newspaper, *Kievskaya
Mysl*. This second period of exile greatly increased his admiration
and sensitivity for European culture but produced in him an
intensely ambivalent attitude towards the role of intellectuals and
*literati* in politics. Though increasingly drawn to bohemian and
intellectual circles, his long-standing distrust of the vacillating
Russian intelligentsia was now aggravated by his perception of
the special status and bourgeois comforts which their counterparts enjoyed in Central European society.

Ironically enough, Trotsky tended to accuse the intellectuals
of the very same vices – personal ambition, individualism, lack of
discipline, indifference to organization, self-styled messianism
and opportunism – with which he was later saddled by his
adversaries in the Russian party.[4] Nevertheless, he distinguished
carefully between the type of the Russian *intelligent* and the
bourgeois intellectuals who joined the labour movement in
Central and Western Europe. Both groups were convinced of
their own intellectual superiority, but only in Russia had the
rootlessness and alienation of the intelligentsia divorced it completely from social realities. The Russian *intelligent* lived off a
borrowed Western culture which he tended to transform into
abstract metaphysical concepts: radical intellectuals in the West
were more organically tied to the programmes and class-interests
of the labour movement, less prone to escape into an ethereal
realm of ideas and doctrinaire schemes to transform society. The
estrangement of the Russian intellectuals from the masses led
them to exaggerate their sense of 'chosenness' and to indulge in
delusions of grandeur.[5] Since the early nineteenth century they
had acted by proxy for weakly-developed or non-existent social
classes. Thus, the aristocratic Decembrists substituted themselves
for the 'rabble', the Populists for the peasantry and the Marxist
intelligentsia for the industrial proletariat.[6] This insight was one
of the main factors behind Trotsky's pre-war critique of the
vanguard élitism cultivated by the Bolshevik Party.

In Western and Central Europe, on the other hand, with its
highly-developed class structures and historic traditions of

political liberty, the danger of substitutionism did not exist. On the contrary, the problem here was the organizational conservatism and inertia of the proletarian mass parties which encouraged a bureaucratic, philistine psychology in the socialist intelligentsia. During his Vienna years, Trotsky, while keenly aware of these defects in European socialism, responded enthusiastically to the more open democratic spirit of the Western labour movements. With all their faults they corresponded more closely to his own vision of a self-directed, grassroots mass movement than the narrow, rigid disciplines of a clandestine party structure as advocated by Lenin. German Socialism especially impressed Trotsky, not only because it was *the* leading party of the Second International but also as the fount of all theoretical wisdom. In his autobiography, he writes:

'For us Russians the German Social Democracy was mother, teacher, and living example. We idealized it from a distance. The names of Bebel and Kautsky were pronounced reverently. In spite of my disturbing theoretical premonitions ... I was undeniably under its spell. This was heightened by the fact that I lived in Vienna, and when I visited Berlin off and on, I would . . console myself: No, Berlin is not Vienna.'[7]

Trotsky's first meeting in Berlin with Karl Kautsky, the 'Pope' of the Second International, was recalled with almost boyish excitement. Like Lenin and all the Russian socialists, Trotsky looked up to the German theoretician as the ultimate authority on questions of Marxist theory. He contributed articles to his periodical, *Die Neue Zeit* (and also to the Berlin socialist daily, *Vorwärts*) and wrote him friendly, deferential letters.[8] Following the outbreak of World War I, and even more after the October Revolution, Trotsky was brutally to settle his accounts with his former 'teacher', the 'renegade Kautsky', as Lenin now called him. Before the war, he had defended Kautsky against the charge of 'dogmatism', arguing that he had 'no rival in his capacity to single out from the empirical chaos of history its *general, fundamental* tendencies'.[9] In the pre-1914 era Trotsky admired this capacity for abstraction and generalization; later he came to see in Kautsky's Marxism 'a finished system' divorced from the living experience of revolution. Kautskyism, he concluded, was a purely theoretical radicalism of a deeply opportunist character which already contained within it the seeds of its 'social-patriotic' degeneration during the First World War.[10] In My Life the verdict pronounced on Kautsky's strategy of wearing out the class enemy was altogether merciless.

'Kautsky's line was that of an increasingly firm adaptation to the existing system. In the process what was 'worn out' was not bourgeois society, but the revolutionary idealism of the masses of workers. All the philistines, all the officials, all the climbers sided with Kautsky, who was weaving for them the intellectual garments with which to hide their nakedness'.[11]

Trotsky's pen-portrait of the veteran socialist leader was even more jaundiced. Kautsky's angular, dry mind, 'lacking in nimbleness and psychological insight' had disappointed him from the outset. 'His evaluations were schematic, his jokes trite.'[12] Such verdicts, delivered long after Trotsky's break with the Second International, must be treated with considerable scepticism. Both Lenin and Trotsky, embittered by Kautsky's severe criticisms of the October Revolution, were naturally reluctant to acknowledge the extent of their intellectual debt to the old master.[13] From his autobiography, one would never guess that Trotsky's closest ties before 1914 were to 'centrists' in the German party (SPD) such as Kautsky, Bebel and Hilferding rather than to the left-wing Marxists like Rosa Luxemburg and Karl Liebknecht. Though Rosa Luxemburg's intransigent character and attitudes to political issues coincided in so many ways with Trotsky, they remained distant before 1914. Similarly, he was not initially much attracted to the passionate idealism of Karl Liebknecht, whom he later bracketed with Lenin and Rosa Luxemburg as the intellectual inspiration for the Fourth International. In 1919, following the brutal murder of Liebknecht and Luxemburg in the aborted Spartacist rising, Trotsky wrote an ecstatic eulogy of these two co-founders of the German Communist Party. Brave warriors of the world proletariat, comrades-in-arms, saint-like heroes who symbolized socialist internationalism in its pristine purity, Karl and Rosa were now mystically transposed into 'magnificent figures who tower over all humanity'.[14]

Trotsky liked to contrast Liebknecht's 'peerless moral stature' and revolutionary courage to the 'honest mediocrity' of Hugo Haase, the centrist politician who succeeded Bebel as leader of the SPD.[15] He had in fact known Haase much better than Liebknecht and valued his considerateness in personal relations yet subsequently dismissed him as 'a provincial democrat without revolutionary temperament or theoretical outlook'.[16] Karl Liebknecht, on the other hand, appeared in retrospect as a giant lost among pygmies whose 'authentic and profoundly revolutionary instinct always directed him . . . on to the correct path.' A genuine revolutionary and sincere internationalist, 'he stood out sharply against a background of the decorous, impersonal and monotonous party bureaucracy.'[17] Trotsky's sketch of Liebknecht revealed his personal preference for dashing men of action over vacillating, Hamlet-like intellectuals. 'His was an impulsive, passionate and heroic nature; he had, moreover, real political intuition, a sense of the masses and of the situation, and an incomparable courage of initiative.'[18]

Trotsky's best biographical profiles of the pre-war leaders of the Socialist International were devoted to its three most important figures, August Bebel, Jean Jaurès and Victor Adler. Each portrait is in its way a minor journalistic masterpiece, capturing a sense of time and place, of social types, national traditions, diverse life-styles and subtle shadings of personality. Trotsky displays a remarkable literary gift, an ability to root individual traits in a concrete atmosphere and cultural milieu, a fascination with political settings and psychological observation. Beyond their artistic qualities these profiles also reveal the young Trotsky's perceptions of the historical structures and traditions of European Social Democracy, their strengths and weaknesses. Perhaps because they deal more objectively with leading contemporaries whom Trotsky had studied with sympathetic attention, they appear more rounded and balanced than his sketches of the lesser figures.

With the death of Bebel and Jaurès on the eve of World War I, Trotsky sensed that an entire epoch of European Social Democracy had passed into history. Its last living links with an earlier, more heroic phase of development had faded. In Bebel's personality was embodied the stubborn, unswerving movement of a new class rising from below – its slow, irresistible growth, concentration on a single goal and its belief that events would lead inevitably to a decisive and triumphant dénouement. The undisputed leader of the German proletariat for nearly half a century, Bebel's qualities reflected a class that 'gets its learning during its spare hours, values every minute, and absorbs voraciously only what is strictly necessary . . .'[19] Completely removed from any rhetorical excesses and aesthetic niceties, Bebel 'knew no such thing as expending mental energy on an object which did not immediately serve some practical purpose'.[20] His spiritual profile was that of a plebeian democrat, a materialist and an irreconcilable supporter of Marxist principles, whereas Jean Jaurès with his poetic imagination and aristocratic features, his eclectic idealism and reformist tactics embodied the inspired flights of the Latin temperament. 'Bebel and Jaurès each in his own way reflected their era but as men of genius they were both a head above it . . . they left the scene opportunely so affording history the opportunity of conducting in a pure form an experiment on the reaction of a catastrophe upon an uncatastrophic consciousness'.[21]

Trotsky's assessment of Jaurès, the French socialist tribune, was notable for its generosity towards a leader who did not hesitate to pursue backstage deals and to indulge in the politics of opportunism. The riddle of Jaurès's political influence in the Third Republic lay in the power of the *revolutionary tradition*, just as the French working class itself represented a force far greater than its level of organization or parliamentary strength. Jaurès, the practical politician and shrewd horse-trader, was at the same time a selfless and ardent enthusiast. He personified the French art of oratorical technique, 'a common heritage which they adopt without effort and outside of which they are as inconceivable as a "respectable" man without formal dress'.[22] But beyond this rich technique, behind this wonderful voice and the profuse, athletic gestures lay 'the *genius's naïveté* of his enthusiasm' which brought Jaurès close to the masses. At once revolutionary *and* opportunist, a figure of action who possessed the élan of the moment, the French leader reflected the contradictions of his society and of his age. His spontaneous extravagance gave spirit, passion and verve to his oratory but by the same token his politics lacked proportion. 'Among his gifts Jaurès lacks one: the ability to *wait* . . . He wants immediately to switch over to the jangling coinage of practical success, to the great traditions and the great opportunities.'[25]

Curiously enough, Trotsky diagnosed this same fault of impatience in Rosa Luxemburg, yet it was one for which he had some indulgence even, as in the case of Jaurès, when it was linked to reformist opportunism. In the political *impatience* of the great French orator he recognized his own inner drives. For this reason he found it easier to forgive Jaurès's gradualist policies, his democratic 'idealism', his republican mystique and integration in the world of bourgeois politics. The genius of Jaurès's passion was revealed in the Dreyfus case, the weakness of his ideology in his advocacy of class collaboration. But this 'athlete of the idea', this supreme incarnation of self-confident creative power and *moral* force could not be judged in terms of a narrow-minded Marxist orthodoxy. Trotsky's excited admiration for Jaurès's oratorical creations, his sensitivity to both the human and the aesthetic qualities of the great French tribune, reveals a dimension that transcends mere politics. Here he found his supreme model, the orator who could simultaneously play on thought, sensibility and will, who stood above his art 'as a craftsman is higher than his tool'. In Jaurès he perceived 'a *human* force of destruction and creation', a devilish and a genuinely divine power of the word made flesh and subordinated to his supreme force – the will to action. The mature Trotsky who was to become *the* spellbinding orator of the Russian Revolution had evidently learnt his art while listening to Jaurès at international socialist congresses and at sessions of the National Assembly in Paris.

'And each time I would listen to him as if for the first time. He did not accumulate set clichés, he never basically repeated himself, each time he rediscovered himself and each time he mobilized anew the many-sided forces of his spirit . . . He would blast crags, roar and shake his audience but he never deafened himself, always kept his guard and astutely captured every comment, snatched it up, parrying the criticism at times without mercy like a hurricane sweeping all resistance from its path and at times magnanimously and tenderly like a tutor or an elder brother.'[24]

But of all the great figures of the Second International, it was Victor Adler, the leader of the Austrian socialists, whom Trotsky knew most intimately. Adler had befriended him when he had first arrived in 1902 as a penniless exile in Vienna and disturbed the *Doktor*'s Sunday rest.[25] It was again Adler (who frequently helped Russian émigrés with money, passports and addresses) whom he consulted before returning to Russia in 1905. Finally, in 1914, it was on his advice that Trotsky left Vienna for Zurich to avoid possible arrest. Politically far removed from this pragmatic master of compromise, Trotsky nonetheless portrayed him sympathetically as a shrewd tactician, a man of great personal warmth and charm, with a powerful, analytical mind.

'Making, as the German expression has it, a virtue out of necessity, Adler learnt how to draw political advantage from the unfavourable Austrian conditions: he developed his rich political intuition to perfection, cultivated an excellent political vision and made tactical improvization a principle guarantee of success.'[26]

Adler's tactical flair derived from a cunning resourcefulness in balancing firmness and moderation within his own party and a finely-tuned sensitivity to the moods of the masses. He knew how to harness the energy and idealism of the Austrian proletariat to the structural necessity for a powerful organizational apparatus, while at the same time overcoming the centrifugal tendencies inherent in a multi-national movement. He knew when to follow the masses and when to lead them 'by dint of his personal superiority, his resources of internal diplomacy and his psychological understanding of men'.[27]

A politician from head to foot, indifferent to all fanaticism and verbal flourishes, Adler was deeply rooted not only in Austria-Hungary but also in the organizational mechanism of which he was the nub. Yet the routinism and creeping bureaucracy, the conservative immobility and inertia that Trotsky sensed in the German and Austrian labour parties gradually sapped even the

journalistic and agitational skills of a Victor Adler. The parliamentary work, the complex administrative and financial under-
takings, the arduous backstage work of negotiation – all these
pressures inevitably produced a trend towards 'opportunist
degeneration'. Adler's opportunism superficially resembled that
of Jaurès but in his psychology, his political style and oratory
he was altogether different. Gifted with an acute analytical mind
and averse to all decorativeness, he was a sceptic who regarded
the craft of the political prophet as 'a thankless one and especially
so in Austria'. Trotsky caught to perfection Adler's sense of
frustration at operating in the hopeless confusion and *schlamperei*
of the late Habsburg Empire, his resigned pessimism at the
follies of human nature. In a moment of self-mocking despair he
has Adler tell him: 'Perhaps it is precisely the fact that I learnt
in good time how to deal with the inmates of a psychiatric
hospital that prepared me for dealing with Austrian political
figures.'[28]

Adler's oratory showed a fine gift for *personal* characterization
and for grasping the inner logic of a situation. His greatest
weapon was the devastating irony with which he exposed the
stupidity of his opponents. No other socialist leader could match
his psychiatric insights and rare ability to play on the 'inner
keyboard' of the human soul. 'As a result,' Trotsky cleverly
observed, 'a conversation with him was not only the highest
pleasure but also a perpetual anxiety.'[29]

Trotsky's pre-war portrait of Victor Adler significantly omitted
any critique of his politics, stressing instead 'the inexhaustible
generosity of his nature' and his remarkable human qualities. By
October 1916 the tone had become sharper following the sensa-
tional news that his son Friedrich Adler (a friend of Trotsky) had
assassinated the Austrian minister-president. Trotsky depicted
the younger Adler's deed as a despairing protest against the
complacent, social-patriotism of his father's Party. Victor Adler
had become 'the first and the greatest victim' of his own Austrian
method of adopting temporizing half-measures instead of a
resolute, offensive policy which could unite the multi-racial
Austro-Hungarian proletariat. The Austrian Socialist Party had
succumbed to the infections of nationalism, to petty careerism

and 'unbridled servility towards the Austro-Hungarian state'.[30] This was not directly the fault of Victor Adler himself who was 'in all respects far above the rest of his colleagues' but rather of the mediocrities, lobby politicians and official bosses around him who had become sworn enemies of any revolutionary initiative or mass action. Nonetheless, Victor Adler's passivity in face of the rampant chauvinism of his collaborators, his tolerance towards the growing nationalist mood had helped to corrode Austrian Social Democracy to its very core. This was the negative side of Victor Adler's ironic scepticism – its lack of a broad political view of the future – which placed him at the opposite pole to Trotsky's own robust optimism.

Among the younger generation of Austro-Marxists whom he learned to know during his stay in Vienna, Trotsky's closest personal friend was Rudolf Hilferding. Subsequently he claimed that there was no moral or political basis for their friendship but this was after their break. It was Hilferding who introduced him to Otto Bauer, Max Adler and Karl Renner, the most talented theoreticians of the Viennese Marxist school. Trotsky's assessment of this group is extraordinarily harsh, even vitriolic, and altogether lacking in the objectivity and balance with which he described the veteran leaders of the Second International. In My Life, all the frustrations and resentments of his Vienna years seem to be transferred to the younger socialist élite he encountered in the coffee-houses of the Imperial capital. He invariably construed their frivolous, easy-going manner as smug complacency and self-satisfaction. He felt that he could detect a tone of philistinism 'in the quality of their voices'. In his reaction to these 'academics' one can sense all the suppressed indignation of a young Russian émigré who had received his Marxist education not at the Imperial University of Vienna but in Tsarist prisons and Siberian exile. Trotsky conceded that the Austro-Marxists were 'well-educated people whose knowledge of various subjects was superior to mine' but they 'represented the type that was furthest from that of the revolutionary'.[31] Late one night, sitting with Karl Renner (future Chancellor of Austria) in a Viennese café, Trotsky was appalled at the 'civility' and cold 'indifference' with which his interlocutor discussed the future prospects of a

Russian revolution. This conversation was enough to convince him that Renner 'was as far from revolutionary dialectics as the most conservative Egyptian pharaoh'.

The Austro-Marxists, Trotsky concluded, might be capable of writing competent theoretical articles but 'to me they were strangers'. In informal talks they revealed either 'undisguised chauvinsm or the bragging of a petty proprietor, or holy terror of the police, or vileness towards women'.[32] They were not revolutionaries but philistines 'who had learned certain parts of Marx's theory as one might study law' and lived off the interest that *Das Kapital* yielded them. They used the same formulas as Trotsky yet gave quite different meanings to identical concepts. They believed neither in revolution nor in war in spite of all their May Day manifestos. This 'ridiculous mandarin attitude of the Vienna academists', combined with their 'shameless' chauvinism, infuriated Trotsky as almost no other instance of social-democratic reformism. With grim satisfaction he noted that 'history had already poised its gigantic soldier's boot over the ant-heap in which they were rushing about with such self-abandon'.[33]

The scarcely veiled hostility behind Trotsky's description of the Viennese Marxists clearly suggests a backward projection of later Bolshevik attitudes. At the time, the soft, cosy *Gemütlichkeit* of the Viennese atmosphere did not grate on Trotsky nearly as much as he implied. No doubt the men with whom he spent his evenings in the Café Central may have seemed somewhat patronizing in their attitudes to the highly-strung, intense young Russian émigré but he nonetheless sought their company, visited their workers' meetings and contributed to their journals. Perhaps the Bolshevik Commissar of later years did not like to think of himself as having hobnobbed with these socialist intellectuals who had singularly failed to live up to his expectations. Nevertheless, if we are to believe his own account, there was one important gain for Trotsky during his Vienna years: he read the correspondence of Marx and Engels and discovered that he was bound to them by a direct inward affinity. It was not so much a theoretical as a 'psychological revelation'. The passage deserves quoting in full for it is indeed an unconscious self-portrait of the mature Trotsky as he wished to be seen by others. 'Marx and Engels were revolutionaries through and through. But they had not the slightest trace of sectarianism or asceticism. Both of them, and especially Engels, could at any time say of themselves that nothing human was strange to them. But their revolutionary outlook lifted them always above the hazards of fate and the works of men. Pettiness was incompatible not only with their personalities, but with their presences. Their appreciations, sympathies, jests – even when most commonplace – are always touched by the rarefied air of spiritual nobility. They may pass deadly criticism on a man, but they will never deal in tittle-tattle. They can be ruthless, but not treacherous. For outward glamour, titles, or rank they have nothing but cool contempt. What philistines and vulgarians considered aristocratic in them was really only their revolutionary superiority. Its most important characteristic is a complete and ingrained independence of official public opinion at all times and under all conditions.'[34]

The young Russian exile in the Café Central who harboured these lofty thoughts would shortly become the leader of a victorious revolution. Its triumph would coincide with the death-agony of that old imperial Vienna whose futility he described with such implacable sarcasm.

## CHAPTER SIX

# RED PETROGRAD

'Had I not been present in 1917 in Petersburg, the
October Revolution would still have taken place –
*on the condition that Lenin was present and in command.* If
neither Lenin nor I had been present in Petersburg,
there would have been no October Revolution: the
leadership of the Bolshevik Party would have prevented it from occurring – of this I have not the
slightest doubt! If Lenin had not been in Petersburg,
I doubt whether I could have managed to overcome
the resistance of the Bolshevik leaders.'

Leon Trotsky, *Diary in Exile*

Trotsky was astonished at the patriotic enthusiasm of the masses
in Austria-Hungary following the outbreak of the First World
War. Yet as he strode along the Ringstrasse in Vienna he thought
he detected in the festive mood of the crowds 'something
familiar to me from the October days of 1905 in St. Petersburg'.[1]
War and revolution were indeed intimately connected for they
forced life from the beaten track, even if their immediate effects
were exactly the opposite. But the speedy capitulation of the
German (and Austrian) Social Democracies in the face of nationalist militarism shook him to the core – already in August 1914 he
recognized that the Second International was dead. In October
1914, while living in Zurich, he wrote his pamphlet *War and the
International* which indignantly repudiated the pro-war policy of
the SPD. 'We owe a great deal to the German Social Democracy.
We have all gone through its school; we have learned from its
successes as well as its mistakes . . .'[2] But in the name of Russian
socialism, Trotsky declared, and 'out of respect to this past, and
all the more so out of respect to the future', it was imperative to

spurn 'the injection of imperialist poison into the German and Austrian proletariat'. The war of 1914 signified the end of an epoch of 'national' parties whose organization, activity and psychology pledged them to the defence of conservative state structures. '... In their historical fall the nation-states have dragged down with them the national socialist parties'.[3] But Trotsky saw no grounds for despair – *'the epoch which we are entering will be our epoch'* – it would create amidst the hellish music of death a new International. The war heralded the inevitable collapse of the nation-state as a self-contained economic arena and disintegration of the capitalist system. It would drive the international proletariat onto the road of socialist revolution to create 'a new, more powerful and stable fatherland – the republican *United States of Europe*, as a transition to the United States of the World'.[4]

Lenin's own theses, elaborated in Switzerland, resembled this prognosis insofar as he expected, like Trotsky, that at the end of the war Europe would be seized by proletarian revolution. But Lenin objected to an ambiguous formula like 'the United States of Europe' and to the implication that the Russian revolution could only be part of a *simultaneous* European upheaval. He now suggested that, because of 'the unevenness of economic and political development', a rising in Russia might succeed before it did in Europe – a hypothesis also foreseen in Trotsky's concept of permanent revolution. Trotsky's rejoinder was to categorically reject that 'national revolutionary messianic mood which prompts one to see one's own nation-state as destined to lead mankind to socialism'.[5] The revolution would have to *begin* on a national basis but it could not be concluded in isolation from the rest of Europe. This was in fact a position which Lenin also shared.

As a result of the war the past differences between Lenin and Trotsky were clearly beginning to narrow, though the latter's collaboration with Martov and the Mensheviks in Paris on *Nashe Slovo* was a continuous source of friction. At the Zimmerwald Conference in September 1915 (the stirring manifesto was written by Trotsky), in spite of some personal antagonism they found themselves in agreement except over Lenin's tactics of revolutionary defeatism. Some of Trotsky's collaborators now began to argue that the Leninists were the only active and consistently internationalist force in the Russian labour movement, able to successfully resist the tide of social-patriotism.[6] These arguments must have impressed Trotsky, though in his autobiography he presents the rapprochement with Lenin as an inevitable result of conclusions which he had reached 'on the basis of my own premises and my own revolutionary experience'.[7]

'In New York at the beginning of March 1917 I wrote a series of articles dealing with the class forces and perspectives of the Russian Revolution. At that very time Lenin, in Geneva, was sending to Petrograd his *Letters from Afar*. And both of us, though we were writing in different parts of the world and were separated by an ocean, gave the same analysis and the same forecast. On every one of the principal questions, such as the attitude towards the peasantry, towards the bourgeoisie, the Provisional government, the war, and the world revolution, our views were completely identical.'[8]

According to Trotsky, Lenin's arrival in Petrograd in April 1917 and the theses he then put forward were a decisive break with the 'Old Bolshevism'. The Bolshevik Old Guard and the editors of the Petrograd *Pravda*, Stalin and Kamenev, were stunned by Lenin's sudden advocacy of an immediate transition to the socialist revolution. For a brief period they even accused Lenin of 'Trotskyism', Kamenev in particular did this openly, others more cautiously behind the scenes. 'I had to argue', Trotsky writes, 'that Lenin had not come over to my point of view, but had developed his own, and that the course of events ... had revealed the essential identity of our views.'[9]

Trotsky does not actually say that the Bolshevik leader adopted the theory of permanent revolution (though Trotskyists have frequently implied this) but rather that in his April theses Lenin had independently advanced a perspective and a strategy which paralleled his own. This is important to remember because in April 1917 Lenin still mistakenly identified 'Trotskyism' with Parvus's old slogan 'No Tsar, a workers' government', and evidently had no first-hand knowledge of the theory of permanent revolution. Significantly, after 1917 Lenin never mentioned the theory, nor did he directly comment on the character of Trotsky's Marxism or even on the latter's conversion to Bolshevism. This silence is curious but it has not prevented many historians (including those far removed from Trotskyism) from assuming without warrant that Lenin accepted the theory, just as Trotsky had adopted the Bolshevik standpoint on Party organization. Early in April 1917, it is true, Lenin wrote that anyone who still used the Old Bolshevik formula of the 'revolutionary democratic dictatorship of the proletariat and peasantry' was out of touch with life. Indeed he even advocated putting such people 'into an archive for the rarities of pre-revolutionary Bolshevism'.[10]

Why then this sudden volte-face? What made Lenin abandon his previous insistence that the bourgeois democratic revolution must be followed through to the end? Lenin was, in effect, claiming that, with the overthrow of Tsarism in February 1917, the bourgeois-democratic revolution was *already completed* and the newly constituted Soviets of Workers Deputies now represented 'the *only possible* form of revolutionary government'. However, these Soviets under Menshevik and Social Revolutionary domination were for the present moment 'defencist' – they supported the Provisional Government and the continuation of the war. The peasantry, also, appeared, at least in its upper layers, to be moving to the right. The revolution could, therefore, only be driven forward by carrying the class war into the villages, winning over the poorer peasantry and abandoning all slogans about a 'democratic' dictatorship. This 'hard' line was in fact close enough to Trotsky[11] and stemmed from Lenin's apparent loss of faith in the revolutionary potential of the peasantry as a whole. This necessarily made any seizure of power more dependent on socialist revolution in Europe as Trotsky had all along maintained.

Nevertheless, Lenin also developed another more democratic policy line, modelled on the Soviets and the historical precedent of the Paris Commune – whose political theory was expounded in *State and Revolution*. Here the role of the Bolshevik Party was scarcely mentioned and the revolution was imagined as a spontaneous upsurge of the majority of the population which would sweep away the old government apparatus, its bureaucracy, army and police. Both strategies, however contradictory, envisaged a 'proletarian dictatorship' in Russia whose goal was to open up a breach in the global front of imperialist capitalism and blaze a trail for workers in other countries. The two-stage theory of revolution was explicitly abandoned though not a peasant-oriented policy which called for immediate and total land distribution. Lenin did now advocate the seizure of power regardless of the level of socio-economic development but he never shared Trotsky's absolute belief in the necessity of a European revolution to save the Russian proletariat from drowning in an ocean of petty-bourgeois *muzhiks*. Lenin's tactical adjustments did not, therefore, mean that he had rallied to the concept of 'permanent revolution' (Trotsky undoubtedly overestimated the extent of the shift), but they did entail an *insurrectional* policy which greatly reduced the disagreements between the two men. Much more dramatic, however, was the extent of Trotsky's movement towards Lenin. He now recognized in the Bolshevik party the *missing link* in his own theory without which the insurrection could not be achieved. Prior to 1917, the anti-Bolshevik Trotsky had looked to the spontaneous action of the revolutionary masses and not to the *vanguard* party as the decisive historical agent of change. But during the October Revolution he was irrevocably converted to Lenin's theory of vanguard action and to the seizure of power by an organized minority in the name of the working class.

The rapprochement occurred gradually in the months following Trotsky's arrival in Petrograd on 4 May 1917. He was still regarded with some suspicion by both Bolsheviks and Mensheviks. His first speech before the Petrograd Soviet created a minor sensation by opposing socialist participation in the Provisional government and proclaiming 'all power to the Soviets'. Trotsky declared that the February Revolution had opened a new epoch 'an epoch of blood and iron, not in a war of nations, but in a war of the oppressed classes against the domineering classes'.[12] He warned the Soviet not to trust the Russian bourgeoisie but to rely on its own revolutionary strength, concluding with a rousing appeal: 'Long live the Russian Revolution as the prologue to the world revolution!'[13] His tone, his slogans and his emphasis on the dual power situation in Russia were already very close to the line being advocated by Lenin and the Bolshevik Party. On May 7, Trotsky met Lenin for the first time since the Zimmerwald Conference. With Trotsky's abandonment of 'conciliationism', their different roads as revolutionary internationalists seemed at last to have converged. But whereas Lenin stood at the helm of a tightly-knit disciplined party, Trotsky had behind him only a very small, though admittedly gifted circle of intellectuals grouped in the Inter-Borough Organization (*Mezhrayonka*). It included men like Ryazanov, Joffe, Uritsky, Volodarsky, Lunacharsky and Manuilsky who were later to rise high in the Bolshevik Party, but it offered no independent base for action.

At a second meeting on May 10, Lenin, ignoring past controversies, generously offered Trotsky and his supporters entry into the Bolshevik Party and positions in its leading bodies.[14] Trotsky was not yet ready to call himself a Bolshevik and proposed instead a merger into a new party which would adopt a new name. This suggestion, the last echo of his long years of resistance to Lenin, reflected that mixture of personal pride, compounded of vanity and the absolute need for intellectual independence, which had hitherto excluded him from the Bolshevik Party. The practical politics of insurrection were soon to sweep aside the old theoretical differences, though they would re-emerge with a vengeance in the aftermath of Lenin's death.

In the next few months before the October rising, Trotsky made his mark primarily as an agitator and speaker at mass meetings in the capital. He immediately established a remarkable rapport with the Petrograd masses and with the sailors at the Kronstadt naval base who faithfully followed and even idolized him. Once again, as in 1905, Trotsky's eloquence, his dramatic flair and gifts of improvisation made him irreplaceable. Anatoly Lunacharsky (the future People's Commissar of Education) whose own talent in this field was considerable and who addressed innumerable meetings together with Trotsky, considered him the equal of Jean Jaurès and 'probably the greatest orator of our times'. The eloquence which was to electrify the Petrograd

masses and the soldiers of the Red Army in the civil war, were
all summed up in this assessment by Lunacharsky:
    'Effective presence, beautiful broad gesture, mighty rhythm
    of speech, loud absolutely tireless voice, wonderful com-
    pactness, literariness of phrase, wealth of imagery, scorching
    irony, flowing pathos, an absolutely extraordinary logic,
    really steel-like in its clarity – those are the qualities of
    Trotsky's speech.'[15]
Lunacharksy was far from blind to Trotsky's faults. He noted
'. . . a tremendous imperiousness and a kind of inability or un-
willingness to be at all caressing and attentive to people, an
absence of that charm which always surrounded Lenin.'[16] Trotsky,
he observed, was ever glancing into the mirror of history, as if
preoccupied with what posterity would think of him. 'Trotsky
treasures his historic role, and would undoubtedly be ready to
make any personal sacrifice, not by any means excluding the
sacrifice of his own life, in order to remain in the memory of
mankind with the halo of a genuine revolutionary leader.'[17]

    Trotsky's prickly, self-centred personality, his magniloquence,
which seemed alien to the whole Bolshevik tradition, still grated
on the Old Guard and obviously made him difficult to work with
in political groups. But as Lunacharsky observed, 'in the ocean
of historic events where such personal features lose their importance, only his favourable side came to the front.' This assessment was almost exactly right. Trotsky more than any other
figure of the Russian revolution undoubtedly thrived on the
presence of the dark, huddled masses before him. The vigour
and élan of his speech received something akin to an electric
charge from this contact, rousing his mental energies in a way
that party debate or purely theoretical discussion never altogether
succeeded in doing. There is a marvellous passage in *My Life*
where Trotsky describes how each new meeting would awaken
such hidden reserves of nervous energy, how he would draw
sustenance from the spirit of the gathered multitudes and arguments would come rushing up from his subconscious to meet
the mood of his listeners. His particular fortress was the Modern
Circus in Petrograd where he usually spoke in the evenings, often
late at night.

'My audience was composed of workers, soldiers, hard-working mothers, street urchins – the oppressed underdogs of the capital. Every square inch was filled, every human body compressed to its limit. Young boys sat on their fathers' shoulders; infants were at their mothers' breasts. No one smoked. The balconies threatened to fall under the excessive weight of human bodies ... The air, intense with breathing and waiting, fairly exploded with shouts and with the passionate yells ... I spoke from out of a warm cavern of human bodies; wherever I stretched out my hands I would touch someone, and a grateful movement in response would give me to understand that I was not to worry about it, not to break off my speech, but to keep on. No speaker, no matter how exhausted could resist the electric tension of that impassioned human throng. They wanted to know, to understand, to find their way. At times it seemed as if I felt, with my lips, the stern inquisitiveness of this crowd that had become merged into a single whole. Then all the arguments and words thought out in advance would break and recede under the imperative pressure of sympathy, and other words, other arguments utterly unexpected by the orator, but needed by these people, would emerge in full array from my subconsciousness. On such occasions I felt if I were listening to the speaker from the outside, trying to keep pace with his ideas, afraid that, like a somnambulist, he might fall off the edge of the roof at the sound of my conscious reasoning.'[18]

In the fiery frenzy of this popular arena where the crowds were 'like infants clinging with their dry lips to the nipples of the revolution', Trotsky was to score many dazzling successes. For a few months even Lenin (whose political genius had not yet fully revealed itself) seemed overshadowed by the brilliance of Trotsky's oratory and his virtuoso mastery of the Russian language. In the open forums and the more democratic milieu of the Soviets, Trotsky's charisma, his articulateness and lightning intelligence flourished as nowhere else. He felt himself borne aloft by a force greater than himself, a mouthpiece of irresistible passions that welled up from the depths of a Russian society convulsed by disorder and chaos, to which he gave form and shape. He had become within a few months the popular spokesman of Bolshevism, whose personal influence on the masses was unrivalled by any other leader. During the 'July Days' when a premature popular rising led to governmental crackdown on the Bolshevik leadership and Lenin fled into hiding, Trotsky wrote a defiant 'Open Letter to the Provisional Government' virtually calling for his own arrest. In the Petrograd Soviet he defended Lenin against the charge of being a 'German agent' and warned that the moderate socialists would themselves become victims of the mounting wave of counter-revolutionary hysteria.

Trotsky was arrested on July 23 and spent some weeks in prison until an attempted coup by the monarchist General Kornilov led to his release. The new coalition government headed by Kerensky could not meet the challenge without Bolshevik help in mobilizing the masses. As a result of the Kornilov affair, the Bolsheviks gained political support and by the end of September Trotsky's prestige was still further increased by his election to the key position of Chairman of the Petrograd Soviet.

In the absence of any national parliamentary institutions, the Soviets, elected in the factories and barracks, played a pivotal role, even more important than in 1905. They represented the working classes, the army and important sections of the peasantry. The mood of the masses of workers and soldiers in the major cities had changed significantly by September 1917 and the Bolsheviks had already obtained a majority in Petrograd and Moscow. There was now strong popular support for a *Soviet* government – one made up of the various socialist parties – committed to peace negotiations, land distribution, workers' control and the calling of a Constituent Assembly. In his presidential address as Chairman of the Petrograd Soviet, Trotsky solemnly pledged that he would conduct its work 'in a spirit of lawfulness and of full freedom for the parties'.[19] At the same time he demanded the transfer of governmental power to the Congress of Soviets.

Trotsky had by now become a member of the Central Committee of the Bolshevik Party and in the next few weeks because of Lenin's enforced absence from Petrograd, he was to play the decisive role in the preparations for the October rising. From his hiding place in Finland Lenin was already urging the party to capitalize on the new mood in the Soviets, in the army and among the peasantry and move over to armed insurrection.[20] Trotsky shared this sense of urgency but he argued that since the Bolsheviks had a majority in the Petrograd Soviet, the insurrection should be carried out in its name. This would give it a broader popular mandate and a cloak of 'constitutional' legality, especially if the coup were timed to coincide with the forthcoming All-Russian Congress of Soviets. Lenin was more preoccupied with the dangers of counter-revolution and of missing a unique historic opportunity. He did not envisage the rising having to begin in Petrograd itself. Nor did he think much of the 'constitutional' niceties.[21] To those in the Central Committee who urged delay he answered with burning impatience 'We must not wait! We may lose everything! . . . History will not forgive delay by revolutionists who could be victorious today, while they risk losing much tomorrow, they risk losing all.' This was the constant refrain of all Lenin's letters from hiding – 'to delay action is the same as death'.[22] His sense of urgency was increased by the attitude of some influential Bolsheviks, led by Kamenev and Zinoviev, who opposed insurrection as a fatal 'adventure' which did not have the support of the majority of the Russian population. They correctly foresaw that elections to the Constituent Assembly would give a majority to the main peasant party – the Social Revolutionaries – and they were sceptical as to the value of international support for the Bolsheviks. Other moderate Bolsheviks such as Nogin and Lunacharsky opposed the idea of an exclusively Bolshevik government which they predicted, could only keep itself in power by means of political terror.

In this confrontation, Trotsky, the newcomer, stood unequivocally with Lenin and their tactical differences over the date of the insurrection ultimately paled into insignificance. But Trotsky, in spite of the popular ascendancy which he had established within a few months, could not alone have carried the Bolshevik Party into the insurrection. Ever since April 1917 it needed all the overwhelming authority of Lenin within the

Party to overcome its hesitations as Trotsky himself stressed when he wrote: 'Thus it is by no means excluded that a disoriented and split party might have let slip the revolutionary opportunity for many years. The role of personality arises before us here on a truly gigantic scale.'[23] But though Lenin was the supreme theoretician and strategist of the Russian revolution, he had relatively little to do with the actual mechanics of the insurrection. His decisive role had been to build the revolutionary organization and to identify the major sources of mass discontent in a war-weary nation, to crystallize its grievances in the immensely popular slogans of Land, Peace and Bread. But in his enforced absence (Lenin had been denounced in July 1917 as a 'German spy'), it was Trotsky who assumed leadership of the Bolshevik Party, developed the plan of attack and dominated the actual proceedings.[24] As Chairman of the Petrograd Soviet he was in a unique position to stage-manage the coup and give it the democratic camouflage it required.

Trotsky realized that only by neutralizing the Petrograd garrison and carrying out the revolution under the mask of defending the national capital from German troops, could Bolshevik objectives be achieved. Petrograd was still exposed to German attack. The Provisional Government was planning to transfer the Petrograd garrison to the front for active duty, the one thing they feared. Trotsky was determined to forestall this plan which involved the departure of pro-Bolshevik regiments and which presaged an eventual showdown with the Soviet. He successfully outmanoeuvred Kerensky, persuading the Soviet on October 9 to prevent the dismantling of the garrison. On the same day, at a session of the Soviet Executive, the Military Revolutionary Committee headed by Trotsky was formed. It was responsible for the defence of Petrograd but just over a fortnight later, it became the supreme directing organ of the revolution. Trotsky surrounded himself with a core of reliable Bolsheviks who acted as his general staff. Through the Commissars of the Bolsheviks' military organization, he could count on preventing the arming of cadets in the military schools and divert necessary equipment to the Red Guards. Bolshevik ascendancy at other decisive points – in the Baltic fleet, the garrisons around Petrograd and in Moscow – greatly facilitated the preparation.

Two days before the coup the key Fortress of Peter and Paul on the Neva, which commanded the Winter Palace, was won over to the Soviet as a result of Trotsky's rousing personal appeal to the soldiers. Without a shot being fired, one hundred thousand rifles were handed over. The authority of the Provisional Government was slipping away rapidly. The regiments of the garrison no longer obeyed its writ but that of the Military Revolutionary Committee. The unforeseen postponement of the Congress of Soviets merely gave more time for the final preparations to be set in motion. In the Petrograd Soviet, Trotsky denied that an armed action was under way, but warned its members that they must guard against an attack by the counter-revolution. The operations already being carried out were, he insisted, purely defensive in character.

The Mensheviks and Social Revolutionaries were taken in by this lofty rhetoric, not yet suspecting that they would soon be faced with a fait accompli. On October 23 the Kerensky Government made a belated effort to fight back, raiding the Bolshevik printing plants and ordering the cruiser *Aurora*, manned by a Bolshevik crew, to put to sea on a training cruise. It was all the provocation which Trotsky needed to launch the insurrection. At an extraordinary session of the Petrograd Soviet he announced that 'this semi-government only awaits the sweep of history's broom'.[25] He countermanded Kerensky's orders to the *Aurora* and declared that 'if the government tries to use the twenty-four or forty-eight hours still left to it in order to stab the revolution, then we declare that the vanguard of the revolution will meet attack with attack and iron with steel.'[26] On the evening of the Congress of Soviets which was to set its seal of 'legitimacy' on the Bolshevik coup, the rising was already in progress. While the citizens of Petrograd slept in peace, one institution after another was being occupied by detachments of soldiers, sailors and Red Guards on orders issuing from Trotsky's headquarters at the Smolny Institute. Resistance was only nominal. There was no street-fighting and scarcely any bloodshed. Railway-stations, the post-office, the telegraph, the State Bank were occupied, the Winter Palace and its staff surrendered.[27] In his report to the

Petrograd Soviet on October 25, Trotsky could already declare
that the Provisional Government no longer existed.[28]

The Congress of Soviets opened the same evening to the sound
of the *Aurora*'s bombardment of the Winter Palace. The Bolsheviks commanded an absolute majority at the Congress but
their seizure of power behind its back aroused the fury of the
Mensheviks and Right Social Revolutionaries. Some of them
walked out in protest at the rising – others, led by Martov who
spoke for the Left Mensheviks, still sought a compromise solution, vainly calling for a coalition government of all the socialist
parties. Trotsky's reply delivered with all the withering scorn and
arrogance of which he was capable, was a tour de force of oratory
designed to justify what was in effect a Bolshevik coup d'état in
Petrograd.

'The insurrection of the masses stands in no need of justification. What is taking place is not a conspiracy but an
insurrection. We moulded the revolutionary will of the
Petrograd workers and soldiers ... The masses gathered
under our banner, and our insurrection was victorious. But
what do they [the other socialists] offer us? ... To give up
our victory, to compromise, and to negotiate – with whom?
With those miserable cliques which have left the Congress
or with those who still remain? But we saw how strong
those cliques were! There is no one left in Russia to follow
them. And millions of workers and peasants are asked to
negotiate with them on equal terms. No, an agreement will
not do now. To those who have left us and to those proposing negotiations we must say: You are a mere handful,
miserable, bankrupt; your role is finished, and you may go
where you belong – to the rubbish bin of history.'[29]

The Bolsheviks had indeed steeled the revolutionary will of
the *Petrograd* workers and soldiers. But were they identical with
the millions of workers and peasants throughout Russia? Were
the Social Revolutionaries and Mensheviks merely 'miserable
cliques' whom nobody in Russia followed? The all-Russian
elections to the Constituent Assembly on November 25, 1917
which gave the Bolsheviks only 175 out of 707 elected members
(just under 25 per cent of the vote) compared to 410 Socialist

Revolutionaries, revealed the falsity of Trotsky's claim. Nor was the Second Congress of Soviets the representative body that the Bolsheviks made it out to be. It excluded for example all the non-soldier peasants, among whom the Bolsheviks were but a drop in the ocean. Lenin and Trotsky were able to legitimize their coup merely by equating the majority principle with one Soviet only – that of Petrograd.[30] There was no doubt that here, left-wing opinion had been racing ahead of other regional and social groupings ever since the summer of 1917. It was here, too, that the leading elements of the Russian proletariat and the élite of the Bolshevik party membership were in fact concentrated. In his *History of the Russian Revolution* Trotsky clearly perceived the link between this decisive role of Petrograd and Lenin's elitist theory of a highly centralized party acting as the vanguard of the proletariat. He was writing about the role of Petrograd in the February revolution of 1917 but his remarks apply no less to the Bolshevik coup in October.

'The revolution was carried out upon the initiative and by the strength of one city, constituting approximately about 1/75 of the population of the country. You may say, if you will, that this most gigantic democratic act was achieved in a most undemocratic manner. The whole country was placed before a fait accompli ... This casts a sharp light on the question of democratic forms in general, and in a revolutionary epoch in particular. Revolutions have always struck such blows at the judicial fetishism of the popular will, and the blows have been more ruthless the deeper, bolder and more democratic the revolutions.

It is often said, especially in regard to the great French Revolution, that the extreme centralization of a monarchy subsequently permits the revolutionary capital to think and act for the whole country. That explanation is superficial. If revolutions reveal a centralizing tendency, this is not in imitation of over-thrown monarchies, but in consequence of irresistible demands of the new society, which cannot reconcile itself to particularism. If the capital plays as dominating a role in a revolution as though it concentrated in itself the will of the nation, that is simply because the

capital expresses most clearly and thoroughly the fundamental tendencies of the new society. The provinces accept
the steps taken by the capital as their own intentions already
materialised. In the initiatory role of the centers there is no
violation of democracy, but rather its dynamic realization.
However, the rhythm of this dynamic has never in great
revolutions coincided with the rhythm of formal representative democracy . . . In all genuine revolutions the national
representation has invariably come into conflict with the
dynamic force of the revolution, whose principal seat has
been the capital . . . The role of the capital is determined not
by the tradition of a bureaucratic centralism, but by the
situation of the leading revolutionary class, whose vanguard
is naturally concentrated in the chief city: this is equally
true for the bourgeoisie and the proletariat.'[31]

Better than any other Bolshevik leader (including Lenin)
Trotsky grasped this decisive role of Petrograd, the scene of
his own greatest triumphs. Almost symbolically, the revolutionary
associations of this most Europeanized of the Bolsheviks lay
with Russia's 'window on the West'. Here, in this occidentalized,
'rational' city on the north-western periphery of Russia, among
its shipbuilders, engineers, sailors, steel and electric workers,
Trotsky felt at home in a way he never did in semi-Asiatic
Moscow, the 'Third Rome' and symbol of Russian national
messianism. In 1905 he had stood at the head of the Petersburg
Soviet whose slogans and fighting methods 'found a mighty
revolutionary echo in the country as a whole.'[32] At that time
there had been no major victory in the provinces to sustain the
initiative of the Petrograd workers and no Bolshevik organization
and leadership to centralize the power of the soviets. Now, in
October 1917, Trotsky himself had harnessed the elemental
aspirations of the Petrograd workers and soldiers to the will of a
small but determined organization of underground revolutionaries. In only eight months the Bolsheviks (numbering less than
25,000 members in February 1917) had catapulted themselves
into a position of exercising exclusive authority over a nation of
nearly 150 million people. They had seized power on behalf of
the working class and in the name of the Soviets which in 1917

enjoyed enormous social authority and expressed that spontaneous plebeian democracy that epitomized the popular character
of the Russian Revolution.

It was still tacitly assumed that these Soviets could at anytime
depose the government if it no longer represented the popular
will. Similarly, the existence of opposition was taken for granted.
But under the hammer blows of Bolshevik centralism the ideals
of the Soviets were soon to be submerged and their role subordinated to that of the ruling party. Under the onslaught of
civil war and foreign intervention in a politically backward
country, strong centralized government was to become a permanent feature of the new 'Soviet' regime, leading almost imperceptibly to the creation of a monolithic state. Only during the
course of the ferocious civil war which followed did the Petrograd
coup – the work of a tiny minority of determined insurrectionists
– first become an all-Russian or national revolution. It raised
Leon Trotsky to the pinnacle of his power as a Bolshevik Commissar and transformed the man of the Soviets into an authoritarian dictator. The prescient prophecies of his youth against
Bolshevik Jacobinism and a 'substitutionist' assumption of power
were forgotten in the intoxication of victory. The warnings of the
Mensheviks and of 'moderate' Bolsheviks inside the highest
councils of the Party were contemptuously brushed aside. Independent voices who sounded the alarm, like Maxim Gorky,
whose weekly newspaper *Novaya Zhizn*, denounced the abuses
of power and 'the maniacs of a beautiful idea' were soon silenced.

Only six weeks after the October coup, Gorky had pointed out
that the term 'Soviet' Republic was already a fiction, empty
words which camouflaged the reality of an 'oligarchic republic,
a republic of a few People's Commissars'.[33] The slogan 'All
power to the Soviets' had been transformed by Bolshevik
bayonets and guns into the dictatorship of a single Party. Freedom
of speech and the democratic liberties for which the Russian
people had fought, were being trampled upon by Lenin and Trotsky's ruthless methods of terror and violence. Even such an
impatient ultra-revolutionary as the German Marxist, Rosa
Luxemburg, for all her admiration of Bolshevik audacity and
courage, delivered a crystal-clear admonition in 1918. Political

life – she observed – and with it, the vitality of the Soviets, were
being suppressed throughout Russia. 'Without general elections,'
Luxemburg warned,

> 'without complete freedom of the press and of meetings,
> without freedom of discussion, life in every public in-
> stitution becomes a sham in which bureaucracy alone re-
> mains active . . . Public life gradually disappears; a few dozen
> extremely energetic and highly idealistic party leaders rule
> . . . Au fond this is the rule of a clique – a dictatorship it is
> true, but not the dictatorship of the proletariat, but of a
> handful of politicians . . .'[34]

In 1904 the young Trotsky had shared Rosa Luxemburg's
opposition to Lenin's ruthless centralism and conspiratorial
tactics. Later he was to hold her memory sacred but now as a
Bolshevik neophyte he could not grasp the real meaning of her
criticism or perceive the gulf that was opening up between
libertarian and authoritarian socialism. One need only read the
minutes of the historic session of the Petrograd Bolshevik Committee held on November 1 1917, a few days after the seizure of
power, to see how quickly the heady flush of victory had blunted
Trotsky's libertarian instincts. The problem at issue was the
argument of the 'moderate' Bolsheviks (led at that time by
Zinoviev, Kamenev, Rykov, Kalinin and Lunacharsky) in favour
of a coalition with the other socialist parties. Lenin predictably
denounced this proposal in the most trenchant language, claiming
that the Soviets were the 'vanguard' of the masses and the Bolshevik Party the 'vanguard' of the Soviets. Any compromise
with the Mensheviks would be 'miserable horse-trading'. 'As for
conciliation', Lenin pointed out, 'I cannot even speak about that
seriously. Trotsky long ago said that unification is impossible.
Trotsky understood this, and from that time on there has been
no better Bolshevik.'[35] (For the rest of his life, Trotsky never
tired of quoting this accolade from Lenin as proof of his im-
peccable Bolshevik credentials!)

Lunacharsky's objections were, however, perfectly reasonable.
He pointed to the Bolshevik land decree (which had been
borrowed from the Social Revolutionary Party) and asked why
state power could not be shared with parties who agreed with

the Bolsheviks on so many issues. The party, he complained, had become 'a party of the soldiery, a party of war', not of the working class.[36] It tried to coerce people to work by force, it used bayonets and terror to clear its way, and arrested those who stood in its path. Trotsky's reply was brutally realistic, proving how far he had absorbed Leninist 'hardness' into his own bloodstream. 'We are told that we cannot sit on bayonets', he reminded the Bolshevik conciliators. 'Lunacharsky says that blood is flowing. What to do? Evidently we should never have begun.'[37] There could be no return to half-way measures, to vacillation and compromise. The 'prejudices' of Lunacharsky were 'a heritage of the petty-bourgeois psychology'. All government was based on force, not conciliation – that was the ABC of Marxism. The Bolshevik task was to rebuild the old apparatus from top to bottom and make it work for the Dictatorship of the Proletariat. 'We will compel these people [the railway unions] to work,' Trotsky thundered. The masses had worked under the former terror of a minority now they would work in the name of class violence organized against the bourgeoisie.[38]

It was an effective if crude performance by the organizer of the October insurrection, the man who was soon to become the Bolshevik Commissar for War. Angelica Balabanoff, (confidante of both Lenin and Mussolini) summed up the psychological transformation of Leon Trotsky into a Bolshevik-Leninist with penetrating feminine intuition. 'He was the neophyte who wanted to outdo in zeal and ardour the Bolsheviks themselves, the neophyte who wanted to be forgiven the many crimes against Bolshevism he had committed in the past – by becoming more intransigent, more revolutionary, more Bolshevik than any of them.'

CHAPTER SEVEN

# BOLSHEVIK COMMISSAR

'The Jesuits represented a militant organization, strictly centralized, aggressive, and dangerous not only to enemies but also to allies. In his psychology and method of action the Jesuit of the "heroic" period distinguished himself from an average priest as the warrior of a church from its shopkeeper ... the Bolsheviks appear in relation to the democrats and social-democrats of all hues as did the Jesuits – in relation to the peaceful ecclesiastical hierarchy ... Opportunities are peaceful shopkeepers in socialist ideas while Bolsheviks are the inveterate warriors.'
Leon Trotsky, *Their Morals and Ours*

The ease with which they had seized power, at least in Petrograd, took the Bolshevik leaders by surprise. Trotsky records in his autobiography the following extract from notes made by his wife, Natalia Sedova, on the days immediately after the October rising: '. . . I dropped into a room at the Smolny and found Vladimir Ilyich [Lenin] there with Lev Davidovich. With them if I remember correctly, were Dzerzhinsky, Joffe and a crowd of others. Their faces were a greyish-green from lack of sleep; their eyes were inflamed, their collars soiled, and the room was full of smoke ... Someone was sitting at a table surrounded by people waiting for orders. Lenin and Trotsky were also in the midst of a waiting mob. It seemed to me that orders were being given as if by people who were asleep. There was something of the somnambulist in the way they talked and moved about.'[1] There is this same dream-like quality as Trotsky reports Lenin hesitatingly, almost shyly whispering to him: 'You know, from persecution and a life underground, to come so suddenly into power . . .' – Lenin pauses, and then finds the right word, not in Russian but German – '*Es schwindelt*' (it makes one dizzy). But a government must be formed at once: Trotsky suggests calling it 'The Council of People's Commissars' – Lenin picks up the title eagerly – 'That's splendid; smells terribly of revolution.'[2] He even suggests that Trotsky should head the new government since he had led the insurrection, but the latter indignantly refuses and Lenin is persuaded to preside over the Council. The discussion becomes even more curious when Trotsky objects on the grounds of his 'nationality' to Lenin's next proposal, that he become Commissar of Home Affairs and direct the struggle against the counter-revolution. 'Was it worthwhile to put into our enemies' hands such an additional weapon as my Jewish origin?' is Trotsky's quizzical response. Lenin dismisses this objection as irrelevant. In the midst of a 'great international revolution', this is a mere trifle.[3]

But Tro+ksy's relucatance finds support among other members of the Central Committee, led by Yaacov Sverdlov, himself a Jew and Stalin's actual predecessor as the Party's General Secretary. The whole episode is almost comically bizarre, yet a highly significant pointer to Trotsky's sense of alienation when suddenly faced with the problem of power. Hitherto, he had made no mention of anti-Semitism as a factor in his revolutionary career. He had no personal memories of suffering racial discrimination either in Yanovka, at school, in the underground struggle or in the international socialist movement. He always insisted that the national question, which was so important in Russian life, had 'practically no personal significance for me'. As a revolutionary Marxist, his internationalism had been reinforced by a knowledge of 'so many different languages, political systems and cultures' that he could feel nothing but contemptuous disdain for national prejudices. Almost apologetically, he remarks that 'if, in 1917 and later, I occasionally pointed to my Jewish origin as an argument against some appointment, it was simply because of political considerations.'[4]

But now suddenly, after leading a victorious insurrection, Trotsky perceived his Jewishness no longer as a peripheral 'nationality question' but as a *personal* conflict-situation. The civil war was looming ahead and he was being asked to assume responsibility for internal security and repressive measures against the enemies of the Bolshevik regime. Should a Jew take up this thankless task, given the depths of Tsarist and White Guard anti-Semitism, not to speak of the Judeophobia endemic in the peasant masses of rural Russia? What makes this momentary hesitation so intriguing is that Trotsky's psychic break with his own petty-bourgeois Jewish background had been an important pre-requisite in his adoption of the revolutionary cause. Many of Lenin's closest associates in the Bolshevik Party including Zinoviev, Kamenev, Sverdlov, Radek, Litvinov, Joffe, Sokolnikov, Uritsky and Lozovsky were also Russified 'non-Jewish' Jews who had broken with their background and repudiated any attachments to the Jewish people. In the name of transcending all tribalism, parochialism and local nationalism, they leant over backwards to disclaim their origins.[5] No other group of revolutionists were so indifferent to 'national prejudices', so absolute in their internationalism as the 'Jewish' Bolsheviks. They had rejected their religious and national tradition in the name of a new secular universalism. Even the legitimate claims of the Jewish proletariat, whether organized in Socialist parties like the Bund or the Poale-Zion, were treated by them with indifference or disdain. The 'Jewish' Bolsheviks were historically a post-ghetto phenomenon: young men, frequently of middle-class or petty-bourgeois origin, whose revolt against social injustices had let them passionately to deny all nationalism. Even among the Mensheviks and Social Revolutionaries (where there were proportionately more Jews than in the Bolshevik Party), there was a similar outlook. With a few exceptions like Axelrod, Martov and Lev Deutsch, they felt anything but Jews. They looked forward to the disappearance of the Jews as a distinct entity, convinced as they were that there would be no place for anti-Semitism in the new socialist order.

Within this Russified Marxist élite, cut off from the masses of the Jewish people, Trotsky stood out not only as a result of his prominence and revolutionary charisma, but because he more than anyone appeared so ostentatiously non-Jewish in his bearing, his style and his concerns. Trotsky might raise the question of his origins out of 'political considerations'. But this did not prevent his galvanizing within a few months the energies of the Russian peasant masses and leading them to victory in the civil war on a dozen fronts. Looking back, he concluded that his misgivings on 'the question of race' had been misguided. Lenin had after all been proved right.

'In the years of the revolutionary *ascendancy* this question never had the slightest importance. Of course the Whites tried to develop anti-Semitism motifs in their propaganda in the Red Army, but they failed signally. There are many testimonials to this, even in the White press. In the *Archives of the Russian Revolution*, published in Berlin, a White Guard writer relates the following striking episode: 'A Cossack who came to see us was hurt by someone's taunt that he not only served under, but fought under the command of a Jew – Trotsky – and retorted with warm conviction: "Nothing of the sort. Trotsky is not a Jew. Trotsky is a fighter. He's ours . . . Russian! It is Lenin who is a communist, a Jew, but Trotsky is ours . . . a fighter . . . Russian . . . our own!" The same motif will be found in *The Horse Army*, by Babel, the most talented of our younger writers. The question of my Jewish origin acquired importance only after I had become a subject of political baiting. Anti-Semitism raised its head with that of anti-Trotskyism. They both derived from the same source – the petty-bourgeois reaction against October.'[6]

There is a grain of truth in Trotsky's explanation but his approach is overly subjective and altogether superficial. The anecdote that he quotes, proved only how much store he set on being regarded as a non-Jew. It evidently tickled his pride to be recognized as a fighter', a 'Russian' who led his men from the front. Far from demonstrating that race was irrelevant, the story underlines how tenaciously popular folk prejudice upheld the idea that Jews were 'aliens', shirkers who did not fight but directed events from behind the scenes. The quasi-automatic association of 'Jews' with 'Bolsheviks' (here projected against Lenin rather than Trotsky) was one of the trump-cards of the Whites and during the Civil War it developed into a murderous

obsession.[7] It led to the greatest modern mass murder of Jews
before the advent of Hitler, a fact which Trotsky passed over in
complete silence. Over 200,000 Jews were massacred in the
Ukraine alone, and many more made homeless by the pogroms.
In the complex civil war waged by the Ukrainian nationalists, the
Makhnovite peasant bands, the Red Army, and the Whites, every
army, even the Bolsheviks, was guilty of murdering Jews. The
troops of the anti-Bolshevik 'Volunteer Army', usually Cossacks,
indulged in by far the most violent pogroms and there is little
doubt that their anti-Semitism was exacerbated (though not
caused) by the presence of Jews in key positions in the Soviet
regime.

White propaganda undoubtedly succeeded in whipping up
hostility to the *Zhid* Bronstein and the Bolshevik armies under
his command.[8] Trotsky himself was more worried about this
than he let on and favoured a greater number of Jews at the battle
front to counter what he described as 'chauvinist agitation' among
Red Army men.[9] Hence it was rather misleading for Trotsky to
claim that anti-Semitism emerged only with the decline of the
revolutionary ascendancy in the mid-1920s. Even in the Kronstadt
rebellion of 1921, there were significant, populist anti-Semitic
motifs which surfaced in the anger of the revolutionary sailors
at the authoritarian policies of Trotsky and Zinoviev. Whereas
Lenin was seen as a Great Russian from the peasant heartland,
Trotsky and Zinoviev symbolized in the eyes of many of the
mutineers everything malevolent about the Soviet regime.[10] In
terms reminiscent of White Guard propaganda, the Jews were
depicted as a new 'privileged class' of 'Soviet princes' who
dominated the Communist Party and were the real beneficiaries
of the Revolution. Of all the Bolshevik leaders, the 'Jew' Trotsky
was singled out as the most blood-thirsty – 'the evil genius of
Russia swooping like a hawk' on heroic Kronstadt – a monster
of tyranny and commissarocracy 'standing knee-deep in the
blood of the workers'.[11]

The course of events already in the first years of the Soviet
regime (and even more under Stalin) reveal that Trotsky's
momentary hesitation at the assumption of power in October
1917 was, in a sense, better grounded than his subsequent

attempts to rationalize the depths of Russian anti-Semitism.[12] The 'Jewish question' was not as easily subsumed under the heading of general nationality problems, as Trotsky and some other Bolshevik leaders assumed. There were, for example, no recriminations against Georgians, Latvians and Poles for their important role in the revolution and in the early years of Soviet power. With Jews, on the other hand, the problem was different, no matter how vehemently they might repudiate their origins. Those, who like Trotsky, had absorbed internationalism into their very flesh and blood, could not adapt so easily to Stalin's new *orthodoxy* of socialism in one country. Signficantly, there were very few Jews to be found in the Stalinist and Bukharinist factions, which unconsciously appealed in the mid 1920s to ancient Russian reflexes of national messianism and self-sufficiency.

Trotsky's own messianism was of a more apocalyptic quality, militant, atheist and supranational in its Marxist form – missionary and salvationist in its underlying content. The quasi-religious fervour and fanaticism with which he inspired the Red Army was more reminiscent of Cromwell's Puritan Ironsides than the domesticated Marxism of the West European Social Democracies. This messianism predicated on a passionate and unswerving faith in the imminence of the world revolution, enabled him to overcome the psychic inhibitions imposed by his residual Jewishness and the reflective intellectuality associated with it. It was a messianism steeled in the Leninist teaching of revolutionary violence rather than in any primal Jewish experience. Indeed, from the moment that he assumed power and became an *armed* prophet, Trotsky broke the last chain linking him to the Jewish tradition which he had spurned from his childhood. Only when stripped of the attributes of power and condemned to lonely opposition, then made the scapegoat for all the failures and defeats of World Communism, did fate cast Trotsky in a more familiar though unwelcome role: that of the wandering Jew and arch-heretic of the theocratic universe institutionalized by the Stalinist Comintern.

Yet it remains true that in the first years of the Bolshevist regime such ambiguities were more easily thrust aside, so immense were the tasks confronting the new rulers of Russia. On

Sverdlov's initiative, Trotsky had been appointed Commissar for Foreign Affairs – the best man, so it seemed, to 'confront' Europe with the apocalyptic message of a victorious revolution. Trotsky himself had little regard for conventional diplomacy and somewhat airily dismissed the very notion of a Soviet 'foreign policy': 'I will issue a few revolutionary proclamations to the peoples of the world and then shut up shop.'[13] But as the Bolshevik Foreign Secretary at the head of the Soviet delegation sent to Brest-Litovsk to negotiate peace with Germany and Austria-Hungary, Trotsky soon found himself sitting 'with the representatives of the most reactionary caste among all the ruling classes'.[14] His brief was to delay the proceedings as long as possible in order to let the European proletariat absorb the facts of the Soviet revolution. Since the October rising, Trotsky had been insistently proclaiming that 'either the Russian revolution will raise the whirlwind of struggle in the West, or the capitalists of all countries will stifle our struggle'.[15] While negotiating with the Germans he now defined the dual aim of Soviet foreign policy: 'to secure the quickest possible cessation of the shameful and criminal slaughter which is destroying Europe, secondly to help the working class of all countries by every means available to us to overthrow the domination of capital and to seize state power in the interests of a democratic peace and of a socialist transformation of Europe and of all mankind.'[16] Trotsky evidently believed that the German revolution (on which he more than any other Bolshevik leader staked such enormous hopes) might break out before the Soviet government had to conclude any treaty with the Central Powers. His famous formula 'neither war nor peace' was intended to provide Soviet Russia with a temporary respite while denying the German army the benefits of a final settlement on its Eastern Front. It was moreover important, Trotsky argued, to deal a decisive blow at the story of a secret Russian connection with the Hohenzollerns. The Bolsheviks must not be accused of collaborating with the Kaiser behind the backs of the German workers. For these reasons, Trotsky favoured capitulation to the exceedingly harsh German terms, only in face of an obvious show of force. He was perfectly aware that Russia could not fight the Germans – the Russian soldiers were already abandoning the trenches in droves – but the prospect of a German rising was worth the gamble of a delay.

Lenin, more pragmatic and above all concerned with securing the fragile Soviet power, was not prepared to take any risks even at the cost of signing a humiliating peace. But he found himself in a minority and threatened to resign in face of continued opposition in the Central Committee. Within the Bolshevik Party, a group of 'Left Communists' led by Bukharin and supported by the left Social Revolutionaries, advocated 'revolutionary war' against the Central Powers and bitterly attacked Lenin's call for an immediate peace. When the Germans broke off the talks and began their offensive, the Bolshevik Central Committee was still deadlocked until Trotsky, with considerable misgivings, voted with the peace faction against revolutionary war.[17] He preferred to sacrifice his own principles and personal ambition rather than risk a split in the party which might lead to bloody conflict and an even more desperate situation. At an emergency Party Congress on March 6 1918 he declared: '... I could not assume responsibility for the split. I had thought that we ought to retreat (before the German army) rather than sign peace for the sake of an illusory respite. But I could not take upon myself the responsibility for the leadership of the party . . .'[18]

This self-restraint was remarkable given his egocentric and imperious temperament but was characteristic of Trotsky's new relationship with Lenin, whose leadership he unreservedly acknowledged. For the next five years, in spite of all their differences in political style and personality, they would become indissoluble partners in the joint enterprise of establishing the Soviet power. Their personal relations were cordial, though perhaps not as intimate as Trotsky believed. They complemented each other, at times almost as if a single mind was at work:[19] yet they were poles apart in character – Lenin almost impersonal in his habits, patient, tactful yet ruthless in controversy – Trotsky more impuslive, highly-charged, yet methodical and systematic in his precision. Looking back in later years, Trotsky would see Lenin's early death not only as a cruel blow to the party but as the direct source of his own tragedy and that of Soviet Russia. Lenin would become his idol and hero-figure in a way that he could never have envisaged in the years before 1914. Trotsky would even come to see himself as the embodiment of Lenin's true policies, the loyal heir and successor of the founder of Bolshevism whose teachings had been usurped and 'betrayed' by Stalin.

Though there was still something assertive in Trotsky's deference to Lenin, they were united on most essentials. After 1917 Trotsky had embraced without hesitation Lenin's teaching on the revolutionary vanguard and the Dictatorship of the Proletariat. For the next six years he was even to outdo Lenin in his Bolshevik *Jacobinism*, in his insistence on ruthless centralism, iron discipline and the cult of authority. Trotsky's over-bearing self-confidence (which Lenin criticized in his Testament) led him to excesses that the more cautious Lenin generally avoided. Harsh, autocratic, arrogant at the zenith of his power, Trotsky's fall would be seen by many as a symbol of Bolshevik hubris. But under Lenin's firm hand, he was capable of such prodigious bursts of energy and zeal – his audacity, impatience and *élan vital* were harnessed so effectively that his defects as a political leader seemed less apparent.

Trotsky's heroic qualities and organizational talents revealed themselves to most effect during the Civil War. As War Commissar he created a model army almost out of nothing though he had no previous military experience except as a war correspondent. The Bolsheviks initially had at their disposal only a small para-military force, consisting of Red Guard members who had fought in the October rising and guerilla bands lacking any training or organization. The difficulties in the way of creating a centralized, disciplined army out of this unpromising material were immense. There was the popular mood of war-weariness and the anti-militarism of the entire Socialist tradition to contend against – the revolutionary ethos of the new egalitarian ideals which led soldiers to demand the right to elect their own commanders and establish local committees. Beyond that, there was the immense organizational task of training and welding together masses of raw peasant recruits who lacked any sense of discipline and order.

Trotsky's methods necessarily involved a frontal attack on all the sacred taboos of the revolution. He opposed the committee system in the army as a force for disintegration and derided the methods of guerilla warfare as 'very abstract' and 'nothing but an idealization of our weakness'; he believed firmly in the 'superiority of central organization and strategy over local improvizations, military separatism and federalism'.[20] Trotsky clamped down on rampant anarchy and disobedience in Communist ranks with particular severity: he warned that 'Communists found guilty of misdemeanours and crimes against the revolutionary military duty will be doubly punished, for offences that may be condoned in a benighted, uneducated man cannot be condoned in a member of the party that leads the working classes of the world'.[21] He had no patience at all with 'the sort of strategist-dilettantism that flooded the party as a result of the revolution' nor with such sacred cows of socialist doctrine as the people's militia. He considered Marxism as irrelevant to purely military problems, rejecting out of hand the notion of a 'proletarian' military strategy, advocated by commanders like Frunze, Tukhachevsky or Voroshilov. War was a *practical art*, a skill, not a science or a theoretical doctrine which could be reduced to Marxist ideological principles.[23] Trotsky was the unrepentant champion of a Regular Army, a consistent patron of military professionalism, who organized his forces according to orthodox rules of hierarchy and command. He strongly defended his use of 'specialists' from the former Tsarist army to constitute the officer corps of the Red Army. It was axiomatic for Trotsky that these officers were as indispensable to military defence as were engineers to industry or trained agronomists to agriculture.[24]

This policy aroused intense suspicion not only among the left Communists and 'democratic centralists' who objected to conventional methods of military discipline but even within the inner Bolshevik hierarchy. Trotsky's adversaries found support among the non-commissioned officers and commanders of the Red Guard and the irregular formations who bitterly resented their subordination to former Tsarist generals, indeed to any centralized authority. At the VIII Party Congress (March 1919) this 'military opposition' crystallized around a programme of support for a partisan against a regular army, for the election of

officers and commissars and greater authority for party cells in
the army. Lenin supported Trotsky's stand (though for some
time he, too, was reserved about the use of ex-Tsarist officers)
and his policy was confirmed but already behind the scenes
political opponents like Zinoviev and Stalin were working to
exploit these difficulties. The focal point of resistance to Trotsky's
command was Voroshilov's Tenth Army, and Stalin, who was
chief political Commissar on this southern front, actively in-
trigued at Tsaritsyn to undermine the War Commissar's authority.
Matters reached such a head, that Trotsky had to threaten
Voroshilov with a court-martial and to insist on Stalin's recall.
In his military work, Trotsky did not hesitate to elbow away
'those who interfered with military success' but in the haste of
the moment he also made many enemies. Those soldiers and
bureaucrats whose pride had been ruffled were quietly picked
up by Stalin who concentrated on accumulating political influence
while Trotsky was covering himself in military glory.

For two and a half years, Trotsky's life was bound up with the
Red Army and his famous armoured train which was a military-
administrative, a political and a fighting institution rolled into
one. In this mobile headquarters, which combined the roles of a
War Ministry and a flying Bolshevik propaganda department,
Trotsky rushed from one front to another, rallying demoralized
soldiers and leaving in his trail a string of victories. The mysterious
train included a secretariat, a printing-press, a telegraph station,
a radio and electric-power station, a library, a garage and a
bath.[25] It was so heavy that it needed two engines. Trotsky's
own office was equipped with comfortable armchairs, wall maps
and nailed-down typewriters. Here he held conferences with local
military and civil authorities, studied the telegraphic dispatches,
dictated *Terrorism and Communism*, his book against Kautsky, and
a spate of pamphlets, battle-orders and articles. For relaxation
he read French novels. 'In those years', Trotsky later recalled, 'I
accustomed myself, seemingly forever, to writing and thinking
to the accompaniment of Pullman wheels and springs.'[26] The
influence of the train on the morale of the Red Army was
immense. 'The arrival of the train put the most isolated unit in
touch with the whole army and brought it into the life not only

of the country, but of the entire world. Alarmist rumours and doubts were dispelled, and the spirit of the men grew firm.'[27] It was as if the rhythm of the armoured train had become a symbol of Trotsky's relentless drive, his unlimited mobility and personal power. It also contained the warning and threat of the drumhead court-martial. At the little town of Svyazhsk, opposite Kazan, during one of the crucial battles of the civil war, Trotsky showed himself implacable towards those who failed in their duties. The commander and commissar of a regiment which had deserted, along with more than twenty soldiers, were sent to the firing squad as an example. Trotsky issued a solemn warning:

'... if a unit retreats without orders, the first to be shot will be the commissar, the second will be the commanding officer. Courageous soldiers will be rewarded according to their merits and will be given commissions. Cowards, scoundrels and traitors will not escape bullets – this I pledge before the entire Red Army.'[28]

By such draconian measures, Trotsky welded together an army out of untrained bands of guerillas, refugees escaping from the Whites, detachments of workers, peasants, Communist loyalists and trade-union volunteers. The Party stiffened all units with its most zealous members and with the help of the Cheka (security forces) tightened discipline, never hesitating to punish desertion with summary firing squads. The Bolshevik commissars attached to the former Imperial officers ensured their loyalty and with it political control over the Army (it was Trotsky who had instituted this system of dual command). In case of treason an officer's family would be executed. Such ruthlessness and intimidatory methods kept the Red Army in the field, and despite occasional mutinies, there were no desertions on a scale comparable to that of the Whites.

Clearly this strict, stern policy paid dividends during the Civil War and without such resolute cultivation of the martial virtues the revolution would not have survived. In defence of the revolutionary fatherland, neither Lenin nor Trotsky had any hesitation in opting for efficiency and bureaucratic centralism, hierarchy and discipline however unpalatable it might be to the revolutionary romanticists in the Party. By May 1918 the Red

Army consisted of about 306,000 men – by December 1920 the command and administrative staff alone numbered 446,729. Between May 1918 and October 1920 the Bolsheviks mobilized almost 5½ million men (at least 800,000 were active combatants), a remarkable feat of organization. Nevertheless, draconian reprisals and the building of an efficient military machine could not alone have transformed the vacillating, unreliable mass of the Russian peasantry into a real army. This also required tireless propaganda and revolutionary example which could create the will to fight in difficult situations. In this sphere Trotsky's speeches and manifestos were irreplaceable. They inspired his troops with the belief that they were crusaders fighting for a better world. 'The strongest cement in the new army', Trotsky wrote, 'was the ideas of the October Revolution, and the train supplied the front with this cement.'[29] Through their ideology and propaganda, the Bolsheviks won the loyalty of the peasantry who feared that the land settlement of 1917 might be reversed by the Whites. Moreover, to many of the peasants, the Bolsheviks appeared as independent Russian patriots defending their country against foreign intervention. The White Armies were more often perceived as undignified puppets of Britain and France. On all these counts, the Red Army, for all its weaknesses and faults, had a clear advantage over its White adversaries. But without Trotsky's insistence on rehabilitating the ex-Tsarist officers who in 1918 constituted more than three-quarters of the commanding staffs in the Red Army, the Bolsheviks would have been doomed to defeat.

Trotsky's supreme moment of glory came during the defence of Red Petrograd, cradle of the revolution and scene of his earlier triumphs. The city was threatened by General Yudenich's troops (supported by the British navy) who had reached its outskirts in October 1918. Trotsky's personal intervention had an instant and electrifying effect on the morale of the population. Proper discipline was restored, desertion from the front radically reduced, all avenues of retreat cut.[30] He penetrated into every detail of the city's defence, giving clear, precise orders, demanding the utmost exertion, providing an inspiring example by his restless energy. When a rifle regiment began to retreat in panic, Trotsky mounted on horseback, and chasing one soldier after another, made them all turn back. He was wounded in both legs but his perserverance inspired the Red Army units to a heroic frenzy. According to one enemy account 'they attacked the tanks with their bayonets, and although they were mowed down in rows, by the devastating fire of the steel monsters, they continued to defend their position.'[31]

On the second anniversary of the October rising, Trotsky was back in Moscow to report that Petrograd had been saved. Elsewhere the White armies were soon in full disarray – in Siberia, on the southern front, in the Ukraine. By the end of 1919 the outcome was no longer in doubt, though Baron Wrangel's forces still had to be dislodged from the Crimea. Trotsky stood at the height of his military glory, the saviour of the Soviet Republic and embodiment of the Revolution. This is how Victor Serge described his majestic entrance at a Congress of the Communist International in 1920.

'No one ever wore a great destiny with more style. He was forty-one and at the apex of power, popularity and fame – leader of the Petrograd masses in two revolutions; creator of the Red Army, which (as Lenin said to Gorky) he had literally "conjured out of nothing"; personally the victor of several decisive battles, at Sviazhsk, Kazan and Pulkovo; the acknowledged organizer of victory in the Civil War; "Our Carnot!" as Radek called him. He outshone Lenin through his great oratorical talent, through his organizing ability, first with the army, then on the railways, and by his brilliant gifts as a theoretician ... He made his appearance dressed in some kind of white uniform, bare of any insignia, with a broad, flat military cap, also in white, for headgear; his bearing was superbly martial, with his powerful chest, jet-black beard and hair, and flashing eye-glasses. His attitude was less homely than Lenin's, with something authoritarian about it ... we have much admiration for him, but no real love. His sternness, his insistence on punctuality in work and battle, the inflexible correctness of his demeanour in a period of general slackness ... the political solutions prescribed by him for current difficulties struck me as proceeding from a character that was basically dictatorial.'[32]

The passionate Zimmerwald anti-militarist had metamorphosed, under the pressure of events, into the Bolshevik Commissar and dictatorial Chairman of the Supreme War Council. As co-founder of the Third International Trotsky spoke to the representatives of the world proletariat assembled in Moscow, in the martial tones of a heroic Red Warrior defending the fortress of Soviet Russia against the predatory brigands and oppressors of all countries.[33] Angrily he denounced 'the wailings of the bourgeois world against civil war and Red Terror as the most prodigious hypocrisy known in history'. To the founding Congress of the International he had unfolded, in April 1919, an aggressive Marxist version of the old church formula *Ex Oriente Lux* ('the light shineth from the East'). 'In our generation the revolution began in the East. From Russia it passed over into Hungary to Bavaria and, doubtless, it will march westward through Europe.'[34] History was taking the line of least resistance, beginning with the most backward countries where the peasantry predominated and mounting upwards 'rung by rung, towards countries more highly developed economically'. The old Marxist schema had been reversed by events. England, the first-born capitalist nation was from the standpoint of proletarian revolution 'the most conservative country' because of its privileged imperial position and flexible parliamentary machinery. But the Russian upheaval had 'dealt a cruel blow to the social power of the European bourgeoisie' which would inaugurate a new revolutionary epoch. The 'birthright' of the Russian proletariat was only temporary. Its dictatorship could not be consolidated until 'the European working class frees us from the economic yoke and especially the military yoke of the European bourgeoisie, and having overthrown the latter, comes to our assistance with its organization and its technology'.[35] There was no trace of Russian national messianism in Trotsky's analysis – the centre of the International would shift westward from Moscow to Berlin, Paris, London – of this he was profoundly convinced. 'For a World Communist Congress in Berlin or Paris would signify the complete triumph of the proletarian revolution in Europe and consequently through the world.'[36]

But the great hopes of world revolution were to crumble

within a few months. The new 'Soviet' Republics in Bavaria and Hungary soon collapsed and the German Revolution was defeated. Trotsky momentarily played with extravagant fantasies of preparing a military thrust against India. In a secret paper to the Central Committee in August 1919, he suggested:

'. . . the road to India may prove at the given moment to be more readily passable and shorter for us than the road to Soviet Hungary. The sort of army which at the moment can be of no great significance in the European scales can upset the unstable balance of Asian relationships of colonial dependence, give a direct push to an uprising on the part of the oppressed masses, and assure the triumph of such a rising in Asia'.[37]

Nothing came of the plan but it was to prove a characteristic of Bolshevik strategy that when prospects of revolution in the West dimmed, they began to look to the colonial areas of the awakening East for new opportunities. For Trotsky this was less typical insofar as his own vision tended to be Eurocentric and permeated with a horror of Russia's *isolation* from the West. He had always seen such a development as fatal to the revolution. It also conflicted with his general opposition to the aggressive military doctrine of exporting revolution abroad 'on the point of bayonets', a viewpoint advocated by Tukhachevsky, the rising young star of the Red Army. During the Soviet-Polish war of 1920, Bolshevism tried to expand through military conquest and failed. Even Lenin deluded himself into thinking that the Polish workers and peasants would welcome the Red Army as 'liberators' and that Germany was in a revolutionary ferment. Among the top Bolshevik leaders only Trotsky opposed the offensive against Poland and the march on Warsaw, though he was obliged to submit to the majority decision. Few realized at the time that the Polish fiasco marked the end of a cycle of world war, revolution and civil conflict and the crystallization of Russian isolation from the West.

The new problems that now confronted the regime lay primarily in the field of civilian reconstruction. A shattered economy had to be rebuilt, its ruined industries and agriculture restored to their pre-war levels. To meet this challenge, the Bolsheviks

promptly nationalized all industry, banned private trade, par-
tially eliminated money exchange, put the city population on
strict rations and dispatched workers' detachments to the countryside to requisition agricultural surpluses. 'War Communism', as
this system came to be called, was in Trotsky's words, 'the
systematic regimentation of consumption in a besieged fortress'.
In 1919–20, like most Bolshevik leaders, Trotsky convinced
himself that these methods could lead rapidly to the creation of a
fully-fledged Communist economy. The time had come to realize
the slogan 'He who does not work shall not eat'. Militarization
of labour was Trotsky's solution to the problem of restoring the
nation's productive forces, reassembling the dispersed working
class, many of who had fled to the countryside, and sending them
back to the factories. To save Russia from economic collapse all
methods seemed justified to Lenin and Trotsky, including com-
pelling and coercing workers according to the dictates of the
political leadership and directing demobilized soldiers to essential
jobs in the economy. Compulsion was allegedly in the 'interests
of the workers themselves' – it would instill those habits of work
discipline, solidarity and cooperation which Russian capitalism
had singularly failed to inculcate in the population. It would
shorten the transition to socialism on the basis of a forced march
towards the complete socialization of the economy, enabling
Russia to leap over the intermediate stages in the modernization
process. The militarization of labour was not merely seen by
Trotsky as an imperative for economic survival but as laying the
groundwork for a fully collective society.

'We are for regulated labour on the basis of an economic
plan, obligatory for the whole people and consequently
compulsory for each worker in the country. Without this
we cannot even dream of a transition to socialism ...
obligation and, consequently, compulsion are essential
conditions for overcoming bourgeois anarchy, securing
socialization of the means of production and labour, and
reconstructing economic life on the basis of a single plan.'[38]

Compulsion and forced labour was not only justified as an
instrument of socialist dictatorship applied by a 'workers' and
peasants state' (Trotsky's facile identification of the Soviet regime

with the proletariat was vehemently rejected even by Lenin) it was allegedly 'progressive' on principle. 'Is it true that forced labour is always unproductive?' Trotsky provocatively asked the assembled Bolshevik trade unionists in April 1920. 'That is the most wretched, vulgar liberal prejudice; even chattel slavery was productive, it was higher than slave labour ... Forced labour did not grow out of the feudal lords' ill-will. It was a progressive phenomenon.'[39] When the Menshevik leader Raphael Abramovich objected that Trotsky's socialism recalled the methods used by the Egyptian Pharaohs to build their pyramids,[40] he glibly replied: 'Abramovich sees no difference between the Egyptian regime and our own. He has forgotten the class nature of government. ... our compulsion is applied by a workers' and peasants' government.' But by 1920 the Russian proletariat no longer had any power of decision or political self-determination. It was not through their Soviets that the policy of labour regimentation had been decided but by an elite leadership which looked on the population as a vast reservoir of labour power which it could direct at will. Trotsky had, it is true, momentarily advocated a change of course in February 1920, following a stay in the Urals, where he noted that the policies of War Communism were not working. He suggested to the Central Committee that a halt should be called to the requisitioning of food products and a measure of economic freedom restored to the peasantry.[41] This anticipation of Lenin's New Economic Policy (NEP) was rejected by the Central Committee and Trotsky dropped the matter, without raising it again. Instead, he became identified in the public mind with the rigorous, unpopular policies of 'War Communism' and insistent advocacy of a single, all-embracing economic plan.

More importantly, Trotsky's policies brought him into sharp conflict with transport workers' unions. As head of *Tsektran* (the Central Transport Commission) Trotsky had unhesitatingly dismissed those union leaders who opposed his high-handed centralizing methods and who insisted on their electoral rights and established voting procedures. With the conclusion of the Soviet-Polish war, the resentment of the union leaders burst forth and this time they won Lenin's approval for their con-

demnation of Trotsky's military-bureaucratic methods. At this
time Trotsky was not only the most extreme opponent of workers'
control over the economy but also the zealous defender of
bureaucratic privileges in the name of efficiency. Stalin's taunt
that Trotsky was 'the patriarch of the bureaucrats', coming from
any other source, would have been amply justified. The Commissar for War saw no role at all for the unions except as an arm
of the State, confined to maintaining labour discipline and increasing productivity.

At the other extreme, the Workers' Opposition, led by
Alexandra Kollontai and Shlyapnikov (who rightly saw in
Trotsky their chief adversary) attacked the new bureaucratic
tutelage over the unions and demanded direct control by the
producers over the economy. Lenin adopted a middle position
in this debate, emphasising party control over the unions but
rejecting Trotsky's call for their complete absorption into the
state. In Lenin's view the unions should be allowed a measure of
autonomy and the right to act as a pressure-group on behalf of
the working-class. Soviet Russia was, according to Lenin, still a
'deformed workers' State' marked by bureaucratic distortions,
not as Trotsky implied, a *monolithic* State where conflicts of
interest between the Party and sectional groups were inconceivable.

At the tenth Party Congress in March 1921 Trotsky revealed
just how far he had come from his pre-October defence of
'proletarian democracy'. He accused the Workers' Opposition of
'fetishizing the principles of democracy', and defended 'the
revolutionary historical birthright of the party', claiming that it
was obliged to maintain its dictatorship 'regardless of temporary
vacillations in the elemental moods of the masses'.[43] The Party
dictatorship stood above the workers' right to elect their own
representatives and the spontaneous inclinations of the masses.
Trotsky's position clearly contained all the seeds of political
despotism, of the ominous development towards the monolithic
bureaucratic system which in a few years he was so trenchantly
to criticize. He had emerged as the foremost Bolshevik apostle of
that *substitutionism* which he had indicted in his youth, i.e. the
complete identification of Party interests with those of the work-

ing class. '... In this "substitution" of the power of the party for the power of the working class there is nothing accidental, and in reality there is no substitution at all. The communists express the fundamental interests of the working class' – he wrote with breathtaking glibness in *Terrorism and Communism*.

This most spine-chilling of all Trotsky's works, composed aboard his armoured train, breathes the imperial arrogance of the military commander in whom the last remnants of moral conscience have been eradicated. Trotsky's central postulate is that as long as class society exists 'repression remains a necessary means of breaking the will of the opposing side'.[44] From this premise he interprets the Red Terror as a direct continuation of armed insurrection which consists of shooting landlords, capitalists and generals seeking to restore capitalism. This State terror is justified if it hastens the destruction of the bourgeoisie, which through internal plots and foreign intervention seeks to strangle the revolution. The form of repression is purely 'a question of expediency' and against 'a reactionary class which does not want to leave the scene of operations', ruthless terror is indeed the most efficient method.

'*Intimidation* is a powerful weapon of policy, both internationally and internally. War, like revolution, is founded upon intimidation. A victorious war, generally speaking, destroys only an insignificant part of the conquered army, intimidating the remainder and breaking their will. The revolution works in the same way: it kills individuals and intimidates thousands ... The State terror of a revolutionary class can be condemned "morally" only be a man who, on principle, rejects (in words) every form of violence whatsoever ... For this, one has to be merely and simply a hypocritical Quaker.'[45]

*Terrorism and Communism* is full of vicious diatribes against 'Kantian-priestly and vegetarian-Quaker prattle' which represent for Trotsky no more than a philosophical or legal mystification designed to chain the proletariat to the chariot of capitalism.[46] Against such sacred taboos of democracy as the sanctity of the individual, equality before the law and universal suffrage, Trotsky proposes his own *mystification* – that the 'class truth of the pro-

letariat' is the supreme law of political struggle. In the name of
the 'will of a class' he justifies the indiscriminate taking of life
wherever this is expedient, the suppression of a free press (the
Mensheviks and Social Revolutionaries are now defined as
'counter-revolutionary') and the rejection of democracy as a
'bourgeois fetishism'. The whole argument is a crude Bolshevik
variation on Rousseau's 'forcing men to be free', a 'bourgeois'
terror on the Jacobin model translated into a primitive, semi-
Asiatic environment. An oligarchy of Commissars identifying
their merciless will with that of a 'historically rising class' stand
beyond the law.

In 1939, with the nightmare of Stalinist totalitarianism before
his eyes, Trotsky was to return unrepentantly to this line of
argument in *Their Morals and Ours*. Indignantly, he tried to
repudiate the argument that there was no 'principled' difference
between Trotskyism and Stalinism, since both followed the
Jesuitical maxim that 'the end justifies the means'. The amoralism
of the Jesuits was for Trotsky a sign of their superiority – they
were 'more consistent, bolder, and perspicacious' – fanatic
warriors of a cause which could not be judged 'with the eyes of
an obtuse and slothful shopkeeper'.[47] The Bolsheviks had been
slandered by democrats and 'peaceful shopkeepers in socialist
ideas' who cravenly avoided the stern imperatives of struggle.
But just as the Jesuit 'warriors of the church' had degenerated
into bureaucrats and swindlers, so too Stalinism had allegedly
betrayed the militant purity of Bolshevism, of which Trotsky
stood as the lonely guardian.

But all Trotsky's broadsides against the 'moralizing Philistines'
cannot alter his own complicity in the ruthless suppression of
opposition – not only from the 'bourgeoisie' – but also from the
Mensheviks, the SRs, the Workers' Opposition, the anarchists
and the peasant guerilla bands in the early years of Soviet power.
The seeds of totalitarianism were already planted in 1920–1 with
the forced labour camps and Chekist terror when Trotsky stood
at the zenith of his influence. Already then, the Soviets had
degenerated into mere appendages of the Bolshevik Party, the
other socialist parties had been outlawed, and factions inside the
ruling party banned. On the eve of the Kronstadt rebellion in

March 1921 which hoisted the banner of a 'Third Revolution' that would restore the crippled 'Soviets' to power, mass discontent in the country was rife. The sailors of the Kronstadt naval base (whom Trotsky had hailed in 1917 as the 'pride and glory of the Revolution') demanded freedom of speech and of the press for workers, peasants, anarchists and the socialist parties. They called for free elections to the Soviets, the liberation of political prisoners of the socialist parties and a review of the cases of all those held in prisons and labour camps. They asked for the abolition of Communist detachments in all branches of the army, in the mills and factories. They called for the equalization of rations for all workers and the right of peasants 'to do as they pleased with all the land . . . provided they use no hired labour'.

The Kronstadt rising was a direct expression of popular disillusion with the tyrannical policies of War Communism and the military-bureaucratic regime which Trotsky had advocated. It was promptly denounced by the Bolsheviks as a counter-revolutionary White Guard plot and the rising was brutally quelled by specially picked shock troops sent across the ice of the Gulf of Finland. Trotsky himself had arrived in Petrograd on March 5 1921 and delivered a ruthless ultimatum to the insurgents. 'Only those who surrender unconditionally may count on the mercy of the Soviet Republic . . . I am issuing orders to prepare to quell the mutiny . . . by force of arms. Responsibility for the harm that may be suffered by the peaceful population will fall entirely upon the heads of the counter-revolutionary mutineers. This warning is final.'[48] The rebels ignored the warning and as War Commissar it was Trotsky who ordered the attack on March 8.

Subsequently he sought to distance himself from the whole affair, claiming in 1938 that he took 'not the slightest part in the pacification of the Kronstadt rising or in the repressions which followed'. In his autobiography it is barely mentioned and in his last work on Stalin, he devotes only one sentence to Kronstadt, referring to 'a few dubious Anarchists and SRs' who 'were sponsoring a handful of reactionary peasants and soldiers in rebellion'. In reply to critics who had resurrected the ghost of

Kronstadt in the 1930s, Trotsky insisted that the sailors of the fortress were no longer loyal revolutionists but had become infected by anti-Communist Makhnovism, the 'anarcho-bandit frame of mind' of the Ukrainian peasant guerillas.[49] All these convenient rationalizations overlooked the mendacity with which the Bolsheviks had branded the insurgents as agents of a White Guard conspiracy and the intransigent brutality with which the sailors' demands had been met. On April 3 1921 Trotsky took part in the victory parade and referred to the massacred rebels as 'blinded sailor-comrades'.

The Kronstadt rising was the nemesis of War Communism and in a sense it symbolized the beginning of Trotsky's own slide from power. Even before the rebellion had been quelled, Lenin introduced his New Economic Policy at the Tenth Party Congress – the 'forced retreat' from the authoritarian methods that had manifestly failed to solve the problems of famine, poverty and economic stagnation. Trotsky was soon to find himself out of place in 'the unheroic atmosphere of the early NEP'.[50] He no longer found the easy, intimate contact with mass audiences of former years. His identification with the authoritarian strand in Bolshevism, his record as a militarizer of labour and as a ruthless disciplinarian led to a slump in his popularity. He had made enemies inside the Party not only with the Workers' Opposition and the Trade Unions but also in the Army and the Politburo where he was increasingly isolated by the intrigues of Zinoviev and Stalin. Even more sympathetic colleagues were irritated by his restless, inventive schemes, his exacting demands, his war on all forms of slackness and inertia. Trotsky lacked the subtlety to deal with those he deemed his intellectual inferiors, never sparing their feelings or pride. As a relative newcomer to the Bolshevik cause he was perceived as a man of the State (!) rather than the party, as a brilliant interloper with no personal following. Only Lenin's authority shielded Trotsky from the threat of Old Guard reprisals and inner-party intrigues. His illness and early death in January 1924 left Trotsky strangely vulnerable.

Deeper social forces also sapped any potential support for Trotsky within the Party. The failure of revolution in the West, the ferocity of civil war, the militarization of the Party and the banning of factions at the 1921 Congress were processes that ineluctably led to the atrophy of the revolutionary spirit in Russia itself. The working class was fragmented, exhausted and rendered apathetic by the ravages of civil war. They had no more stomach for the messianic leadership-style that Trotsky offered with all its attendant sacrifices, risks and complications. The Party, too, was weary of the forced march to socialism under a would-be 'saviour' who appeared to offer only the regimentation of a bureaucratic utopia or the distant music of world revolution.

## CHAPTER EIGHT

# AGAINST THE STREAM

'A Bolshevik is not merely a disciplined man; he is a man who in each case and on each question forges a firm opinion of his own and defends it courageously and independently, not only against his enemies, but inside his own party. Today, perhaps, he will be in the minority in his organization ... But this does not always signify that he is in the wrong. Perhaps he saw or understood before the others did a new task or the necessity of a turn. He will persistently raise the question a second, a third, a tenth time, if need be ...'

Leon Trotsky, *The New Course*

During the period of War Communism, Trotsky had been the main architect of the system of authoritarian economic controls which were now temporarily relaxed as a result of Lenin's New Economic Policy. Trotsky's proposals for compulsory labour service had been governed primarily by criteria of efficiency and an organizational model derived from his military experience. He had envisaged a perfectly functioning bureaucratic system using efficient accounting techniques, recruiting bourgeois specialists to restore industrial operations and replacing factory committees by qualified engineers and technicians. 'We must know exactly what property we possess, how much raw material and grain, what means of production, what work force, and precisely what their skills are. And all these must be arranged like the keys of a piano, so that every economic instrument acts properly ...'[1] Labour power was to be transformed into the basic lever of economic recovery, since capital resources were scarce, technical equipment worn out and the Russian economy completely isolated from Europe. Trotsky's policy of military discipline in the factories, his advocacy of the system of *udarnost* (shock work) – a kind of organized inequality which offered incentives to the most productive workers – was predicated on the assumption of a prolonged period of isolation where Russia might have to become self-reliant, building its own machinery and equipment.[2]

Trotsky's proposals for the 'statification' of organized labour by administrative decree, which aroused so much antagonism, were as much a logical deduction from his *isolationist* assumptions as an expression of his personal horror of anarchy. Equally, his measures to shake up the union hierarchy and remould the psychology of the working-class by use of shock techniques, political commissars on the railways and military cadres in industry, were all governed by a similar perspective.[3] Since aid from Europe was not forthcoming and scarce resources had to be concentrated in key growth sectors, labour was to be treated as a 'free' factor of production and applied on a very extensive basis. For the sake of Russia's 'leap into the future', central planning took precedence over workers' democracy. There were to be no concessions to consumer psychology. But by the end of 1921 Trotsky's concept of labour armies had passed into history, though ironically enough it was Stalin who, on a far more ruthless scale, was to realize many features of Trotsky's economic strategy in the industrialization of the 1930s.

Lenin was critical of Trotsky's excessive reliance on administrative statism and anxious in his last years to find correctives to the growing bureaucratism of the regime. His sharp disagreement with Trotsky over the trade-union debate arose out of his recognition that the concept of a 'workers' state' was an abstraction. The trade-unions, he argued, had to be in a position to defend the workers against the *actual* Soviet state which suffered from 'bureaucratic deformations'. But there was another aspect to Lenin's thinking: the belief that Western capitalist interests would help promote Soviet recovery, providing the country with large quantities of consumer goods in return for access to Russia's raw materials. Through separate deals with foreign capitalists, Russia could import machine technology and finance its reconstruction. This policy of concessions (which Trotsky initially

viewed with suspicion) was an important plank in Lenin's NEP
which envisaged a mixed economy with many state capitalist
elements. Trotsky was out of sympathy with this conception. He
still thought of Soviet Russia as a 'besieged fortress' and feared
that foreign concessions were a Trojan Horse which would
undermine the socialist economy and lead to a collapse of the
political superstructure.

With the advent of NEP, Trotsky was clearly out of his
element and it was no accident that his political decline coincided
with the new turn in policy. In contrast to Lenin, who considered
the idea of a single, all-embracing economic plan in the conditions
of 1921 as a 'bureaucratic utopia', Trotsky was obsessed by the
need for a 'Dictatorship of Industry'. Lenin's New Economic
Policy envisaged the market as the centre of gravity around which
the unity of industry and agriculture was to be attained in the
first stage of economic recovery. It was a forced retreat to
prepare the conditions for the industrial 'electrification' that
would follow, once a degree of stability had been achieved. But
Trotsky did not grasp the strategy behind this tactical retreat,
enamoured as he was with abstract schemas and a concept of
central planning that was not adapted to Russian conditions in
the early 1920s. Trotsky was determined to defeat the NEP by
strengthening the socialist against the private sector, industry
against agriculture. At the XII Party Congress (April 1923) he
argued that, if unchecked, the NEP would lead to capitalist
restoration. Large-scale industry would be unable to compete
with small producers unless the planning principle was extended
to the whole economy, the tempo of industrial growth raised,
and income redistributed in favour of industry. The market was
to be overcome by gradually swallowing and eliminating it.

But Trotsky's call for more power to the State Planning Commission (Gosplan) was received with little enthusiasm. He was
attacked for ignoring the *smychka* (union of proletariat and
peasantry) and the importance of currency stabilization. Bukharin,
especially, argued the necessity to fortify the *smychka* in order to
reinforce peasant buying power and to expand rural incomes if
socialist construction was to be financed by taxes on the nepmen
and capitalist elements in the countryside. Bukharin's agrarian,

cooperative socialism with its concessions to the *kulaks* (wealthy
stratum of peasants) was anathema to Trotsky. But it was more
in line with the mixed economy flowing out of NEP and undeniably more responsive to the popular mood of the mid 1920s.
  By 1925 Bukharin and Stalin had succeeded in identifying NEP
with the idea that Soviet Russia might succeed in building
socialism in one country. They could draw not only on the
indefinite delay of the international revolution, which necessitated
a new perspective, but also on Lenin's last writings which
envisaged the possibility of a distinct Russian path to socialism.
In his article, *On Cooperation*, Lenin had written that Soviet
Russia had all that was 'necessary and sufficient' to build a
complete Socialist society. The social ownership of the means of
production, the class victory of the proletariat over the bourgeoisie, and its alliance 'with the many millions of small and very
small peasants' were the basis for a system of cooperatives which
would provide all the pre-requisites for Socialism.[4] Bukharin
argued that his reformist gradualism with its perspective of a
dual private-public economy, the preservation of civil peace and
emphasis on trade inducements to the peasantry, was a logical
continuation of the NEP. Stalin seized on the Bukharinist position
and gave it a *personal* stamp by focusing on the 'one country'
theme. Soviet Russia would blaze the trail to socialism even without help from outside. It had the material and human resources
to sustain a policy of self-reliance, provided the contradictions
between the proletariat and peasantry could be resolved. Russia
must become an economically independent unit, producing its
own machinery and equipment, and not a mere appendage of
the world capitalist economy.
  This had also been Trotsky's position in 1920–1 but by 1925
he had swung over to 'economic integrationism', the theory that
accommodation with the West and reintegration in the world
economy was essential if Soviet Russia was to overcome her
capital scarcity.[5] Trotsky now insisted that Russia could not
finance its own industrialization without foreign aid and concessions. A closed national economy would impose enormous
limitations on its development. He argued that Russia was a
component part of the global economy, subject to its laws and

that protectionism would lead to a decrease in the *tempo* of its growth and accumulation of capital resources.[6] Trotsky exactly reversed his earlier position of hostility to consumer interests and now favoured investment in the consumer goods industry, the standardization of products and specialization of factories to mitigate scarcities. He warned against bureaucratization and attempting to install socialism by administrative decree in terms reminiscent of his own critics in 1920-1. By 1925 Trotsky was arguing that 'only by way of the greatest initiative, individual activity, persistence and resilience of the opinion and will of the many-millioned masses, who sense and know that the matter is their own concern . . is it possible to build socialism'.[7]

Such reversals of position were typical of most of the leading contenders in the power-struggle that was opening up. At the same time there were genuine disagreements about economic policy and the best path to socialist modernization. The one consistent strand in Trotsky's standpoint was his opposition to any concessions made to 'the renascent *kulak* stratum' whom he regarded as a potential source of counter-revolution. His insistence on the speedy and rational organization of industry was designed to counter the growth of private capital and the demands of the rural petty bourgeoisie – the kulaks, middlemen and retailers who, he felt, were being pandered to by the Bukharinists. Since 1923 Trotsky and the Left opposition had concentrated their fire against this neo-populist trend of support for the strong farmers, because they saw in it the danger of a *muzhik* thermidor – i.e. the restoration of private capitalism. Trotsky was convinced that only an optimal planning strategy which harnessed the industrial resources and investment capital of Europe to finance Soviet industry could secure the road to socialism. Between 1924 and 1926 it was this perspective rather than the theoretical postulates of permanent revolution which preoccupied Trotsky. Politically, however, it was still an extremely unpopular programme, as out of tune with the mood in the Party as Trotsky's earlier, rigorous advocacy of War Communism.

Stalin's slogan of 'socialism in one country' appealed much more to the sense of cautious optimism about Russia's domestic prospects and a general desire to avoid international complications. Even though Trotsky had not preached 'permanent revolution' in the mid 1920s as a policy line for the Soviet regime, Stalin had little difficulty in branding him with its newly-acquired stigma. He painted Trotsky and his followers as 'anti-Leninists' who lacked faith in the strength and capacities of the Russian proletariat, who disbelieved in the *internal* forces of the Russian revolution.[8] Their attitude supposedly fostered a 'spirit of capitulation' based on a doctrine of 'permanent hopelessness' – i.e. Russia would have to 'vegetate in its own contradictions' and rot away while waiting for the world revolution.[9]

The picture was greatly overdrawn but there was just enough basis for it in Trotsky's own writings to make it plausible. Although he had never disputed the need to *begin* the task of building socialism, Trotsky's approach to domestic industrialization did suggest that this could only offer a temporary respite. He had frequently said that as long as revolution in the West was delayed and Russia remained a backward country surrounded by capitalist enemies, there was no solution to its social contradictions.[10] In the 1920s Trotsky continued to believe that revolutionary Russia could not maintain itself in isolation, faced by a conservative Europe. In the new preface (written in 1922) to his book, *1905*, he defended his old theory of permanent revolution arguing that 'the contradictions in the position of a workers' government in a backward country with a peasant majority can be solved only on an international scale on the arena of the world proletarian revolution'.[11] The international perspective of 'permanent revolution' was not the foundation of Trotsky's economic strategy (as the Stalinists maintained) but the theory was consistent with his emphasis on the decisive significance of the world market.

In contrast to his adversaries, Trotsky constantly underlined the extent of Russia's industrial lag behind the West – 'the present immense production superiority of world capitalism as compared to us'.[12] In *Whither Russia?* (1925) he observed that this economic superiority of the bourgeois states resided in their higher productivity of labour, their superior techniques and their ability to produce 'cheaper and better goods than socialism'.[13] According to Trotsky it was a 'fundamental law of history' that victory would *ultimately* go to the system that raised society to the higher economic level. In other words, the historic issue between capitalism and socialism would be decided 'by the comparative coefficients of labour productivity'.[14] According to the economic indices, American capitalism was still far ahead of the USSR and Trotsky used the comparison to argue for a more rapid tempo of Soviet industrialization. But his adversaries, led by Stalin, casuistically denounced such arguments as 'defeatist' and a denial of the very possibility of socialist construction in the USSR. Trotsky's theory of permanent revolution, even though it did not refer to contemporary conditions, was deliberately pushed into the foreground to account for his 'pessimism'. In this way Stalin and Bukharin sought to capitalize on the new isolationist mood and the need for self-reliance which they correctly sensed was dominant in the Party. They appealed to a general desire for stability, tranquillity and consolidation of the internal front.

Their programme appeared more sanguine and realistic to those who now had a stake in the success of the new Soviet order. Russia's isolation was a fact but need not imply, (so the Stalinists argued) that it was doomed to wait for rescue from the world revolution. Nor did it mean that Soviet Russia was turning its back on socialism as a universal goal. On the contrary, Stalin suggested, in building a socialist society the USSR would give great impetus to the world revolution. Trotsky was thus manoeuvred into the position of appearing as an alarmist lacking faith in Russian capacities, who offered no positive hope that the sacrifices of the October revolution and the Civil War were not in vain.

While economic policy was a major substantive issue in the inner-party leadership struggle, it was not the prime cause of Trotsky's defeat. This contest took the peculiar form it did, largely because Trotsky's non-Leninist past provided a chink in his armour that could be exploited by his adversaries. The Bolshevik Old Guard had never really trusted Trotsky and their irritation was only increased by the speed with which he had risen in the Party after 1917. His military supremacy, his authoritarian role in the Civil War and the trade-union debates, stamped him in their eyes as a potential Bonaparte. Stalin's progress, on the other hand, had been far less spectacular. He had been nominated as General Secretary of the Party in April 1922, without anyone foreseeing what enormous organizational power this would allow him to wield. In contrast to the highly educated émigrés who returned with Lenin from abroad and assumed the reigns of power in 1917, Stalin was a committee-man (*Komitetchik*). An organizer whose practical experience had been acquired in the Russian underground, he lacked the intellectual breadth of leaders like Trotsky, Zinoviev, Kamenev and Bukharin. But the very limitations which Trotsky stressed in Stalin's make-up – his narrow political horizons, his stubborn empiricism, his lack of creative imagination or theoretical sophistication – were also sources of political strength. In a conversation held in 1925 with his former deputy in the war-commissariat, Sklyansky, Trotsky had described Stalin as 'the outstanding mediocrity in the Party'. But this was only a half-truth, though it was undoubtedly an opinion shared by many in the upper echelons of the Bolshevik hierarchy. As the debates of the mid-1920s showed, Stalin could hold his own against more sophisticated opponents, demonstrating considerable political skills and a sure mastery of Leninist texts. His plain, down-to-earth, plebeian manner and reputation for cautious moderation led his rivals to underestimate him as a dull, plodding empiricist. The significance of the fact that he was already *organizationally* master of the party by 1923 was lost on his adversaries, on all except the dying Lenin, who saw the danger and desperately sought to avert its potential consequences.

Trotsky, on the other hand, was remarkably blind to Stalin's capacities and incapable of uniting the Bolshevik Old Guard against him. Always awkward and uncertain in factional combat, Trotsky conducted the struggle on the plane of 'ideas' and precisely for this reason failed to perceive Stalin as his main adversary. When he belatedly organized an 'Opposition' it was not directed primarily at Stalin but at Zinoviev, Kamenev and Bukharin – ideologues like himself. The latter allied themselves with Stalin at various times not only because they also misjudged him but out of fear of Trotsky. Stalin's cautious realism and close identification with the Party apparatus, seemed more reassuring than the arrogance of Trotsky, his heroic postures, and his rigid adherence to Marxist 'principles'. For his part, Trotsky not only underestimated the immense social force of the apparatus which Stalin controlled but made no effort to win allies in the Politburo or in the lower echelons of the Party. Although the Politburo functioned through Party secretaries largely appointed by Stalin and his henchmen, this did not *automatically* ensure his dominance. Had Trotsky been able to win the allegiance of the Old Guard or at least to secure allies in the Party leadership, he might have been able to avert his total political isolation and consequent defeat. Trotsky's passivity in this regard has always puzzled historians yet his own account provides many revealing clues to his behaviour.

In *My Life*, Trotsky concedes that in 1922–23 'it was still possible to capture the commanding position by an open attack on the faction then rapidly being formed of nationalist socialist officials, of usurpers of the apparatus, of the unlawful heirs of October, of the epigones of Bolshevism. The chief obstacle was Lenin's condition.'[15] In other words, Lenin's incapacitating stroke was the decisive factor which in Trotsky's opinion prevented any action against the apparatus-men and the bureaucrats. Otherwise, the 'bloc of Lenin and Trotsky' *against* the Central Committee would have been victorious at the beginning of 1923 in overthrowing the Stalin bureaucracy. Independent action by Trotsky himself was ruled out since this would have been interpreted 'as my personal fight for Lenin's place in the party and the state'.[16] The very thought of this idea made Trotsky shudder – it would have brought such 'demoralization in our ranks that we would have had to pay too painful a price for it even in case of victory'.[17] Thus the outcome of the whole struggle is ultimately made to hang on the uncertainty of Lenin's physical condition. A healthy Lenin would have removed Stalin from the post of General Secretary and crushed him politically at the Twelfth Party Congress. Trotsky, on the other hand, could not act decisively alone, as if the very notion of exercising power in his own name was distasteful to him. The question of the succession was not related to any act of *will* on his part but solely to the impact of outside forces – whether of Lenin, the Party or the tide of history itself.

Such irresolution undoubtedly disillusioned Trotsky's potential followers who looked to him for leadership in the struggle that was developing within the Party. It seemed as if Trotsky was bewildered by the very nature of the contest which was more about control of the levers of power than about such grand ideas as 'the future of the revolution'. Perhaps, too, he was overwhelmed by a sense of helplessness. He fully realized that he was isolated in the Politburo and was still reluctant to appeal openly to Opposition groups whom he had previously alienated by his authoritarian stance. He held back, vainly hoping for Lenin's recovery and refusing to wield the weapons and raise the issues which the dying leader now handed him in order to attack Stalin – the Georgian question, the nature of the party regime, the indictment of the bureaucracy. Trotsky declared himself in favour of preserving the status quo and against removing Stalin, contenting himself with paper victories and promises that there would be radical change in policy.

At the XII Party Congress in 1923 the ruling triumvirate of Zinoviev, Stalin and Kamenev (united solely by their antagonism towards Trotsky) were still vulnerable. None of them enjoyed Trotsky's prestige or renown in the mind of the Party, the masses or the Communist International. At the Congress, Trotsky, along with Lenin, still received extraordinary tributes from the party cells, trade union organizations, workers' and student groups from all over the country. He still shone in the reflected light of Lenin's charisma as the 'second great leader of the Russian Revolution'. In March 1923 an article in *Pravda* by Karl Radek had eulogized Trotsky as the 'Organizer of Victory', the creator and driving force of the Red Army, a *vozhd*' (leader) of the party.[18] 'The Revolution changed to a sword the pen of its best publicist . . . The Marxist Trotsky did not see merely the external discipline of the army, the cannon, the technique, but he also saw the living persons who serve as instruments of war . . .' Only a man with such organizing genius, Radek wrote, 'only a man as pitiless to himself as Trotsky, only a man who knows how to speak to the soldier as Trotsky spoke, could become the standard bearer of the armed workers.'[19] (Thirteen years later, this same Radek was to attack the 'Fascist' and 'super-bandit'

Trotsky as the organizer of the 'assassination of the best leaders of the proletariat'!)[20]

But in early 1923 the glowing testimonials to Trotsky's achievements already had a double-edged effect. They fuelled still further the whispering campaign against him as a potential Bonaparte. It is true that the Army (and possibly the GPU) would probably have supported Trotsky if he had so wished. He still enjoyed the sympathy of its professional officers, of many of its party cells and of intellectuals in the Political Administration of the Revolutionary Military Council. But Trotsky had always accepted the authority of the Politburo over the Army and made no attempt to secure its support. Military action from above, could, in his view, only have accelerated the establishment of that 'bureaucratic Bonapartism' against which the Left Opposition were to fight for so many years.[21] Trotsky's refusal to have recourse to a military coup was consistent enough with his general principles. But 'principles' alone cannot explain his extraordinary reticence at the XII Party Congress. Lenin had asked him to take up the defence of the oppressed Georgians who were vehemently protesting at their brutal treatment by Stalin and his associates. Armed with Lenin's theses on the 'national question' Trotsky could have sat in judgement over Stalin's 'errors'. Yet he made no attempt to participate in the debate on the national question (only Bukharin took up the defence of the Georgians), allowing Stalin instead to make a hypocritical condemnation of 'Great Russian chauvinism'. This was precisely the 'rotten compromise' that Lenin had feared and it revealed how isolated Trotsky evidently felt his position to be.

Trotsky's behaviour during this period was that of a man who did everything *except* to concern himself with the Succession. Already in 1922 he had refused Lenin's offer to become Deputy Chairman of the Council of People's Commissars – an action which disadvantaged him greatly. It was as if he wished to dissociate himself from any attempt to claim Lenin's mantle. The very idea of becoming the head of state seemed to inhibit and almost paralyse him. Already an outsider in the top party hierarchy who lacked a power-base except in the Army and the masses, Trotsky's room for manoeuvre was objectively limited. But it was his psychological sense of isolation, his inability to see himself as *the* Bolshevik leader, which proved even more crippling. Trotsky's own account of this process is both perceptive and revealing. He admits that he felt increasingly out of place in the post-revolutionary mood of moral relaxation, self-satisfaction and trivial gossip. He took no part in the amusements of the new governing stratum because he found them so philistine and boring:

'The visiting at each other's homes, the assiduous attendance at the ballet, the drinking-parties at which people who were absent were pulled to pieces had no attraction for me. The new ruling group felt that I did not fit in with this way of living and they did not even try to win me over. It was for this very reason that many group conversations would stop the moment I appeared, and those engaged in them would cut them short with a certain shamefacedness and a slight bitterness towards me. This was, if you like, a definite indication that I had begun to lose power.'[22]

Clearly, Trotsky's sense of being an outsider within the ruling élite, one whose puritanical, austere life-style was out of tune with the new psychology of Soviet officialdom, reinforced his sense of bewilderment and isolation. The heroic tensions of the underground struggle, revolution and civil war had unwound – 'the nomads of the revolutions passed on to settled living' – and everyday routine was swamping the Old Bolshevik spirit.

'The out-and-out philistine, ignorant, and simply stupid baiting of the theory of permanent revolution grew from just these psychological sources. Gossiping over a bottle of wine or returning from the ballet, one smug official would say to another: "He can think of nothing but permanent revolution." The accusations of unsociability, of individualism, of aristocratism, were closely connected with this particular mood ... The revolt, against the exacting theoretical demands of Marxism and the exacting political demands of the revolution gradually assumed in the eyes of these people, the form of a struggle against "Trotskyism". Under this banner the liberation of the philistine in the Bolshevik was proceeding. It was because of this that I lost power, and it was this that determined the form which this loss took.'[23]

Much of this rings true, at least on the psychological level, and it also fits in neatly with Trotsky's theory of the Russian Thermidor. According to this version, as the October revolution receded into the past and prospects of salvation from abroad dimmed, there was a definite shift in the psychology of the Soviet ruling stratum. Self-satisfied mediocrity at all levels thrust itself forward in the form of a new conservatism. This trend found supreme embodiment in Stalin, the representative figure of the bureaucracy. Nevertheless, as an explanation of Trotsky's defeat, this theory too conveniently ignores his own serious errors and underestimates Stalin's political skills. Trotsky's whole conduct of the inner-party struggle was so replete with hesitations, ambiguities, strategic and tactical blunders that to a very large extent he dug his own grave. Trotsky never appeared to grasp the extent of the social vacuum existing in Russia after the Civil War. The atomization and disintegration of the working class had virtually excluded it as a political factor in the 1920s. The passivity of the masses corresponded to the growing autonomy of the political apparatus and ensured that the leadership struggle would be confined to the summits of the Party where Trotsky was more easily outmanoeuvred. Yet, in spite of the crippling of the Soviet proletariat, Trotsky persisted in believing in its revolutionary, fighting potential and in underestimating the autonomous power of the new political institutions.

It is true that Trotsky protested in *The New Course* (1923) at the abuses of bureaucratic power but he did not challenge the bases of its existence. At the XII Congress when the Workers' Opposition attacked the General Secretariat and called for disbanding the Triumvirate, Trotsky remained impassively silent. His critique of the bureaucracy when it came, was halting, qualified and lacked Lenin's trenchant sharpness. Nor did Trotsky attack the single-party system, let alone call for a restoration of the free soviet institutions of 1917. He fully supported the Bolshevik monopoly of power, sharing the assumption of the Triumvirs that the Party was the custodian of the working class, though he did demand free competition for political trends *within* the Party. Inevitably, Trotsky's call for the application of democratic rules within a monolithic structure strained credibility. He had vehemently defended the early restrictions – both political and economic – on proletarian democracy, e.g. the appointing of functionaries from above (*naznachenstvo*), the establishment of the Cheka, the suppression of internal debate, of trade unions, factory committees and soviets. Now, at the end of 1923, he suddenly attacked the 'old course' as the product of a regime of apparatus cliquism, bureaucratic smugness and servility. The Party, Trotsky declared, was living on two levels: 'the upper storey where things are decided, and the lower storey, where all you do is learn of the decisions'.[24] The rank and file, he complained, had no right of participation, the specific weight of factory cells and of the industrial workers in the party had declined. At every level – central, regional and local – a process of bureaucratization was detaching the leadership from the masses, narrowing horizons, sapping the revolutionary spirit and ossifying the Party. 'The task of the present', Trotsky wrote, 'is to shift the centre of party activity towards the masses of the party.'[25]

The problem with this analysis was that it ignored all those measures by means of which Bolshevik policy had enclosed the workers in their current apathetic and cynical passivity. The party apparatus was already too powerful to make Trotsky's call for *inner-party democracy* anything more than a pious wish. Nor were Trotsky's warnings to the Old Guard that it stood in danger of 'degeneration' liable to arouse a sympathetic echo in those whom he addressed. On the contrary they merely solidified the natural tendency of the party secretaries, bureaucrats and *apparatchiks* to unite around Stalin. Although Trotsky as yet rejected any analogies with the Thermidorean degeneration of the Great French Revolution, he did remind the Bolshevik Old Guard of what had happened to the Marxist leaders of the Second International. Here, too, his ground was poorly chosen, for it enabled his adversaries to recall his own 'Menshevik' past. Nevertheless, Trotsky's critique had its valid aspects. He saw the danger that the Party would merge into the bureaucratic apparatus of the State and that *political* leadership would decline into organizational fetishism, order-giving, passive obedience, careerism and sycophancy. He recognized in the state apparatus 'the most important source of bureaucratism' and traced its underlying causes to the backwardness and 'lack of culture of the broad masses'.[26] Trotsky looked to student youth as the most important 'barometer' and check on these bureaucratic tendences – a fact which alarmed the Triumvirs, who promptly accused him of trying to incite the young cadres against the Old Guard.[27] Trotsky had, in fact, argued that only active collaboration with the new generation could prevent the ossification of the Party and instill in youth the will to fight for its views with conviction and independence of character. Careerist functionarism and bureaucratic lick-splittlery had even spread to the Army where it was beginning to corrupt the young. The history of the Red Army was being written in pompous, bombastic tones as if there were only heroes and victories to celebrate. 'Supreme heroism, in the military art as in the revolution', Trotsky protested, 'is veracity and the feeling of responsibility.' It could not be cultivated by encouraging sycophancy, spurious docility and lying to please superiors.

Trotsky also stressed that the spirit of Leninism was totally alien to the functionary arrogance and bureaucratic cynicism pervading the Party hierarchy. It was being turned into a petrified orthodoxy by conservative elements in the apparatus who had no sense of Leninist revolutionary initiative, 'victorious war cunning' and freedom from all formalistic prejudices. 'Lenin cannot be chopped into quotations suited for every possible case', Trotsky insisted, 'because for Lenin the formula never stands higher than the reality, it is always the tool that makes it possible to grasp the reality and dominate it.'[28] Leninism was a policy of swift tactical orientation, abrupt turns (*Krutye povoroty*) and the search for concrete truth, which reduced inertia, routinism and moralizing doctrinalism to a minimum.

Trotsky's call for a 'new course' looked to new blood and new ideas injected by mass participation, to counteract the institutionalized conservatism of the apparatus. He still believed that bureaucratism was a 'tendency' that could be arrested, though by 1926 he privately recognized that the mood of the masses themselves was disillusioned, cautious and sceptical.[29] There was some support for his position in Party cells in the larger factories, in the army and among the student youth but much of his critique could be recuperated by the bureaucracy. Trotsky had seen in the weakness of 'proletarian' cells in the Party a prime cause of its ossification. The Triumvirs promptly swamped the Party with 240,000 workers (the so-called 'Lenin levy') – mainly raw and easily manipulable recruits – whose numerical weight helped smash the Left Opposition. Trotsky's programme had, in any case, relatively little appeal to the industrial working class and lacked a broad socio-economic basis of support in the Party. His following came mainly from among the higher party intellectuals and young student groups rather than from the rank and file.

The Triumvirs, backed by the Old Guard, moved to the offensive in December 1923, during Lenin's last illness, to brand Trotsky as an anti-Leninist whose outlook was alien to the Party. In an unsigned article in *Pravda* (December 28, 1923) Bukharin developed Trotsky's past differences with Lenin and exposed his 'errors' as deviations from Bolshevism. Zinoviev denounced Trotsky as an 'outspoken individualist' who had no understanding for economic relations in Russia and underestimated the peasantry. At the XIII Party Congress in 1924 Stalin systematized the six 'errors' of Trotsky. He had elevated himself above the Central Committee and its decisions; he had failed to declare himself for or against the Central Committee; he had opposed the apparatus to the Party; he had driven a wedge between the youth and the Old Guard; he had broken with the organizational line of Bolshevism by exalting the role of intellectuals and students; he had asserted the admissibility of groupings (*gruppirovka*).[30] Trotsky was thus branded as an outsider in the Bolshevik family who had violated party unity and discipline.

In his reply to these and other accusations Trotsky was calm, moderate, even conciliatory, though this availed him nothing. There was a note of stoical resignation and fatalistic pathos in his declaration of loyalty to the Party.

'In the last instance the party is always right, because it is the only historic instrument which the working class possesses for the solution of its fundamental tasks . . . One can only be right with the party and through the party

because history has not created any other way for the
realization of one's rightness. The English have the saying
"My country, right or wrong". With much greater justification we can say: My party, right or wrong . . .'[31]
This declaration contains yet another clue as to why Trotsky
made no real thrust for power against the Triumvirs. He persisted
in defending a disembodied idea of the Party while his opponents
used his acceptance of Lenin's ban on factionalism as a way of
castrating him politically. Much as he had clung to the fiction of
'conciliation' in the pre-war era, so now he held on to a spurious
idea of Bolshevik 'unity' which was being turned against him.
Now, as then, he had no faction or power-base in the Party and
appeared out of touch with inner-party affairs. Like most other
Oppositionists he was still psychologically conditioned by the
doctrine of *partiinost* (party-mindedness) and belief in the historical
infallibility of the Party even though he rejected its current
policies.

   Zinoviev and Stalin exploited to the full this misplaced sense
of loyalty, dispersing the ranks of the Opposition, sending some
of its leaders abroad and rigging elections to the Party Congress.
They invented the spectre of 'Trotskyism' as an internally consistent ideology which negated Leninist teachings on the Proletarian Dictatorship, ignored the peasantry as a revolutionary
force and sought to discredit the leaders of Bolshevism as well
as the authority of the Party. 'Trotskyism' was presented both as
a variety of Menshevism (to link it with Trotsky's non-Bolshevik
past) *and* as a form of revolutionary adventurism! The death of
Lenin in January 1924 greatly accelerated this process and seemed
to completely paralyse Trotsky, who was already suffering from a
persistent low fever and periodic bouts of listlessness and apathy.
Whether Trotsky sought to escape into illness from the orgy of
denunciation which was now being orchestrated against him by
the Party apparatus or whether the flood of mockery and falsification temporarily incapacitated him, he found himself completely
at a loss. The Lenin-cult was being cynically utilized as a pretext
to stifle all dissent and criticism of the leadership and in particular
as a weapon against 'Trotskyism' which was subjected to daily
vilification. 'Lenin's death freed the conspirators and allowed

them to come out into the open. The process of personal selection descended a rung lower. It now became impossible to obtain a post as director of a plant, as secretary of a party local, as chairman of a rural executive committee, as bookkeeper or typist, unless one had proved one's anti-Trotskyism'.[32] At every social level, the new careerism made itself felt, but above all in the selection of responsible workers in the Party and State.

Ironically enough, Trotsky himself had participated in the Lenin-cult which was now being used against him. On Lenin's death he had written in *Pravda*: 'The party is orphaned. The working-class is orphaned. Just this is the feeling aroused by the news of the death of our teacher and leader.'[33] His farewell article even struck a mystical note. 'In each of us lives a small part of Lenin, which is the best part of each of us.' Nevertheless, in spite of such eulogies, he was opposed to the dogmatization of Lenin's teachings as a system of *orthodoxy* rather than a theory of revolutionary praxis. Trotsky tended to overlook the doctrinaire aspects in Lenin, his scholastic taste for polemical textualism, which Stalin was to develop to such a fine art. Stalin's mastery of this body of teaching was to stand him in good stead in the inner-party debates of the 1920s.

The most powerful ideological weapon against Trotsky was, however, not so much his alleged 'deviations' from pure Leninism as his own personal biography. Trotsky had provided a pretext for this assault with his memoir (*On Lenin*) and his tactless introduction to *Lessons of October* (1924). In the former work, Trotsky presented his relationship to Lenin as a partnership of equals, in which the Bolshevik leader often leant on him for advice and support, especially against dissenters in the Old Guard. The reaction was predictably indignant. Zinoviev and others accused Trotsky of glorifying his own role in the October revolution. Stalin claimed that he had maligned the dead leader as 'the most bloodthirsty of all bloodthirsty Bolsheviks' and 'some kind of Blanquist dwarf'. In *Lessons of October*, Trotsky's polemic against the Old Bolsheviks (especially Kamenev and Zinoviev) was much more provocative. He accused them of right-wing tendencies, of adopting a fatalistic, temporizing, 'Social Democratic, Menshevik attitude to revolution', of trying to contain it within the framework of bourgeois society. Stalin was barely mentioned though he was implicated in the general attack on 'conciliationism'.

The onslaught against Trotsky that ensued was unprecedented in its tone of slander and open vilification of his Bolshevik credentials and revolutionary biography. Zinoviev recalled Trotsky's pre-war work *Our Political Tasks* and described it as 'the most vulgar Menshevist book which the history of Menshevist literature has ever known'.[34] Trotsky was trying to dilute Bolshevism and reduce it to a 'broad Labour Party' with freedom for various tendencies and factions. For fifteen years he had fought against the Bolsheviks and now once more 'he is giving expression to everything in the party which is not Bolshevik'.[35] Kamenev (Trotsky's brother-in-law) dredged up the full catalogue of Trotsky's black spots and errors before 1917, describing him as the agent of Menshevism in the working class'. Assembling a vast array of hostile quotations from Lenin, he portrayed 'Trotskyism' as hostile to the peasantry and organically incompatible with Bolshevism. In the controversies over Brest-Litovsk, the trade unions, economic planning and the party regime, Trotsky had simply continued his pre-war anti-Leninist line. Stalin went furthest in punctuating Trotsky's 'special role' in the October Revolution and the Civil War (his first effort in rewriting history) and emphasized the irreconcilable opposition between 'permanent revolution' and Leninist orthodoxy.[36] He accused Trotsky of minimizing and seeking to dethrone Lenin and of failing to understand the monolithic character of Bolshevism.[37] Most damaging of all, he quoted from some of Trotsky's hostile pre-war comments about Lenin, which stunned many in the party who had been unaware of the extent of their past differences.[38] The campaign achieved its objectives by the sheer volume of slander and the overwhelming power of the party apparatus.

At the beginning of 1925 Trotsky resigned as President of the Revolutionary Military Council and in the next two years he was gradually stripped of all his positions and remaining influence. He kept his silence when the Central Committee voted to suppress Lenin's testament (which called for the removal of

Stalin as General Secretary) and he failed to demand that the will be respected. Belatedly joining forces with Zinoviev and Kamenev in 1926 (he had waited a full year before making any move to exploit the divisions among the Triumvirs) he rejected the creation of a new Party out of the United Opposition. The Opposition still hoped to avoid a schism, believing that the Party had not yet undergone a decisive qualitative degeneration. This 'legalist' attitude notwithstanding, it was unable to operate as an accepted tendency within the Party. The ban on factions meant that the Opposition had to organize clandestine meetings in private houses, forests, even cemeteries – it was almost completely cut off from any appeal to the masses. In October 1927 the Central Committee expelled Trotsky and Zinoviev and the last demonstration of the Opposition was isolated and crushed on November 7, 1927, the tenth anniversary of the October Revolution. Trotsky was exiled to Alma-Ata and in 1929 deported from the Soviet Union. His followers were also driven into exile in Siberia and those who did not capitulate, were later imprisoned and eventually murdered in the Great Purges.

The programme of the Left Opposition as formulated in 1927 suffered a more ambiguous fate. Of its main planks, the first three – central planning, the industrialization of Soviet Russia and the collectivization of agriculture – were realized by Stalin though by far harsher, more brutal methods than Trotsky had envisaged. The remaining demands – for workers democracy, independence of the soviets, freedom of criticism, freedom of factions, greater social equality, the restoration of the workers' right to strike, abolition of the state monopoly of alcohol – were buried in the débris of Stalin's autocracy. The Left Opposition's call for 'proletarian democracy' fell on a barren soil of apathy and indifference in the face of bureaucratic intimidation. The ghosts of Kronstadt and the Workers' Opposition (which Trotsky had helped to smash) and the lack of political consciousness in the working class revenged themselves before the eyes of a nation driven into silent apathy. Refusing to appeal to the non-party masses and blocked in all their efforts to reach the rank-and-file by the vigilant Party machine, the Left Opposition was doomed to impotence. The masses could not follow the subtleties of the

economic debate or the scholastic disputes over 'Socialism in One
Country' and 'permanent revolution'. Though Trotsky re-
covered much of his old fire and oratorical power as total defeat
loomed nearer, he was hurling his thunderbolts into a void.
Nevertheless he went down bravely, with the defiant courage of
an old revolutionist.

  'I have never known him greater and I have never held him
  dearer', wrote Victor Serge, 'than I did in the shabby
  Leningrad and Moscow tenements where, on several
  occasions I heard him speak for hours to win over a handful
  of factory workers . . . He was still a member of the Politburo
  but he knew he was about to fall from power and also, very
  likely to lose his life. He thought the time had come to win
  hearts and consciences one by one – as had been done before,
  during the Tsar's rule. Thirty or forty poor people's faces
  would be turned towards him, listening, and I remember a
  woman sitting on the floor asking him questions and
  weighing up his answers. This was in 1927.'[39]

Trotsky still believed at this time that he was fighting to save
the Bolshevik Party from itself – that it could be reformed from
within. While denouncing its stifling of criticism and strangulation
of inner-party democracy he clung to the fiction that it was the
agent of historic progress and guardian of the Revolution  He
saw his own small Opposition group as the embodiment of the
true Leninist tradition and the 'yeast of the revolutionary future'.
Though he recognized that the proletariat was 'far less receptive
to revolutionary prophets and to broad generalizations than at
the time of the October Revolution' he still nourished illusions
that the mass of class-conscious workers could be roused to
fight for the Left Opposition programme. His close friend and
fellow-Oppositionist Christian Rakovsky diagnosed the passivity
of the Soviet working class more accurately. The nature of the
Party, he wrote from exile in August 1928, had changed since
the Lenin-enrolment brought into it a mass of members who had
'no conception of what the party-regime formerly was'. The most
energetic members of the working class had risen to responsible
positions and become beneficiaries of the new social differentiation. They had changed 'subjectively' and 'objectively' – they

constituted a different social type from the generation of 1917. Those who had remained workers were cowed by unemployment, without experience of class-struggle, disillusioned with the results of the revolution and impotent to resist authority. Hence nothing could be expected from them nor was there any hope of reforming the bureaucracy from within.[40]

Trotsky was too much the political activist to accept such a pessimistic prognosis. He was moreover psychologically incapable of cutting himself adrift from the Soviet regime and the Party which had made him a world figure and still provided his spiritual anchor. He would continue for many years to fight against the stream, from within the world Communist movement, even as it hounded and persecuted him. The arch-heretic of the Party refused to give up the banner of Marx and Lenin and the dream of world revolution – turning against his accusers the very charge of 'betrayal' with which they had excommunicated him. In December 1928 Trotsky wrote defiantly to the Central Committee of the Party and the Presidium of the Communist International: 'The greatest historical strength of the opposition in spite of its apparent weakness, lies in the fact that it keeps its fingers on the pulse of the world historical process, that it sees the dynamics of the class process clearly, foresees the coming day and consciously prepares for it.'[41]

CHAPTER NINE

# MAN OF LETTERS

'For relaxation I read the European classics. As I lay
in my prison bunk I absorbed them with the same
sense of physical delight that the gourmet has in
sipping choice wines or in inhaling the fragrant
smoke of a fine cigar. These were my best hours . . .'
Leon Trotsky, *My Life*

Ever since his youth in Odessa, Trotsky had dreamed of becoming
a writer. According to his own account he had never even
connected the question of his future career with government
work, in spite of the 1905 events.[1] As a professional revolutionary
he had always subordinated his literary work to political tasks,
yet when the Bolsheviks seized power he tried initially to stay
out of government and offered to direct the press. Later, from
his Turkish exile he wrote with manifest sincerity: 'In prison,
with a book or pen in my hand, I experienced the same sense of
deep satisfaction that I did at the mass meetings of the revolution.
I felt the mechanics of power as an inescapable burden, rather
than as a spiritual satisfaction.'[2] Now, during the years of wandering and exile, Trotsky's pen was to become his sole weapon,
much as it had been before 1917. In the title of one of Trotsky's
best-known works, *Literature and Revolution*, one finds these two
intimately connected sides of his political persona almost symbolically expressed – the man of letters and the committed
activist. The two voices are not always in harmony, they co-
habited at times uneasily in the soul of a man restlessly interrogat-
ing history and seeking to divulge from its 'objective' processes
a theoretical guide for his own will-to-action. The man of letters
is fascinated by the dialectic of the individual and society, the

human and the impersonal, the lived experience and the scientific law, the conscious and unconscious processes of history. With the eye of the artist he seeks to combine the psychological portrait with political analysis, the concrete image with the abstract idea, the autonomy of the creative imagination with the disciplines of Marxist theory.

At its best, Trotsky's writing with its intense narrative drive, its lyrical power, its sense of dynamic movement and historical imagination achieves this synthesis in a manner almost unique in socialist literature. Trotsky is able at such moments not merely to provide a coherent theory of the events he is describing, to capture the global historical forces at work, but to *communicate* the feeling of living through them. Sometimes, he overreaches himself, straining too hard for rhetorical effect or falling into hyperbole and exaggeration. At other times, as in his memoir *On Lenin* or in his biography of Stalin he is blinded by passion – whether in the direction of hero-worship or of demonologizing a remorseless adversary. On such occasions the voice of the embattled participant distorts the vision of the writer and critic, driving him to excesses of self-justification.

There are countless vignettes of political adversaries scattered throughout his writings which sometimes reveal more about their author than his subject. They remind one that Trotsky could wield his pen like a sword, using the sharpest edge of his slashing polemical wit to decapitate those opponents whose personality and politics offended his sensibility. Yet here, too, there are occasional flashes of chivalrous magnanimity – even the malicious, sarcastic tone rarely degenerates into crude, personal abuse, almost as if Trotsky were observing some un-written code of revolutionary honour. The man of letters is generally aware of the human content behind the political struggle where the Bolshevik commissar had been only too ready to consign the vanquished to the rubbish-bins of history. The dramatic pathos of Trotsky's writing derives perhaps from the feeling which it generates of gigantic forces locked in combat for possession of his own political soul. The frenzied drumbeat of revolutionary impatience ever ready to storm the gates of the Promised Land wrestles with the calmer voice of humanity and reason waiting stoically for the impersonal tides of history to turn again.

Amidst all this thunder and turmoil, Trotsky remained curiously reticent about his inner life, his sexual experiences, his feelings towards his children, his personal friendships and hatreds. Only in his *Diary in Exile* do we glimpse something of the sufferings, the agony, the bitterness of personal defeat and persecution, of that 'hell-black night' into which fate plunged him and his family. In *My Life* Trotsky manifestly preferred the genre of public autobiography, steadfastly maintaining that all 'the more or less unusual episodes in my life are bound up with the revolutionary struggle and derive their significance from it.'[3] While conceding that he was obliged to treat events not according to their objective significance but in relation to his personal life, he eschewed anything of a purely private character. Trotsky, to the end of his life, refused to measure the historical process by the yardstick of personal fate. 'I know no *personal* tragedy. I know the change of two chapters of the revolution.'[4]

There was a certain grandeur in this affirmation of a proud revolutionary but also a fatal self-deception that runs through even his greatest literary and political achievements. One has only to read carefully his epic *History of the Russian Revolution* to see the source of this flaw. The work was written in exile at the very moment that Stalin was establishing the foundations of his totalitarian dictatorship in the Soviet Union. Disregarding, for the moment, the ominous turn which the revolution had now taken, Trotsky turned back to the glorious days of October, to recapture the excitement and soaring passions of the Bolshevik victory. For all its masterly evocation of the masses in action, its images of heroism and drama, its sense of a new historical epoch, the *History* follows a predictable pattern. The triumphant proletariat under the leadership of Lenin and the Bolshevik Party is presented as the executor of a pre-determined plan, the conscious instrument of the objective laws of history. There is no room for doubt, hesitancy or self-questioning. October 1917 emerges as the consummation and embodiment of the Bolshevik myth, the vindication of historical necessity. For all its flashes of brilliance and literary power, the *History* often reveals a curious blindness to the uncertainties and imponderables of the Russian Revolution. It was as if Trotsky's critical faculties were switched off at the very moment that he was confronted with the fundamental dilemma of his political career – whether or not the seeds of the Stalinist nightmare were already contained in the October victory.

The revolutionary who knew 'no personal tragedy' lacked the necessary detachment to step back and test the premises of his own doctrine with its facile assertion of historical inevitability. It is not so much that the *History* lacked 'objectivity' or failed to meet the highest standards of 'scientific' accuracy. Though the very opposite of an impartial spectator, Trotsky was on the whole scrupulously attentive to historical evidence and indulged in no *conscious* distorting of the facts.[5] Nor can it be said that he exaggerated his own role in the events he was describing – if anything he understated it. The problem lay rather in his Marxist methodology – the insistence that he was interpreting 'the verdict of the historical process'[6] – and in his personal identification with the outcome of the events he was describing. The *History* for all its powerful evocation of the Russian masses forcibly entering the centre of the stage and assuming control of their destiny, consecrates a myth which lies at the heart of all Trotsky's post-October writings. The actions of the Bolsheviks allegedly embody the general will, just as the Leninist party personifies the will of history. In that sense, the October Revolution *is* Trotsky's supreme drama for it marks the point where the particular and the general merge and dissolve in a self-contained totality. Its finest moments are ironically when it leaves the realm of history and becomes dramatized actuality rather than a spuriously 'objective' exercise in predestination.

Considered in this light, primarily as a work of dramatic literature, the *History* is indeed an epic narrative. It is full of profound insights into individual psychology and collective behaviour, into the peculiarities of Russian society, the changing consciousness of the masses and their interaction with the political parties. Short, sharp sketches of particular leaders such as Lenin, Zinoviev, Martov, Chernov or Kerensky blend with striking crowd scenes, theoretical observations on insurrectionary tactics with convincing evocations of the mood of the army units.[7] Almost casually, Trotsky captures the effect of the war on the workers and soldiers, the 'molecular work of revolutionary thought' gradually penetrating the masses and raising their collective consciousness. But he is too certain of the course that events will take to resist the temptations of historicism. 'To the question, Who led the February revolution? we can then answer definitely enough: Conscious and tempered workers educated for the most part by the party of Lenin.'[8] The vision of the dramatist is ultimately subordinate to the demands of the Bolshevik myth.

This was, however, less true of Trotsky's first major work, *1905*, written before he had identified himself with the Leninist Party. *1905* lacks the broad canvas of the *History*, its richness of detail and sustained narrative power. Nevertheless, in some ways it is a more authentic, persuasive work vividly recreating the sense of a *lived* experience that combines both triumph and defeat. The accounts of the strike movement in Petersburg, of the trial of the Soviet, the descriptions of Trotsky's exile and his dramatic escape from Siberia are full of colourful impressions, a sense of narrative movement and flashes of humour which enlivens the reportage. We need not recapitulate here the historical analysis of the driving forces of the 1905 revolution but will focus rather on the literary qualities of the work. Take for example this abbreviated extract from Trotsky's description of the general railway strike which was spreading over the country, having broken out of its local and trade boundaries:

'Where the telegraph refused to serve it, it cut the wires or overturned the telegraph poles. It halted railway engines and let off their steam. It brought the electric power stations to a standstill and where this was difficult it damaged electric cables and plunged railway stations into darkness ... It penetrated into lift systems ... It halted goods trains wherever it found them, while passenger trains were usually run to the nearest junction or to the place of destination ... [it] closed down industrial plants, chemists' and grocers' shops, courts of law, everything ... It used every possible means. It appealed, convinced, implored; it begged on its knees ... it threatened, terrorized, threw stones, finally fired off its Brownings. It wanted to achieve too much: the blood of fathers, the bread of children, the reputation of its own strength. An entire class obeyed it; and when a negligible fraction of that class, corrupted by the very forces it was fighting, stood in its path, it is scarcely surprising that the strike roughly kicked the obstacle aside.'⁹

Trotsky's personification of the strike movement lays bare its inner dynamic, building up a cumulative assault on the senses reminiscent of Eisenstein's rhythmic film-montage. The dialectic of image and abstract idea is almost cinematic in its effects like many passages in *1905*. In contrast to some other writings of Trotsky, the author does not overwhelm his material but *shows* us in graphic terms the self-generating progress of the movement itself. But the strike not only paralyzes the motor and sensory nerves of the country (railways and telegraphic communications) it organizes colossal meetings, animates political life, confronts the troops. The whole of urban Russia is brought to its feet and attaches the villages to itself 'by the iron bond of rails'. Thus the strike not only personifies the decisive role of the railways and confirms the hegemony of the urban proletariat, it creates the very conditions for revolution by pitting the army against the popular masses.

Another scene, almost overpowering in its emotional intensity evokes the obverse side of the picture – the mobilization of counter-revolutionary pogromists in the name of the Tsar and the fatherland. The revenge of the old order in the form of the Black Hundred gangs is conjured up by Trotsky with a searing indignation and narrative skill it would be difficult to surpass. Recruiting their battalions from every alley and slum, among petty shopkeepers, beggars, publicans, police spies, professional thieves, dumb *muzhiks* and brothel doorkeepers, the pogromists burst into Russia's townlets, transforming them into living hells. Their basic props are 'the Tsar's portrait, a bottle of vodka, a tricolour flag'. The ragged Black Hundred army, embittered by ignorance and poverty, is organized around a disciplined nucleus 'receiving its slogans and watchwords from above'. The scene is set by pogrom proclamations, special articles in local newspapers, sinister rumours, the arrival of visiting 'specialists', the drawing up of a general strategic plan. The hungry mob is called from the suburbs, a special service is held where 'the bishop makes a solemn oration'. Here now is part of Trotsky's description.

'A patriotic procession starts out, with the clergy in the front, with a portrait of the Tsar taken from police headquarters, with many national flags. A military band plays without cease. At the sides and at the rear of the procession march the police. The governor salutes, the police chief publicly embraces the leading members of the Black Hundreds. Churches along the way of the procession ring their bells . . . To start with a few windows are smashed, a few passers-by beaten up; the wreckers enter every tavern on their way and drink, drink, drink. The band never stop playing "God Save the Tsar", that hymn of the pogroms . . . The doss-house tramp is king. A trembling slave an hour ago, hounded by police and starvation, he now feels himself an unlimited despot. Everything is allowed him, he is capable of anything, he is the master of property and honour, life and death. If he wants to, he can throw an old woman out of a third-floor window together with a grand piano, he can smash a chair against a baby's head, rape a little girl while the entire crowd looks on, hammer a nail into a living human body . . . There exists no tortures, figments of a feverish brain maddened by alcohol and fury at which he need ever stop. He is capable of anything, he dares everything. God save the Tsar'.[10]

Having described the hideous savagery of the pogromists, Trotsky now shows us the face of their victims.

'Here is a young man who has seen the face of death: his hair has turned white within an instant. Here is a ten-year-old boy who has gone mad over the mutilated corpses of his parents. Here is an army doctor who went through all the horrors of the siege of Port Arthur, but who, unable to stand a few hours of pogrom in Odessa, has sunk into the eternal night of madness . . . The victims, bloodstained, charred, driven frantic, still search for salvation within the nightmare. Some put on the bloodstained clothes of people already dead, lie down in a pile of corpses and stay there for a whole day . . . Others fall on their knees before the officers, the policeman, the raider, they stretch out their arms, crawl in the dust, kiss the soldiers' boots, beg for mercy. In reply they hear only drunken laughter. "You wanted freedom? Here, look, this is it." [11]

Images of unimaginable suffering, of pain, degradation and death fuse into an indictment of the 'whole infernal morality of the pogrom policy'. The Jews are never specifically mentioned. Yet somewhere deeply lodged in Trotsky's subconscious there must be an awareness that the pogrom epitomizes more than anything the inferno of atavistic Russian barbarism on which he had declared war.[12] But the pogrom mentality of Tsarism, of the nobility, the bureaucracy and the Black Hundred thugs represents only one pole of Russian society – its other side is the instinct for *revolutionary* violence. Sometimes it is elemental and chaotic as in the peasant riots where 'political nuances were washed away by the wave of class hatred' that razed the old country houses to the ground.[13] On other occasions as in the scenes of mutiny in the army and navy, elements of order begin to crystallize within the chaos but are outpaced by the march of events. A sailors' orchestra plays the 'Marseillaise' at the head of a revolutionary demonstration, workers come in their thousands to soldiers' meetings, there are handshakes, embraces, fraternal greetings. As in the *History of the Russian Revolution*, the crowd sequences are graphically orchestrated, rhythmic, multiform and full of fervent emotion.

No less striking is the description of the Trial of the Soviet, with the court building placed under martial law and transformed into a military encampment. But inside the courtroom, piercing the wall of gendarmes in blue uniforms – newspapers, letters, sweets and flowers appeared in the dock. 'There were flowers in buttonholes, flowers held in hands and on laps, finally flowers simply lying on benches. The president of the court did not dare remove these fragrant intruders.'[14] From the Trial we move to the wilderness of Siberia and Trotsky's animated letters to his wife describing their route, the climate, the peasants, the country-side, the friendly attitude of the soldiers' escort. Trotsky's mind turns to thoughts of escape and anguish at the prospect of con-

finement inside the Arctic circle. 'Obdorsk! A miniscule point
on the globe . . . perhaps we shall have to adapt our lives for
years to Obdorsk conditions. Even my fatalistic mood does not
guarantee complete peace of mind. I clench my teeth and yearn
for electric street-lamps, the noise of trams and the best thing in
the world – the smell of fresh newsprint.'[15]

*1905* is full of countless incidents, personal touches or snatches
of dialogue which interrupt the political narrative, yet illuminate
the broader canvas of events. It already shows Trotsky as an
accomplished creative writer who did not live by 'politics' alone.
This receptivity to the wider areas of human experience is equally
apparent in his literary criticism which was relatively free of any
sectarian narrowness. Trotsky's tribute to the greatest of all
Russian writers, Leo Tolstoy, written in 1908 for the novelist's
eightieth birthday, is a case in point. He sees Tolstoy as an
*aristocrat* in the deepest recesses of his creativity, who in the wrath
of repentance had renounced 'the false and worldly-vain art of
the ruling classes' to become the philosopher of the simple life.[16]
Landlord and *muzhik* represented the two sacred poles of his
creative universe – everything in–between he regarded with
patrician contempt.

> 'His whole heart was fixed in a way of existence where life is
> reproduced changelessly from one generation to the next,
> century after century; where sacred necessity rules over
> everything; where every decision and action depends on the
> sun, the rain, the wind, and the green grass growing, where
> nothing comes from one's own reason or from an individual's
> rebellious volition. . . . Everything is predetermined, every-
> thing justified in advance, sanctified.'[17]

Though Tolstoyan aesthetic pantheism with its deeply conservative spirit was alien to Trotsky's whole way of thinking, he
nevertheless acknowledged that the Russian writer's titanic
creativity formed an epic whole 'where everything breathes the
spirit of inner necessity and harmony.'[18] The mystical, quietist
idealism of Tolstoy remained far removed from revolutionary
socialism, yet in his work there breathed not only true artistic
genius but also an indestructible spirit of moral courage'.[19]

There is a passage in Trotsky's review which also expresses

one of the leitmotifs of his own revolutionary politics, his disgust at the barbarous crudity and creative nullity of traditional Russian society. 'How miserable, in reality, is this Old Russia, with its nobility disinherited by history, without any brilliant past of hierarchical estates, without the Crusades, without knightly love ... without even romantic highway robberies.'[20] The observation was historically striking, even apt, insofar as it focused on the contrast between the past richness of European civilization and the primitive backwardness of Russian society. Yet it ignored those contemporary trends which were already transforming Russian society and underestimated the importance and talent of its indigenous intelligentsia. In his literary criticism, even more than in his politics, Trotsky exhibited a tendency to deprecate Russian cultural achievements and to idealize the West which inevitably ruffled the edges of national pride. His immense admiration for French literature for example, which began while in prison in 1906 and remained with him to the end of his life, reflected a very subjective taste for elegant, refined language more than any general theory of art.

Trotsky never crystallized any specifically Marxist approach to aesthetic problems. But his judgements, especially on post-revolutionary Russian literature, did reveal a definite tension between the demands of ideology and a personal inclination towards cultural openness. This is particularly evident in *Literature and Revolution*, Trotsky's most important excursion into the field of literary criticism. Written in 1922–23 at the height of the power-struggle in the Bolshevik Party, it is often penetrating and sometimes merely trite in its phrasing but always merciless in its polemic. No doubt, Trotsky relished this vacation from politics but, as he makes clear in his introduction, he also attached great importance to cultural problems. 'The development of art', he wrote, 'is the highest test of the vitality and significance of each epoch.'[21] The most important practical insight in *Literature and Revolution* is Trotsky's recognition that the tempo of cultural change is considerably slower than that of political revolution and that any attempt to call a new culture into existence by edicts and commands would be self-defeating. All through history, Trotsky reminds us, 'mind limps after reality' and 'the

nightingale of poetry, like that bird of wisdom, the owl, is heard
only after the sun is set.'[22] Art required special conditions in order
to flourish – comfort, even abundance and not the poverty, want
and illiteracy of post-war Soviet Russia. A new Socialist culture
could, therefore, only be *prepared* but not brought about by the
proletarian dictatorship. This was the basis of his theoretical
attack on the doctrines of *Proletkult* which was already demanding a monopoly for 'proletarian art' in the USSR. Trotsky warned
against such trends:

> 'It is fundamentally incorrect to contrast bourgeois culture
> and bourgeois art with proletarian culture and proletarian
> art. The latter will never exist, because the proletarian regime
> is temporary and transient. The historic significance and the
> moral grandeur of the proletarian revolution consist in the
> fact that it is laying the foundations of a culture which is
> above classes and which will be the first culture that is truly
> human.'[23]

But if 'proletarian culture' was a chimera, did this mean that in
the transition period the Bolshevik Party was to adopt an eclectic
position towards art? Trotsky seemed somewhat evasive on this
problem. On the one hand he claimed that 'the domain of art is
not one in which the Party is called upon to command'[24] yet in
the same breath he also insisted that there was no question of
following 'the liberal principle of *laissez-faire* . . even in the field
of art'.[25] Trotsky wanted both a 'watchful revolutionary censor-
ship' and a broad, flexible policy free of any partisan malice. He
asserted that 'a work of art should, in the first place, be judged by
its own law, that is, the law of art', yet he simultaneously argued
that only Marxism could shed light on how and why certain
artistic tendencies developed in a given period! Nevertheless, in
spite of these definite limits to his open-mindedness, Trotsky did
protect 'fellow-travellers' in literature and defend the relative
autonomy of cultural activity from the more dogmatic advocates
of 'proletarian' ideology. He had too strong an appreciation of
tradition and the need for continuity in literary culture to accept
the proposition that politics and art should form a monolithic
whole.[26] In *Literature and Revolution* he attacked those ideologues
who approached bourgeois *belles lettres* from the standpoint of

narrow class interest. The working class, he countered, could only be enriched by the heritage of aristocratic and bourgeois culture which would heighten its subjective consciousness. 'What the worker will take from Shakespeare, Goethe, Pushkin, or Doestoevsky, will be a more complex idea of human personality, of its passions and feelings, a deeper and profounder underding of its psychic forces and of the role of the subconscious, etc.'[27]

Elsewhere in a public debate with members of the Na Postu group, Trotsky returned to this theme of Marxism and tradition. Dante's Divine Comedy, he pointed out, was not a mere historical document which expressed the psychology of the Florentine petty bourgeoisie in the thirteenth century. Its real importance and value as a work of art lay in its timeless and universal quality, in the fact that it gave intense, powerful expression to moods and feelings which raised it above the limitations of its social milieu.[28] All great literature from the Psalms to Shakespeare, Byron, Pushkin and Goethe had this 'eternal' quality and it was therefore harmful and futile to approach it in the spirit of pseudo-Marxist class determinism. 'There is no proletarian class standpoint in Pushkin', Trotsky ironically teased his audience, 'not to speak of a monolithic expression of Communist feelings. Of course, Pushkin's language is magnificent ... but, after all, this language is used by him for expressing the world-outlook of the nobility. Shall we say to the worker: read Pushkin in order to understand how a nobleman, a serf-owner and gentleman of the bedchamber, encountered Spring and experienced Autumn?'[29] Such an absurdly reductionist approach, Trotsky insisted, entirely missed the point. Pushkin's poetry had lasted precisely because it was so saturated with the artistic and psychological experience of the centuries.

Trotsky's attitudes to post-revolutionary Russian literature also reveal a persistent conflict between his sense of the complex web of inter-relations and power of tradition which underly the artistic creativity of a given epoch and his own impatient hunger for a work that would somehow capture and fully encompass the revolutionary Zeitgeist. Driven by his feeling for tradition, yet even more by his own obsession with the spirit of dynamism and change, Trotsky analyzes in turn the literary 'fellow-travellers', the Symbolists, the Imagists, the Futurists, Formalists, Cosmists and Proletkult writers, yet nowhere can he discover such a definitive work. Nevertheless his insights into individual writers, though sometimes overly harsh and impatient, have a crisp and penetrating quality. He does not disguise his distaste for the mysticism of Andrey Biely or Vasily Rozanov but he is sympathetic to an Imagist poet like Sergey Yessenin or to a 'realist' like Boris Pilnyak.[30] Nevertheless, Pilnyak, like Vsevolod Ivanov, Alexander Blok, Yessenin and so many of the writers analyzed in *Literature and Revolution* are accused of lacking artistic perspective because they are unable to merge wholeheartedly with the Revolution. Again and again, Trotsky attributes this failure to the class background of the literary 'fellow-travellers' who do not see that the Russian revolution is a revolt 'in the name of the conscious, rational, purposeful and dynamic principle of life against [its] elemental, senseless, biologic automatism...'[31]

Of all the competing tendencies it is Futurism that comes closest to forming the dynamic new art, for which Trotsky was restlessly searching. Nevertheless his approval is carefully qualified. He begins by observing that Futurism had 'obtained its most brilliant expression' in backward societies like Italy and Russia rather than in Germany or America. For all its oppositional character it had originated as a *bohemian* current of protest in the tradition of earlier romantic rebellions against bourgeois morality and philistine life. In Italy it was no accident that it had merged with the Fascist movement which also came to power by 'revolutionary' methods, by tempering and arming the masses.[32] In Russia it was more fortunate since the seizure of power by the proletariat occurred while the Futurists were still a persecuted group and pushed them forward. In the struggle against the old vocabulary and syntax of poetry, against impressionism and symbolism, the Futurists had undoubtedly played a progressive role – just as they had innovated in the field of rhythm and rhyme.[33] They stood for urban technique, scientific organization, the machine, for willpower, courage, speed, precision and 'for the new man, who is armed with all these things'. In all these respects their aesthetic 'revolt' was closely connected with the social revolution.

Nevertheless, Trotsky maintained, the Russian Futurists were at their *weakest* artistically precisely where they spoke as Communists. They could not organically assimilate Bolshevism because of their own spiritual past. Their greatest talent, the poet Vladimir Mayakovsky, whose sympathies were entirely with the Russian Revolution, embodied all the strength and weaknesses of the Futurist movement. His 'subconscious feeling for the city, for nature, for the whole world, is not that of a worker, but of a Bohemian . . . the impudent and cynical tone of many images . . . betrays the all-too-clear stamp of the artistic cabaret, of the café . . .'[34] Mayakovsky had grasped the *dynamic* quality of the Revolution but he lacked the sense of measure to do it justice. For all his violent enthusiasm the thing most lacking in his works was precisely 'action'. His weighty images often paralyzed the sense of movement through their hyperbolism, by shrieking instead of speaking, destroying pathos by their histrionic shouting and hoarseness. His verbal athleticism was marred by an 'individualistic and Bohemian arrogance', the poet was too much in evidence.

'At every step Mayakovsky speaks about himself, now in the first person, and now in the third, now dissolving himself in mankind. When he wants to elevate man, he makes him to be Mayakovsky . . . [He] has one foot on Mont Blanc and the other on Elbrus. His voice drowns thunder; can one wonder that he treats history familiarly, and is on intimate terms with the Revolution? . . . the proportions of our worldly affairs vanish, and it is impossible to establish the difference between a little thing and a big. That is why Mayakovsky speaks of the most intimate thing, such as love, as if he were speaking about the migration of nations. For the same reason he cannot find different words for the Revolution. He is always shooting at the edge, and as every artilleryman knows, such gunning gives a minimum of hits and tells most heavily on the guns.'[35]

No less interesting than such passages where Trotsky shows his ability to evoke a poet's distinctive 'voice', is his shrewd distinction between proletarian revolutionism and the exaggerated Futurist rejection of the past. 'We Marxists live in traditions',

Trotsky declares, 'and we have not stopped being revolutionists on account of it.'[36] Even the Russian revolution appeared as the embodiment of a familiar tradition, internally digested' – a tradition going back to 1905, to the Paris Commune, 1848 and beyond that, to 1789. The political revolutionist as a psychological type is declared ultimately imcompatible with the Futurist 'who is a revolutionary innovator of form' yet a bohemian nihilist in his attitude to tradition.[37] Trotsky's sensitivity to the past was undoubtedly an important factor in his resistance to Futurist fantasies and to the concept of a 'proletarian' culture. Yet, ironically enough, at the end of his book he launches into a wildly utopian rhapsody about the Communist future which would strike any reader today as exceeding the most naive delusions of the Futurists.

'Life will cease to be elemental and, for this reason, stagnant. Man will learn to move rivers and mountains, to build peoples' palaces on the peaks of Mont Blanc and at the bottom of the Atlantic ... More than that. Man at last will begin to harmonize himself in earnest. He will make it his business to achieve beauty by giving the movement of his own limbs the utmost precision, purposefulness, and economy in his work, his walk and his play ... The human species, the coagulated *homo sapiens*, will once more enter into a state of radical transformation and will become an object, in his own hands, of the most complicated methods of artificial selection and psycho-physical training ... Man will make it his purpose to master his own feelings, to raise his instincts to the heights of his consciousness, to make them transparent, to extend the wires of his will into the hidden recesses of his personality, and thereby ... to create a higher social-biologic type, or, if you please, a superman.'[38]

A Faustian vision of the new collective 'Superman'! Having first rationalized the economic system, Communism would then subordinate all unconscious processes to human will – driving out the 'dark elements' from politics, from family life and the deepest recesses of the soul. Sexual selection, 'the dark laws of heredity', the 'morbid and hysterical fear of death' – all would succumb to the self-mastery of Communist man in the glorious future. 'The forms of life will become dynamically dramatic. The average human type will rise to the heights of an Aristotle, a Goethe, or a Marx. And above these heights, new peaks will rise.'[39]

Such passionate, visionary social idealism which was characteristic not only of Trotsky but of a whole generation of Russian socialist intellectuals, inevitably rings hollow in the light of Gulag and other examples of twentieth-century barbarism. It has all the traits of an inverted religious psychology, of a materialist, atheist, messianism which worships science, technology, social utility and the limitless extension of human reason and will over nature. All spheres of human life must be organized and rationalized by Communist man in the name of the higher social collectivity. For all its idealism and intense messianic drive, this is a domineering pyschology expressing an aggressive will-to-power that can and has been all too consistently perverted. Trotsky's utopian vision of the Communist 'Superman' tends to transform man himself into something superhuman by deifying the social collectivity. It contains within itself the seed of what the religious philosopher Berdyaev once described as 'a burning idolatrous fanaticism'.

Nevertheless, in his writings on cultural problems, Trotsky did at times demonstrate an appreciation of the elemental, irrational forces in human nature and a recognition that authentic art cannot survive without spiritual freedom. In the 1930s he vehemently attacked the absurdities of Stalinist 'socialist realism' which had bred 'an epoch of mediocrities, laureates and toadies'.[40] He had nothing but contempt, even physical disgust for the Soviet art produced under Stalinist totalitarianism 'in which functionaries armed with pens, brushes and scissors, under the supervision of functionaries armed with Mausers, glorify the "great" and "brilliant" leaders, who are actually devoid of the least spark of genius or greatness'.[41] Against such attempts to stifle the human spirit, Trotsky now stood unequivocally by the formula 'complete freedom for art'.[42] In his 1938 Manifesto for a 'Free Revolutionary Art' written together with the French surrealist André Breton, Trotsky demanded 'the independence of art – for the revolution. The revolution for the complete

liberation of art.'[43] He now saw both art and socialism as part of
*one* rebellion against the status quo, against established con-
vention, scepticism, snobbery, ideological conformity and totalitarian oppression. Both art and revolution fulfilled an emancipa-
tory mission but the ultimate criterion for the artist was not his
politics but faith in his inner self and in his struggle for truth.

No less significant was Trotsky's defence of psychoanalysis
against efforts to totally suppress it in favour of the Pavlovian
experimental method. Although Trotsky admired Pavlov's
teaching, he was even more attracted to Freud's heroic, iconoclas-
tic cast of mind, the imaginative sweep of his theories. Already
in pre-war Vienna he had read the works of Freud and Alfred
Adler and attended psychoanalytic gatherings. The man of
letters, the artist in Trotsky, rebelled against the notion that the
subtlety of the human mind and of poetic creation could be
reduced to Pavlov's theory of conditioned reflexes. He tried
courageously to defend Freudian psycho-analysis as a materialist
teaching, complementary to the Pavlovian behaviourist school
and consistent with Marxism. 'Both Pavlov and Freud think that
the bottom of the soul is physiology. But Pavlov, like a diver,
descends to the bottom and laboriously investigates the well from
there upwards; while Freud stands over the well and with
penetrating gaze tries to pierce its ever shifting and troubled
waters and to make out or guess the shape of things below.'[44]
Again, in a speech in Copenhagen in 1932 Trotsky returned to
this metaphor of the diver 'descending to the bottom of the
ocean'; through 'the inspired hand of Sigmund Freud' psychoanalysis had 'shed light on the most mysterious driving forces of
the soul' and sought to subject them to human reason and will.
There was clearly an analogy here between Trotsky's categorical
rejection of attempts to ban psychoanalysis and his insistence
that mastery of the art of the past was a necessary precondition
for building a new society and a new culture. Both art and
science constituted different ways in which man tried to find his
bearings in the world. The art of the past had made man more
complex and flexible, it had raised his consciousness to a higher
level. To repudiate this heritage meant to impoverish man
spiritually. Attempts to outlaw psychoanalysis equally ignored

the complex and contradictory character of spiritual culture –
here, too, Trotsky sensed an implied assault on the human personality.

Precisely this concern for 'individual opinion, individual
criticism, individual initiative' (Berdyaev) is what marked off
Trotsky, the man of the letters and the revolutionary, from the
mystical and inhuman collectivism of the orthodox Communist
creed. In *Problems of Life* (1923) he wrote:

'But the Revolution is, in the first place, an awakening of
human personality in the masses – which were supposed to
possess no personality. In spite of occasional cruelty and the
sanguinary relentlessness of its methods, the Revolution is
before and above all the awakening of humanity, its onward
march, and is marked by a growing respect for the personal
dignity of every individual . . .'[45]

This faith in personal conscience, in human reason and artistic
freedom and the conviction that the 'awakening of human
personality' remains the final goal of socialism saved Trotsky
from the ultimate abyss of surrender to the totalitarian juggernaut.
His tragedy was that of a classical revolutionary who still believed
there was a role for personal freedom and responsibility in the
new order he had misguidedly helped to found.

CHAPTER TEN

# SOVIET THERMIDOR

'... Stalin represents a phenomenon utterly exceptional. He is neither a thinker, a writer nor an
orator. He took possession of power before the
masses had learned to distinguish his figure from
others during the triumphal processions across Red
Square. Stalin took possession of power, not with
the aid of personal qualities, but with the aid of an
impersonal machine. And it was not he who created
the machine, but the machine that created him ...
The machine had grown out of ideas. Stalin's first
qualification was a contemptuous attitude toward
ideas.'

Leon Trotsky, *Stalin*

Long before 1917 Trotsky had been fond of employing analogies
from French revolutionary history as a warning against dangers
which he saw as confronting Russian Social Democracy. In 1904
he had prematurely denounced Lenin as the 'Russian Robespierre'
and argued as if his Jacobin tactics were the original sin of
Bolshevism. In the early 1920s Trotsky himself emerged as the
most 'Jacobin' of the Bolsheviks and in the eyes of many of his
adversaries even as a potential Bonaparte. Having been defeated
in the political contest with Stalin, Trotsky now resurrected the
ghost of 'Thermidor' from the history of the great French
Revolution as a warning-signal against the 'degeneration' of the
Soviet regime.

The 'Thermidorian chapter' of French history had opened on
July 27 1794 (the 9th of Thermidor according to the short-lived
republican calendar) with the execution of the *revolutionary*
Jacobins, beginning with Robespierre and Saint-Just. In Marxist

terms, 'Thermidor' was a triumph of the bourgeoisie and signified the decline of the egalitarian ideals of the revolution. This political precedent played an important role in internal Bolshevik debates – nothing was guaranteed to make the ruling circles angrier than the charge of promoting 'Thermidorian' tendencies and thereby repeating the disasters of the French revolution. In the early 1920s the 'democratic centralists' had already argued that Thermidorian elements had achieved ascendancy in Soviet society and the state apparatus. At the time Trotsky (then still in power) had dismissed this as a false alarm though he was worried by the dangers of a capitalist restoration implicit in the New Economic Policy. By 1927 Trotsky had no doubt that the right-wing faction in the Bolshevik party, led by Bukharin, Rykov, Tomsky and Kalinin, did represent a major Thermidorian danger to the Russian revolution. The bureaucratic 'centrist' faction led by Stalin, was still perceived by Trotsky as very much a secondary threat.

In a speech in June 1927 before the Praesidium of the Central Control Commission which charged him with making 'factional' speeches and organizing Oppositional demonstrations, Trotsky dwelt extensively on the Thermidorian analogy. In the Great French Revolution, Trotsky pointed out, 'there were two great chapters, one of which went like this (*points upward*) and the other like that (*points downward*)'.[1] In the first chapter, the French Jacobins (the 'Bolshevik-Leninists' of that era) had guillotined the Royalists and Girondists; but in the second chapter the Thermidorians and Bonapartists (the 'Right-wing Bolsheviks' of the period) had exiled and shot the Jacobins. The implication of Trotsky's analogy was clear. He now unequivocally identified himself and his Left Opposition with the Jacobins, with Robespierre (and therefore with Lenin) and the current Soviet ruling faction with the Thermidorians who had destroyed the revolution. The Bolshevik Central Committee, dominated by right-wing elements, had begun the 'second chapter' of the Russian Revolution by disarming the revolutionary vanguard (i.e. Trotsky's Left Opposition) and stifling those who fought against Thermidor. The rank and file had been reduced to silence, the Party was beginning to 'purge' the Opposition and institute a reign of

terror from above. 'The Jacobin clubs', Trotsky warned, 'the
crucibles of revolution became the nurseries of future functionaries of Napoleon. We should learn from the French Revolution.'[2] The Russian Revolution was on course for a Bonapartist
dénouement based on the re-emergence of the 'bourgeois classes',
but Trotsky did not yet argue that it had perished.[3] There were
important differences from the French Revolution which,
Trotsky believed, were historically favourable to Soviet Russia.
Firstly, the Russian Revolution had been led by the proletariat
whose revolutionary potential made possible the transition to
socialism. Secondly, Russia was surrounded by more advanced
capitalist countries where revolutions could be expected in the
near future. Thirdly, the inevitability of this 'rising revolutionary
curve' would save the Soviet Union, provided a correct internationalist policy was pursued.[4] If it could hold out for a few
years the USSR would eventually be 'taken in tow by the great
historical tugboat of the international revolution'.[5]

The great danger that Trotsky saw, lay in the centrist back-
sliding in *internal* policy, the blandishments to the kulaks, the
reinforcement of the bureaucracy, the introduction of 'capitalism
on the instalment plan'.[6] This was the road to Thermidor but
Trotsky did not believe in 1927 that it could be implemented by
the Stalinist 'centre' which, he was confident, would melt away
at the first major crisis. Stalin's easy defeat of the Bukharinist
right-wing in 1928–29 and his sharp turn to the Left evidently
took Trotsky by surprise. Though Stalin had banished him from
the USSR at the beginning of 1929, Trotsky initially refused to
see his regime as 'Thermidorian'[7] and argued that with the defeat
of the Right, the *kulak* danger was receding. His basic premise
was that the victory of Thermidor entailed the surrender of the
conquests of October to the enemy classes, a process which
could not be consummated without civil war. Only such an
eventuality would signify 'the first victorious stage of the counter-
revolution, that is the direct passage of power from one class to
another'.[8] As long as Stalin maintained his left turn and control
of the most important means of production remained in the
hands of the 'workers' state', there was no Thermidor. According
to Trotsky what had emerged in the Soviet Union was a system

of 'dual power' analogous to that which existed on the eve of the
October Revolution between the Provisional Government and
the Soviets. Stalinism was supposedly 'Kerenskyism' in reverse –
'the last form of the rule of the proletariat' just as Kerensky's
government had been the last form of bourgeois rule in Russia.
The outcome of the struggle between the socialist elements and
the restorationist, proprietor classes was uncertain; but the main
danger still lay more to the Right than in the Stalinist bureauracy.
In Trotsky's opinion, the latter had no real programme or social
base and would lose out in a contest with the *kulaks*, nepmen
and peasant masses who were already being forced into the
*Kolkhozes*. Against this *muzhik* Thermidorian danger Trotsky
was prepared to critically support the Stalinist apparatus, as long
as it pursued the left course.

Trotsky's analysis of the internal situation in Soviet Russia at
the end of the 1920s was clearly far removed from reality. He
seriously underestimated the power of the bureaucracy and its
autonomy, the degree to which it had created its own social
support, independent of other class forces which it kept fragmented and powerless through terror and repression. He saw
only its weaknesses not its strengths – such as its ability to
balance the aspirations of various classes and create its own
vested interests and privileges. The Thermidorian analogy misled
him into thinking that the 'film of revolution' was running
*backwards* from Bolshevism to capitalism with the *kulaks* and
nepmen at the end of the road. In fact the film was moving *for-
wards* towards industrialization, a planned economy and collectivization at an unimaginable cost in human lives. It was Stalin
who was actually liquidating the threat of a *kulak* 'Thermidor'
along with private farming and the remnants of the bourgeois
classes. Trotsky kept looking for the rebirth of a 'new bourgeoisie' at the very moment when its roots were being systemati-
cally extirpated! Far from being a representative of the wavering
'centre', Stalin was, in fact, pursuing an independent course,
whose durability and power were predicated on a ruthless war
by the Soviet State against the Russian peasantry. Bukharin,
much more clearly than Trotsky, saw where this 'revolution from
above' was leading – to the emergence of an autocratic police-

162      TROTSKY: FATE OF A REVOLUTIONARY

state that would adopt an ideology of permanent terror to justify
the 'military-feudal exploitation of the peasantry.'⁹ But Trotsky
and his followers remained unmoved in 1928–29 by Bukharin's
prophetic warnings that Stalin was the new 'Genghis Khan'.
Trotsky's whole assessment of Stalin was vitiated by his
insistence on seeing him as nothing more than a mediocrity,
carried to power on the back of an impersonal Thermidorian
process. In his biography of Stalin, Trotsky recalled telling his
friend Ivan Smirnov in 1924:

'The dialectics of history have already hooked him and will
raise him up. He is needed by all of them – by the tired
radicals, by the bureaucrats, by the nepmen, the *kulaks*, the
upstarts, the sneaks, by all the worms that are crawling out
of the upturned soil of the manured revolution. He knows
how to meet them on their own ground, he speaks their
language and he knows how to lead them. He has the
deserved reputation of an old revolutionist, which makes
him invaluable to them as a blinder on the eyes of the
country. He has will and daring. He will not hesitate to
utilize them and to move them against the Party . . . Of
course, great developments in Europe, in Asia and in our
country may intervene . . . But if everything continues to go
automatically, as it is going now, then Stalin will just as
automatically become dictator.'¹⁰

In fact, there was nothing *automatic* about Stalin's elevation nor
was it true that he embodied a purely conservative, counter-
revolutionary force. Trotsky's picture had, moreover, a strong
element of personal rationalization, it was in a sense an *apologia
pro sua vita*. If Stalin's success was the inevitable consequence
of underlying social forces, then Trotsky's defeat could not have
been averted. Trotsky could preserve his own image of Stalin
as an untutored Asiatic, devoid of intellect or creative imagination, only if his victory was perceived as a temporary aberration
of the 'dialectics of history'. The theory of Thermidor which
reduced Stalin to a mere instrument or personification of bureaucratic reaction undoubtedly performed this unconscious,
apologetic function for Trotsky. Moreover, if the 'dialectics of
history' had raised Stalin up, they would just as surely cast him

down. 'The vengeance of history', Trotsky observed, 'is more terrible than the vengeance of the most powerful General Secretary. I venture to think this is consoling.'[11]

Trotsky's Thermidorian theory contained a more important *methodological* weakness which also explains why he could see a potential ally like Bukharin as his main enemy rather than Stalin. Trotsky's Marxism was predicated on the assumption that the dialectic of social forces was decisively important and he completely failed to take account of the primacy of politics in certain circumstances.[12] The domestic and international situation of the Soviet Union in the 1920s and 30s was a classic illustration of this phenomenon, which largely explained both Trotsky's defeat and the rise of Stalinism. The passivity and atomization of the Russian working class made Trotsky's Opposition programme seem largely irrelevant and unrealistic to the Party and the masses. Even his industrialization policy (though it anticipated Stalin in certain aspects) offered no real solution to the problem of the peasantry: the rallying of many of his followers, like Radek, Preobrazhensky, Smirnov and Pyatakov, to Stalin in 1929, already suggested its *political* weakness. While Trotsky insisted that Russia was still too poor and backward to embark on socialist construction alone, Stalin was stressing the need to infuse the Communist Party and the Russian people with a sense of confidence and purposeful activity. Stalin could always invoke the threat of a national emergency, the ominious international situation and the fear of a capitalist counter-revolution to win over those among Trotsky's followers who wished to play a part in the great upheaval that was beginning.

Trotsky never appeared to fully grasp what was at stake in the collectivization programme. In 1929 he still did not dream that 25 million private smallholdings would be liquidated by force in a few years. In 1930 he welcomed the 'global historical significance' of the new Soviet successes in industrial development as proof of 'the immense possibilities inherent in socialist economic methods'; but he also attacked what he erroneously called the 'ultra-left *zigzag*' with its exaggerated tempo of industrial expansion and administrative arbitrariness. With regard to collectivization, he supported it as a principle. Nevertheless, Trotsky argued that a sufficient technological base did not yet exist for collectivized agriculture and that violent measures would not increase productivity but lead to a collapse from within.[13] He believed that collectivization would only succeed on a 'voluntary' basis but Trotsky failed to suggest how Soviet power could have survived, had Stalin actually adopted a more gradualist path. The brutal offensive unleashed in 1929 had already reached a point of no return; it was a kind of caricature of Trotsky's 'permanent revolution' carried out by the State in a deliberately fostered climate of civil war and within a purely national framework. Trotsky's response to this primitive, autocratic 'revolution from above' was to argue that the supreme test of socialism was the standard of living of the workers, and that 'proletarian democracy' was the pre-requisite of economic progress. Stalinist methods based on the 'reactionary national-socialist utopia' of socialism in one country were bound to fail and could only aggravate the poverty, backwardness and isolation of the USSR. The Soviet economy could not develop in isolation from foreign trade, capital and technology. All attempts at artificial insulation in an underdeveloped country would, therefore, merely increase Russia's subordination to the capitalist world.

Trotsky's critique of Stalinist 'planomania' emphasized the lack of two-way communication between the Party and the people, the disharmony between supply and demand, the absence of any local initiative or material incentives. Ironically, enough, he now appeared in the guise of a common-sense *reformist* – arguing for capitalist methods of monetary accounting, the need for a stable currency, for interaction between the state, the market and 'soviet' democracy. Stalin, he suggested, was ignoring the objective, material limitations of a backward country, expanding industry too quickly and trying to transform agriculture all at once, without attention to the market or popular needs. In 1933 Trotsky even took up the old argument of the Workers' Opposition for greater trade-union independence. His critique overlooked the fact that Stalin had borrowed many of Trotsky's 'War Communist' methods of 1920 (including *udarnost* and the statification of the unions) and applied them on a broader, more ruthless scale. Trotsky did nonetheless see an analogy between the confrontations of 1920–21 and the recurrent danger of a peasant Thermidor or 'petty-bourgeois counter-revolution.'[14] The ruin of the *smychka* (union) between the proletariat and the peasantry, the expropriation by force of the products of the rural economy were one source of this danger; the preponderance of the peasantry and the fact that it had acquired 'an organization for resistance' in the *Kolkhoz* was allegedly another; the bureaucratic stifling of workers' democracy and the defeats of the international revolution were a third factor bringing the Stalin dictatorship closer to Thermidor.

Nevertheless Trotsky still insisted that the Stalin regime was not yet a true form of 'Bonapartism' because the proletariat supposedly remained the *ruling class*. The existing social inequalities were a capitalistic remnant that had not undermined the nationalized property on which the regime was founded. Trotsky defined the Stalinist apparatus as 'centrist', fulfilling a dual role – that of defending the proletarian dictatorship at home (though by faulty methods) – and facilitating the victory of counter-revolution abroad (e.g. Germany, France and Spain). Precisely because Stalinism was a 'parasitic growth' on the trunk of the October Revolution, its inevitable demise was approaching rapidly. As a result of bureaucratic blundering, economic disasters, openly coercive methods and rising mass discontent, the inner contradictions of the regime were ripening to exploding point.[15]

Following the German fiasco in 1933 and Trotsky's orientation towards a new International, the question of the 'class nature of the Soviet state' became even more pressing. In an article in October 1933 Trotsky still asserted that the proletariat was 'the spine of the Soviet state' even though government was in the hands of an 'irresponsible bureaucracy'. The Soviet regime was not Bonapartist 'because the bureaucracy derives its privileges not from any special property relations peculiar to it as a "class", but from those property relations that have been created by the October Revolution and that are fundamentally adequate for the dictatorship of the proletariat.'[16] But though he refused to define the Soviet bureaucracy as a new *exploiting class*, Trotsky did recognize that it had *politically* expropriated the workers, who had lost all control over the state and economy. He also conceded that 'no normal constitutional ways remain to remove the ruling clique' – it was no longer possible to reform it from within.[17] The bureaucracy could only be overthrown by direct action or rather by 'measures of a police character' designed to remove a malignant growth on the proletarian dictatorship.

By the end of 1934 Trotsky began to revise his earlier conception of Thermidor in the light of Kirov's assassination, the mounting terror and purge trials as well as the Popular Front tactics of the Comintern. He now recognized Stalin as the 'Soviet Bonaparte' and suggested that the Thermidorian process was anchored to the social foundations of the October revolution – i.e. it was a *reaction* within the revolution which did not require the overthrow of the new property relations. Trotsky defined his earlier mistake as being rooted in the assumption that the French Thermidor was necessarily 'counter-revolutionary': in fact it had not restored feudal property anymore than Napoleon Bonaparte had attempted to overthrow the social conquests of the French Revolution.[18] Similarly, in Soviet Russia the ruling bureaucracy was still materially bound up with 'the results of the consummated national revolution' and the upsurge in nationalized productive forces.[19] Thus, despite its 'monstrous bureaucratic degeneration' the Soviet state remained the historical instrument of the working class which would prepare the conditions for its future emancipation.

The dominance of the bureaucracy was a product of the social contradictions between the city and village, the proletariat and the peasantry, the Soviet state and its capitalist environment. It had raised itself up over the masses, and the need for discipline within the hierarchy had led 'to the rule of a single person, and to the cult of the infallible leader'.[20] Stalin was the 'leader of bureaucratic "leaders", their consummation and personification'. But how then could such a dictatorship still be exercised by the proletariat? If, as Trotsky conceded, power had been wrested from the hands of mass organizations – the party, the Soviets and the working class had all been strangled – surely this constituted a dictatorship of the bureaucracy? Trotsky's refusal to accept this diagnosis led him into irreconcilable contradictions. He insisted that in spite of everything the 'social content of the dictatorship of the bureaucracy is determined by those productive relations which were created by the proletarian revolution'.[21] Hence the Soviet Thermidor had not liquidated the *social* essence of the workers' state! What had allegedly occurred, beginning in 1924 (the onset of the Soviet Thermidor) was the transfer of power 'from the hands of the revolutionary vanguard into the hands of the more conservative elements among the bureaucracy and the upper crust of the working class'.[22] A broad, privileged upper stratum was created which constituted itself as a 'parasitic caste', *not* as a new ruling class. This bureaucratic caste had concentrated power in the hands of a single person and turned into a 'Soviet Bonapartism' which was analogous to the Consulate and the First Napoleonic Empire, rather than to declining bourgeois or fascist Bonapartism.[23] Thus Stalinism did not represent a bourgeois counter-revolution but rather a contradictory, transitional regime between capitalism and communism.

'Stalin guards the conquests of the October Revolution not only against the feudal-bourgeois counter-revolution, but also against the toilers, their impatience, and their dissatisfaction; he crushes the left wing which expresses the ordered historical and progressive tendencies of the unprivileged working masses; he creates a new aristocracy, by means of an extreme differentiation in wages, privileges, ranks, etc. Leaning for support upon the topmost layer of the new social hierarchy against the lowest – sometimes vice versa – Stalin has attained the complete concentration of power in his own hands.'[24]

But Soviet Bonapartism, like other forms of bureaucratic dictatorship, was, according to Trotsky, inherently unstable and doomed to collapse. Obsessed as he was by the danger of a 'bourgeois restoration' and the impossibility of the USSR surviving without a revolution in the West, Trotsky failed to see how securely entrenched the Stalinist system already was, in spite of the upheavals wrought by the Great Purge. This mistaken prognosis was in fact closely related to his dubiously Marxist myth that the workers 'owned' social property in the USSR. In both cases Trotsky's 'sociologism' led him to overlook completely the primacy of politics. A *politically expropriated* working class in the Soviet Union was necessarily one that had also lost its social and economic power. The existence of nationalized property did not give the proletariat any control over the state or strengthen its social position. On the contrary, as Trotsky himself acknowledged, the working class had been tremendously weakened under Stalinism – reduced to prostration and virtual enslavement along with most other social groups. Nationalized property, far from being, as Trotsky believed, an instrument of social emancipation, had been transformed into a weapon of exploitation and oppression, a justification for police terror against the workers and peasants. To describe Soviet Russia in these circumstances even as a Bonapartistically 'degenerated workers' state' was to remain the prisoner of Marxist categories that had become irrelevant. This framework of analysis could not adequately explain why under a Marxist regime, the State had become more omnipotent than ever. The answers to this enigma were more likely to be found in the logic of Bolshevism itself and in pre-1917 Russian history than in analogies drawn from the course of the great French Revolution.[25]

But Trotsky, blinkered by his theory of Thermidor, tended to overlook the specifically Russian features of the Stalinist regime. To be sure he recognized the decisive importance of Russian economic backwardness but not the specific weight of its cultural and political heritage. He continued to believe that beneath the Stalinist veil there was a 'socialist' essence rooted in public ownership of the means of production, which had to be defended at all costs. This was the whole basis of his pseudo-dialogue with the Soviet state which co-existed uneasily with his denunciations of the 'parasitic' bureaucracy that had usurped the October Revolution. As Lenin's disciple and co-founder of the state, he was too committed to defending the *regime* (though not its abuses) to examine the deeper roots of the Stalinist phenomenon. His critique of Stalinism drew back at the year 1924 (the beginning of Thermidor) as if to go beyond this date was to descend into an abyss. Stalin had to be placed *outside* the Bolshevik tradition embodied by Lenin and Trotsky, just as the Thermidorian analogy had to define him as a non-revolutionary. Whereas Lenin and the Bolsheviks were a necessary and logical result of Russian history, Stalinism was an aberration, a revenge of Russian backwardness on the Revolution. It could not have arisen organically out of Leninism and the institutionalized one-party state which was forged between 1917 and 1924. To admit such a possibility would have meant for Trotsky a degree of detached questioning both of his own past and the glorious 'communist future', of which he was manifestly incapable.

Classical Marxism was unable satisfactorily to explain how and why a 'workers' state' (even a degenerated one) could produce such monstrosities as the Great Purges, the cult of Stalin's infallibility and the Moscow show trials. Trotsky did his best to expose the lies and fabrications on which this 'Tower of Babel' was built; his rebuttals were often lucid and always rational, but he, too, had no real answer. He might point to 'the abyss between the bureaucracy and the people', the monstrous inequalities in the USSR or Stalin's fear of the masses, as underlying causes of the Moscow trials. But to describe the repression and terror as the last stage in a 'Thermidorian' process seemed flimsy and irrelevant in the face of the murder of millions of ordinary Party members and working people. Nor did the trials signify 'the death agony of Stalinism' as Trotsky assumed – they proved to be nothing less than a lobotomy performed on the body politic to prepare it for further rigours.

Trotsky did have something to offer in the face of what he once described as 'the most dastardly of all the police metaphysics in the history of mankind' but it was not so much 'scientific' Marxism as personal courage, revolutionary defiance, the dignity of a free man and a volcanic output of moral indignation. One has only to read his strangely moving testimony before the Dewey Commission in *The Case of Leon Trotsky* (1937) to be struck by the contrast between his personal integrity and burning hatred of totalitarian deceit and the inadequacy of his historical analysis of the Stalinist phenomenon. But with all its limitations, Trotsky's critique did recognize some features of the totalitarian masquerade earlier than his contemporaries. Precisely because he was so deeply implicated in Stalin's great charade yet an irreconcilable adversary, Trotsky could cut through the bogus judicial play 'in which the chief actors play their role at pistol point'.[26] He understood better than most liberals in the 1930s how effectively the massiveness of the 'frame-ups', signed and sealed by the firing-squads, could crush the authority of reason. Hence in his closing address to the Dewey Commission he set about exposing 'the Tower of Babel of slanders and falsifications' on which the moral authority of the Stalin bureaucracy and the Comintern apparatus rested.[27] He showed how the logic of the struggle against 'Trotskyism' had driven Stalin along the road of gigantic judicial amalgams and predicted (again over-optimistically) that 'the first great breach in this Tower of Babel will necessarily cause it to collapse entirely and bury beneath its debris the authority of the Thermidorian chiefs'.

Trotsky's most sustained analysis of Stalinism, *The Revolution Betrayed*, was completed before the first Moscow trial in 1936, but already contained the essence of his subsequent response to the purges and the judicial 'frame-up system'. Trotsky saw in the deification of Stalin 'the sum total of the collective pressure of a caste which will stop at nothing in defence of its position'.[28] The infallible leader was needed to personify the impersonal bureaucracy, to create a national symbol and the illusion of stability in a regime rent by the social contradictions of its own making. Soviet Bonapartism, precisely because it lacked mass support, had resorted to the glorification of state power, to a sham democratic constitution, to the 'plebiscite' and increasing reliance on the bureaucracy and police. In all these respects it was symmetrical to Fascist Bonapartism and both regimes ultimately owed their birth to the same cause – the delay in the world revolution.[29] In both cases, 'in spite of a deep difference in social foundations', Stalinism and Fascism expressed the victory of a political system that was severed from and stood above society with its contending classes. In its drive to *monopolize* all power, Stalinism had resorted to systematic terror both as a means of oppression and of self-preservation, necessary to safeguard the privileges of the bureaucratic elite. The antagonism between the 'new aristocracy' and the masses had to be disguised by a fictitious aura of formal legality behind whose mask the trials and purges could proceed. In its hysteria and paranoic fear of the masses the Stalinist regime proceeded to castrate social classes, to uproot and destroy all independent areas of public activity, to create a faceless, uniform society. In order to forestall the social degeneration unleashed by the Thermidorian processes, Stalinism was driven to assert even more rigidly its political monolithism and ideological purity, symbolically enshrined in the infallible 'leader'.

Trotsky's analysis clearly foreshadowed some aspects of the modern theory of 'totalitarianism', a term he used quite freely with regard to both Stalinism and Fascism. But he stubbornly refused to see in Stalinism a *legitimate* product of the October Revolution. The Stalinists might usurp the name of the 'Bolshevik' party but a river of blood allegedly divided the two phenomena. The Bolshevik revolution had been a social upheaval in the interests of the masses whereas Stalinism terrorized the masses in the interest of a privileged minority. According to Trotsky it had trampled on Marxism, on the revolutionary vanguard, on the soviets and on the Bolshevik Party itself. It had emancipated the party machine from rank-and-file control and transformed the bureaucracy into the lord, not the servant of society. The basis of this bureaucratic domination lay in 'the poverty of society in objects of consumption, with the resulting struggle of each against all'. In conditions of scarcity the Soviet bureaucracy could act as policeman and arbiter – this was the veritable starting-point of its power.[30] Here was a problem that neither Marx nor Lenin had foreseen; and in a sense Trotsky was correct in viewing it as the revenge of Russian backwardness on a revolution that had been isolated from the more advanced capitalist countries of Europe. The bureaucratization of the Soviet state was rendered almost inevitable by such factors as crushing material want, cultural backwardness and the inherited burdens of the Russian past.[31] The destitution caused by civil war and foreign intervention, the lack of material assistance from the West, the ebb of the revolutionary spirit had all facilitated the rise of a 'new commanding caste' on the wave of decline. But the political conclusions which Trotsky drew in the 1930s from this social analysis were often confused and contradictory.

We have already seen that Trotsky rejected the thesis that the Soviet bureaucracy constituted a 'new class'. In *The Revolution*

*Betrayed* he insisted that the bureaucracy had 'no independent property roots', no independent position in the process of production. 'The individual bureaucrat cannot transmit to his heirs his rights in the exploitation of the state apparatus. The bureaucracy enjoys its privileges under the form of an abuse of power . . . Its appropriation of a vast share of the national income has the character of social parasitism'.[32] Hence the privileges of the bureaucracy had not changed the *basis* of Soviet society. On the other hand, the Soviet regime was clearly not socialist. Hierarchical relations of production had been preserved, there was no workers' participation, social inequality and favouritism were being sustained under new labels.[33] If it was neither 'capitalist' nor 'socialist' then Stalinism must be a transitional regime with a *dual* character – socialist in its property forms and bourgeois in its system of distribution.[34] The development of productive forces was preparing the economic basis for socialism but the accelerating process of despotic, bureaucratic consolidation contained within it the seeds of the final death-sentence of Thermidor – the restoration of the old bourgeois classes. This dual character of Soviet society still left open the direction in which it might move but Trotsky could conceive of the alternatives only in terms of either capitalism *or* socialism. The possibility that the USSR might continue to ossify or else undergo a mutation into some new hybrid form of despotism escaped him. The prevailing bureaucratic domination would in his view have to resolve itself in terms of his Thermidorian model.

But if the USSR, as Trotsky himself argued, was undergoing 'degeneration' from within and Stalinism had already become the 'scourge' of the international workers' movement, why then defend it? Many of his followers posed this question and for forty years this dilemma, more than any other, has racked and split the Trotskyist movement. Yet Trotsky ultimately stopped short of a complete rupture with the Soviet Union. The war had to be waged on two fronts – against Stalinism as if there was no capitalist encirclement, and in defence of the USSR, as if there was no Stalin. The USSR was still the land of October where the proletariat had seized power, and even in its 'degenerate' form it was a bulwark against 'world capitalism' and the spread of

Fascism. The threat of a new world war (against which Trotsky warned throughout the 1930s) made the 'unconditional defence' of the USSR seem imperative; moreover the Soviet Union had retained in his view the essential pre-requisite for socialism – i.e. nationalized property, and therefore it remained a 'workers' state' in spite of all its bureaucratic deformations.

Nevertheless, by 1936, Trotsky was arguing that only a popular workers' rising led by the Opposition under the Bolshevik-Leninist banner, could resolve the internal crisis of the Soviet regime. 'There is no peaceful outcome for this crisis. No devil yet voluntarily cut off his own claws. The Soviet bureaucracy will not give up its positions without a fight. The development leads obviously to the road of revolution.'[35] The overthrow of the Bonapartist autocracy would however be confined 'within the limits of political revolution'.[36] The basis of the social structure would remain intact but the rotten superstructure would be swept away. In its place Trotsky envisaged a regenerated socialist democracy with genuine freedom of elections, a revival of 'Soviet' parties, a resurrection of the trade unions, a new emphasis on economic equality, the abolition of ranks, freedom for art and science and the right to free criticism. Foreign policy, too, would return 'to the tradition of revolutionary internationalism'.[37]

This utopian vision of a restored proletarian democracy did not prevent Trotsky from continuing to defend the *actual* Soviet Union as if there was no Stalin – a contradiction which increasingly alienated some of his American followers – the most important group in the newly constituted Fourth International. Partly under the influence of an Italian ex-Trotskyist, Bruno Rizzi, it was already becoming fashionable to argue that the world was not moving towards socialism but to a new form of 'bureaucratic collectivism' which underlay such diverse political façades as Fascism, Stalinism and the American New Deal.[38] In this perspective, the bureaucratization of the Soviet Union signified the first stage in the emergence of a new exploiting society where the bureaucracy totally dominated the State and its economy. Trotsky did not exclude this possibility and took up the challenge it provided to his views, in an article entitled 'The USSR in War'.[39] It was conceivable, Trotsky admitted, that humanity was entering 'the epoch of the declining society of totalitarian bureaucracy' and not that of socialist revolution. If Rizzi's hypothesis was correct this would mean that all the revolutionary potentialities of the world proletariat and of the socialist movement were bankrupt, since no more favourable conditions for world revolution could be expected in the future. Should the proletariat actually fail to fulfil its historical mission 'nothing else would remain except openly to recognize that the socialist programme, based on the internal contradictions of capitalist society, ended as a utopia.'[40]

This pessimistic prognosis did not signify Trotsky's resignation from the struggle. Even assuming the blackest hypothesis, a new minimum programme 'for the defence of the interests of the slaves of the totalitarian bureaucratic society' would have to be formulated. But Trotsky's article did reveal that his unquestioning faith in the socialist future had been badly shaken by the cumulative shocks of his personal life, the ominous threat of Fascism and world war, the Nazi-Soviet pact and the reinforcement of Stalinism. It could no longer be ruled out that the regime of the USSR might be the prelude to a new epoch of totalitarian domination. The Soviet invasions of Poland and Finland in 1939 brought into the open the implications of such untimely thoughts and aggravated the splits among his American followers, led by James Burnham (who abandoned Marxism) and Max Schachtman. Whereas Trotsky quickly stifled his own doubts and fell back on the old formula of 'unconditional defence' of the USSR, Schachtman and his followers now saw in Soviet foreign policy an imperialist design which was no different from that of the West.

The 'Russian question' unequivocally exposed the Achilles heel of Trotskyism. For if the Soviet working class had been expropriated of all *political* rights and internal reform of the bureaucracy was impossible, why call the USSR a 'workers' state'? Furthermore, how could one continue to defend a regime which played a counter-revolutionary role in the world arena? Trotsky's own analyses of the Stalin-Laval pact, of the Comintern role in the Spanish Civil War, and of Russian flirtations with Hitler culminating in the Nazi-Soviet pact, had all along remorselessly insisted on the bankruptcy of the Stalinist policy. Now the Soviet annexations of the Baltic lands, eastern Poland and part of Finland seemed to confirm the worst fears.[41] Yet Trotsky, after years of denouncing the crimes and betrayals of Stalinism (which he attributed to the false dogma of 'socialism in one country'), appeared in 1940 to be justifying Stalin's imperialist conquests abroad. He even described the Soviet occupation of Poland as 'progressive' for it had abolished private property, and destroyed the power of the Polish landowners and bourgeoisie. How could the counter-revolutionary Soviet bureaucracy suddenly be playing a revolutionary role abroad? How could the export of Stalinist totalitarian domination on the bayonets of the Red Army be approved by any serious defender of 'proletarian democracy'?

These were bewildering questions which Trotsky bequeathed to the Fourth International without resolving them. He had dared to imagine the *unthinkable* – that the future belonged to totalitarianism rather than to world socialist revolution – and then drawn back from the abyss into a pure act of faith. The Second World War *must* bring a new dawn, heralding the 'regeneration' of the workers' state and the overthrow of world capitalism. By this leap of faith Trotsky proved only that he could not cut the umbilical cord which tied him to USSR any more than he could abandon his belief in the working class as the historic agency of revolutionary change. To admit otherwise would be to call into question the entire Marxist view of capitalist and socialist societies. In that case Marxism would become just another ideology and its programme a mere utopia.

## CHAPTER ELEVEN

# THE RISE OF NAZISM

'Fascism has opened up the depths of society for politics. Today, not only in peasant homes but also in the city skyscrapers there lives alongside of the twentieth century the tenth or thirteenth. A hundred million people use electricity and still believe in the magic power of signs and exorcisms. What inexhaustible reserves they possess of darkness, ignorance and savagery! Despair has raised them to their feet, fascism has given them a banner. Everything that should have been eliminated from the national organism in the course of the unhindered development of society comes out today gushing from the throat; capitalist society is puking up the undigested barbarism. Such is the physiology of National Socialism.'

Leon Trotsky, *What is National Socialism?*

Leon Trotsky's analysis of National Socialism (and of fascism in general) stands out in the Marxist literature of the 1930s as one of the more lucid attempts to dissect 'this stupendous phenomenon of social psychopathology'.[1] Trotsky was by no means the first Marxist writer to produce a coherent definition of fascism but he perceived more clearly than most of his contemporaries the inner dynamics of the movement and some of its potential consequences.[2] But his insights into the fascist phenomenon, even at their most illuminating, were limited by the framework of his Marxist ideology and overconfidence concerning the revolutionary temper of the European working classes. While fully alive to the political threat that fascism represented he had an inadequate grasp of its deeper emotional sources and *positive* appeal. More specifically, he indulged in romantic illusions concerning the capacity of the proletariat (and the Western Communist parties) to resist, let alone overthrow a totalitarian dictatorship once it had seized the reins of power. Trotsky was convinced that Fascism and National Socialism would be unable to stem the endemic processes of capitalist degeneration – that the *Bonapartist* tendencies in both movements signified their isolation and inevitable downfall. Committed as he was to the view that fascism served the interests of big capital, Trotsky overlooked the extent to which the political power structure (the Party, the secret police, the bureaucracy etc.) constituted an autonomous factor.[3]

This failure adequately to perceive the primacy of politics and the technical efficiency of totalitarian methods of domination revealed the same limitations that were previously apparent in his analysis of Stalinism. These limitations were reinforced by a dogmatic insistence on organically identifying fascism with the last-ditch struggle of moribund capitalism. Nevertheless, Trotsky's writings on National Socialism were perhaps his most important intellectual achievement in exile and stand favourable comparison with the theories of other Marxist thinkers like August Thalheimer and Otto Bauer. Though he failed to provide a complete explanatory model for the rise of fascism, his appraisal of the cynical folly behind the Stalinist strategy in Germany remained second to none. As he wrote in his pamphlet *What Next?* in January 1932, 'It is not enough to understand only the "essence" of fascism. One must be capable of appraising it as a living political phenomenon, as a conscious and wily foe.'[4]

Trotsky's first analyses of fascism date back to the period following Mussolini's victory in Italy in 1922. At that time there was considerable confusion in the ranks of the Russian Bolshevik Party and in the Communist International concerning the rise of the fascist movement. Lenin, for example, evidently did not take Mussolini's victory too seriously, remarking at the end of 1922 at the Fourth Congress of the Comintern that 'the fascists in Italy will render us a great service by explaining to the Italians that their country is not yet sufficiently enlightened and insured

against the Black Hundreds'.[5] Zinoviev (President of the Comintern till his removal by Stalin in 1926) was, if anything, even
more flippant, referring to fascism as an historical 'comedy'. In
1923 Hitler's botched Beer-Hall Putsch in Munich gave momentary substance to Zinoviev's opinion that the fascists were 'fools'
with no more prospect of success than the White counter-
revolution had experienced in Soviet Russia.[6]

There was however another view in the Comintern which
took Italian fascism and its early German imitations more
seriously. For example, in 1923, the veteran German communist,
Clara Zetkin, described the fascist victory in Italy as the worst
setback for world Communism since the October Revolution.
She defined Fascism as 'an extremely dangerous and terrible
enemy', the strongest and most concentrated expression of 'the
general offensive of the world bourgeoisie'. It was a mistake to
identify Italian fascism with such counter-revolutionary 'feudal-
capitalist' regimes as the Horthy government in Hungary. It was
'a movement of the hungry, the poor, of men torn from their
background and disillusioned', including within its ranks a
substantial section of the proletariat.[7] Karl Radek (the Comintern
expert on Germany) agreed with Zetkin that fascism constituted
'a broad, though contradictory popular movement'. He even
advocated a nationalist course for the German Communist Party
(stressing national liberation from the chains of the Versailles
Treaty) in order to split the fascist ranks and recruit broader mass
support for the proletarian movement.

Trotsky did not participate to any significant degree in these
early debates on fascism. But there is evidence that he considered the German Communists to have 'enormously overestimated the power of fascism' in 1923 in order to justify what
he called their 'historic capitulation' in a revolutionary situation.[8]
Trotsky's comments on fascism in the mid 1920s suggest that he
regarded it as a transitional phenomenon, one of several methods
employed by the declining bourgeoisie in times of crisis to forestall its inevitable demise. In *Where is Britain Going?* (1926) he
dismissed Mussolini's regime as 'a dictatorship with a broken
nose', the 'dictatorship of a prematurely rotten, impotent,
thoroughly corrupted Italian bourgeoisie'.[9] In contrast to Bol-

shevism, it did not represent the mighty pressure of a new historic class but a retarded attempt to preserve a decadent social order. In the same book he predicted the development of Fascist tendencies in the right wing of the British Conservative Party, faced with the prospect of a Labour Government and an increasingly militant working class.[10] 'In a country which has grown poorer during the last few years, where the situation of the petty and great bourgeoisie has greatly worsened, and which has chronic unemployment, there will not be a shortage of elements for the formation of Fascist corps. There can be no doubt that, by the time the Labour Party is successful in the elections, the Conservatives will have at their back not only the official State apparatus, but also unofficial bands of Fascists.'[11] Trotsky was certain that if a Labour Government attempted to put through measures such as the nationalisation of the coalmines – 'the police, judiciary, army, and militia will be on the side of the disorganizers, saboteurs and Fascists'.

This prediction was as exaggerated as Trotsky's assessment of Marshal Pilsudski's coup d'état in Poland (May 1926). He described the Polish events as directly analogous to Italian fascism. In a speech to the Polish Commission of the Executive Committee of the Communist International on July 2, 1926 he remarked: 'Pilsudski as well as Mussolini worked with extraparliamentary means, with open violence, with the methods of civil war; both were concerned not with the destruction but with the preservation of bourgeois society. While they raised the petty bourgeoisie on its feet, they openly aligned themselves, after the seizure of power, with the big bourgeoisie.'[12] Behind this over-simplified comparison stood Trotsky's basic thesis in the 1920s that fascism was a weapon of self-defence for the decadent bourgeoisie when more sophisticated parliamentary methods had failed – a 'plebeian' solution which was used only in the last resort.[13] The big bourgeoisie liked fascism as little 'as a man with aching molars likes to have his teeth pulled', Trotsky ironically informed the Polish comrades, but in the final analysis it had become reconciled with the inevitable. Fascism, in its Italian and Polish variants, was a petty-bourgeois caricature of Jacobinism set in motion to act as the gendarme of capital.

Only at the beginning of the 1930s did Trotsky attempt a more
precise definition of fascism which differentiated it from the
various forms of 'counter-revolutionary' dictatorship then
flourishing in Europe. In a letter to an English comrade on
November 15 1931 he pointed out that the Primo de Rivera
dictatorship in Spain (1923–1930), contrary to the official Comintern line, was not fascist. 'The dictatorships of Spain and Italy
are two totally different forms of dictatorship. It is necessary to
distinguish between them. Mussolini had difficulty in reconciling
many old military institutions with the fascist militia. This
problem did not exist for Primo de Rivera.'[14] In the same letter
Trotsky significantly conceded that Italian fascism was a 'spontaneous movement of large masses, with new leaders from the
rank and file. It is a plebeian movement in origin, directed and
financed by big capitalist powers. It issued forth from the petty
bourgeoisie, the slum proletariat, and even to a certain extent
from the proletarian masses; Mussolini, a former socialist, is a
"self-made" man arising from this movement.'[15] Trotsky's re-
assessment of Italian fascism was made under the pressure of
Hitler's growing strength in Germany and the urgent need to
reorient Communist strategy in the country which held the key
to Europe. To this end, Trotsky pointed to the Italian experience
as a vital lesson which revealed the consequences that would
ensue if the 'proletarian vanguard' failed to conquer power.

The most important factor in the victory of Italian fascism had
been the disruption of the workers' councils movement after it
had seized and occupied the factories in September 1920. According to Trotsky, the Italian socialist leaders had taken fright at
the fascist backlash and 'betrayed' the movement in the vain hope
of pacifying bourgeois public opinion.

'To the last hour, they restrained the workers with might
and main from giving battle to Mussolini's bands. It availed
them nothing. The Crown, along with the upper crust of the
bourgeoisie swung over to the side of fascism. Convinced
at the last moment that fascism was not to be checked by
obedience, the social democrats issued a call to the workers
for a general strike. The reformists had dampened their
powder so long ... that when at last they finally with a

trembling hand did apply a burning fuse to it, the powder
did not catch'.[16]
Once in power, Mussolini, though proceeding cautiously, set
about implementing one of the basic objectives of the fascist
State – 'the complete strangulation of all independent mass
organizations.'

The German Social Democrats were repeating the error of
their Italian comrades, only more ponderously and with less
temperament. They looked for their salvation to Field-Marshal
Hindenburg just as Turati and his socialist party had vainly
looked to King Victor Emmanuel and to the Italian State for
protection. The German Communist Party had also learnt
nothing from its Italian predecessors who stubbornly dismissed
fascism as mere 'capitalist reaction' and ignored its organic
traits as a mass movement that mobilized the petty bourgeoisie
against the proletariat. With the exception of Antonio Gramsci,
the Italian communists had not even allowed for the possibility
of a fascist seizure of power. Yet the far more experienced KPD
(German Communist Party) had proved totally incapable of
learning from the tragic events in Italy.

Trotsky saw in Italian fascism a forerunner and model for the
Nazi Party, considering the two movements as identical in their
social content and political methods. Both fascism and Nazism
were 'counter-revolutionary' in their essence, though led by
exceptional agitators and popular tribunes. However meagre
their 'ideas', the victorious leaders of reaction had nevertheless
'displayed initiative, roused the masses to action, pioneered new
paths through the political jungle'.[17] Trotsky was particularly
struck by Mussolini's enterprise, tenacity and gift of improvization. 'Agile and inordinately ambitious, he smashed his socialist
career in his greedy quest for success. His anger at the party
became a moving force. He created and destroyed theory along
his way. He is the very personification of cynical egotism . . .'[18]
Hitler, on the other hand, was a 'pretentious misfit with a sick
psyche' who exhibited traits of monomania and messianism. He
had risen to the top by vilifying Jews and Social Democrats,
creating along the way a 'theory' full of countless contradictions,
'a hodge-podge of German imperial ambitions and the resentful

daydreams of a declassed petty-bourgeois.'[19] He lacked Mussolini's mental boldness and the early Marxist training which had enabled the Italian fascist leader to grasp more clearly the inter-relationships between social classes.

Thus, in common with many contemporaries, Trotsky regarded Mussolini as very much the superior partner and tended to underestimate the structural and ideological differences between the two movements. Indeed, he initially anticipated that Hitler's party, if it achieved power, would follow an identical pattern of 'degeneration' to that of Italian fascism. Trotsky argued in 1932 that under Mussolini, the Fascist party had already become bureaucratized and had strangled its chief support, the petty bourgeoisie, in the vice of the bourgeois State. Only 'historical inertia' enabled it to keep the proletariat dispersed and hence to stay in power. In the long run he was convinced that its bureaucratization would lead to the overthrow of the fascist regime. Trotsky expected Nazism to follow this model. Hitler would begin by smashing the workers' organizations but would discard his 'socialistic' slogans and petty-bourgeois followers once he had assumed control of the state. Nazism, to be sure, owing to the 'acuteness of social contradictions in Germany' was far more ruthless and dynamic but this only meant that it would 'wear itself out sooner than its Italian precursor'.[20] Inevitably, it would be transformed from a 'people's movement' into a bureaucratic-police apparatus. In Trotsky's apocalyptic scheme of things, this meant not the strengthening of fascism but 'the beginning of its end'.

Though Trotsky shared certain assumptions with the theoreticians of the Comintern – notably the thesis that fascism ultimately served the interest of finance-capital – his dialectical interpretation of events was far more sophisticated than the arid formalism of Stalinist dogma. He did not regard fascism as an inevitable product of 'objective conditions' such as the world depression, the cyclical crises of capitalism and mass unemployment. Nor did he hesitate to expose, with all the polemical wit at his command, the catastrophic consequences of the Stalinist theory of 'social fascism' which helped to pave the way for Nazism. It was in the course of this attack on this grotesque ideological dogma and the policies which flowed from its sanctification that Trotsky evolved his own definition of fascism.

The theory of 'social fascism' had been originated by Grigory Zinoviev in the early 1920s as a continuation of the Leninist tradition of irreconcilable hostility to social democratic 'opportunism'.[21] It was picked up by Stalin in an article of 1924, which respectfully echoed the President of the Comintern. 'Social Democracy', Stalin asserted, 'is objectively the moderate wing of fascism ... They are not antipodes, they are twins.'[22] The theory was not enshrined as official Communist dogma until the Sixth World Congress of the Comintern in 1928, which announced the end of capitalist stabilization and predicted the coming death-agony of the capitalist system. Trotsky rejected both the terminology of the new ultra-left turn and the tactical line followed by the KPD leadership in response to directives from Moscow. The German Communist Party was henceforth to concentrate its fire on the 'fascist social democrats' and the reformist trade unions. The Social Democrats were now depicted as the most active elements in the so-called 'fascisization' process of the Weimar Republic, as the treacherous agents of the bourgeoisie and the main class-enemies of the proletariat. Victory over Nazism, according to this aberrant theory, could not be achieved without the total destruction of the SPD. Nazi gains in the elections of September 14 1930 (their vote jumped spectacularly from 810,000 to 6,409,000) were dismissed by the KPD as 'the beginning of their end'. Ernst Thaelmann, the leader of the KPD, confidently announced in April 1931 to the Executive Committee of the Communist International that the Nazi electoral success (of 1930) 'was in a certain sense Hitler's best day, and that afterwards will not come better days but worse'.[23]

Trotsky was not deceived by this complete misreading of the situation. He interpreted the gigantic growth of National Socialism as a consequence and response to two central factors: 'a deep social crisis, throwing the petty-bourgeois masses off balance, and the lack of a revolutionary party that would today be regarded by the popular masses as the acknowledged revolutionary leader.'[24] It was fascism, not Communism which held the initiative in the German situation and to underestimate its forces would be a catastrophic mistake.

'*Fascism has become a real danger* as an acute-expression of the helpless position of bourgeois regime, the conservative role of the Social Democracy in this regime, and the accumulated powerlessness of the Communist Party to abolish it'.[25] While the KPD concentrated their fire on the Social Democrats, the Nazis were preparing to liquidate all those material and moral positions that the German workers had managed to secure under bourgeois democracy. Trotsky had no doubt that a National Socialist victory would mean the extermination of the flower of the German proletariat and the destruction of its independent organizations from the most revolutionary to the most conservative. This prescience gave a dramatic urgency to Trotsky's warnings. In December 1931, he wrote:

'Worker-communists, you are hundreds of thousands, millions; you cannot leave for anywhere; there are not enough passports for you. Should fascism come to power, it will ride over your skulls and spines like a terrific tank. Your salvation lies in merciless struggle. And only a fighting unity with the Social Democratic workers can bring victory.'[26]

It was a case of foresight barred from any effective action. Trotsky was prophesying to those who continued to slander and deride him as a 'panic-monger' and 'adventurist'. In September 1932, Thaelmann (echoing Willi Muenzenberg) even called his advocacy of a united front with the Social Democrats 'the most criminal theory that Trotsky has construed in these last years of his counter-revolutionary propaganda'.[27] While denouncing opponents like Trotsky, the German Communists did not hesitate to campaign along with the Nazis to remove the SPD-led government of Otto Braun and Carl Severing in Prussia. They even adopted as their own, the Nazi slogan of a 'people's revolution', and called on the Nazi masses to join in with them in a common struggle against the Versailles treaty, the Young Plan and the government of finance-capital.[28] This method of imitating the class enemy which wiped away 'the ideological demarcation between Marxism and fascism' was for Trotsky a classic illustration of the inconsistent, unprincipled and bankrupt

Stalinist policy in Germany. One could not fight Nazism with its own weapons by 'borrowing the colours of its political palette, and trying to outshout it at the auction of patriotism'.[29] The KPD's flirtation with the phraseology of petty-bourgeois nationalism, its vacillations, its bureaucratic 'monolithism', its empty talk of 'social fascism' prevented it from making significant inroads into working-class support for the Social Democrats. Trotsky recognized early on that the Communists lacked sufficient strength in the trade unions, the factory committees and the German proletariat as a whole, to wage a war on two fronts. What alarmed him most was that their leadership failed to see Nazism as a deadly danger to the working-class. Instead it claimed that 'fascism' already ruled under the Catholic Chancellor Bruening and that both capitalism and Social Democracy would have to be overthrown first, before the Nazis could be repelled. In other words, the premise was 'that Hitler will add nothing new; that there is no cause to fear Hitler; that Hitler will only clear the road for the communists'.[30]

This strategy revealed to Trotsky 'an utter misunderstanding of mass psychology and of the dialectics of revolutionary struggle', for once Hitler had gained power no amount of speeches about the future 'Soviet Germany' would sweep him away. The false strategic conceptions of the KPD leadership and the Stalinist bureaucracy were demoralizing the German proletariat and sapping its will to resist fascism. As a consequence the wavering petty bourgeoisie was swinging over in droves to the side of National Socialism 'because the proletariat, paralysed from above, proved powerless to lead it along a different road'. The absence of resistance 'heightened the self-assurance of fascism and diminished the fear of the big bourgeoisie confronted by the risk of civil war ... Thus the triumphal procession of Hitler over the bones of the proletarian organization was assured.'[31]

Trotsky did not expect a correct revolutionary strategy from the German Social Democrats who continued to maintain their blind confidence that the Weimar Constitution and the norms of bourgeois legality would suffice to hold Hitler back. As a bourgeois party 'which is good for nothing at all under the conditions of social crisis', except vain appeals to the state apparatus, the police and even the Reichswehr, the SPD also had its historic responsibility for Hitler's victory.[32] Trotsky did not disguise his contempt for 'the politicians of reformism' who by prolonging the agony of the capitalist regime and depriving the proletariat of its capacity to lead the petty-bourgeois masses had strengthened the mass basis of fascism.[33] The SPD had tolerated Bruening, von Papen and General Schleicher in order to preserve its own organizational apparatus and because it had feared the Communists more than fascism. But Trotsky emphasized that there was nonetheless an irreducible conflict of interest between the Social Democrats and the Nazis which the KPD had failed to exploit, and it had thereby sabotaged the possibility of joint proletarian action against Hitler. Once in power, the Nazis would not hesitate to destroy not only the proletarian vanguard but also the bourgeois-parliamentary regime on which Social Democracy itself depended.

The fundamental mistake of Thaelmann and the KPD leadership was their failure to differentiate between the Papen-Schleicher regime (which Trotsky defined as 'Bonapartist') and fascism. 'By disregarding the social and political distinctions between *Bonapartism*, that is, the regime of "civil peace" resting upon military-police dictatorship, and *fascism*, that is, the regime of open civil war against the proletariat, Thälmann deprives himself in advance of the possibility of understanding what is taking place before his very eyes.'[34] The task of German Bonapartism was 'to avoid civil war by amicably disciplining the National Socialists and chaining the proletariat to police fetters'.[35] The German big bourgeoisie like its counterparts in Italy, France and other European countries still feared the 'surgical intervention of fascism' – it preferred to rely on the army and police to hold the balance between the Nazis and the proletariat. The 'Bonapartist' dictatorship was in essence a bureaucratic, *pre-fascist* government in the interests of the propertied classes who were still trying to avert the revolutionary convulsions of civil war with all its attendant risks and uncertainties. The German Junkers, industrialists and bankers would only place themselves in Hitler's hands if the extra-parliamentary Bonapartist combination failed to neutralize the two irreconcilable camps. This acute conceptual distinction allowed Trotsky to make a far more perceptive analysis of the situation than the Stalinists who confused the 'Bonapartist' regime with fascism *already* in power. Trotsky understood that even in February 1933 the Nazis were only one of several armies at the disposal of the possessing classes – the Reichswehr, the police and the Stahlhelm were not yet in Hitler's hands. The Nazis, he pointed out, could only achieve complete victory if they successfully provoked the semblance of civil war, in order to forcibly suppress the workers' organizations.[36] Bonapartism was therefore a warning-signal to the proletarian vanguard of the *imminence* of fascism, its last opportunity to gather momentum for the conquest of power. If it failed to seize the opportunity, the Bonapartist dictatorship would give way to a more stable fascist regime of the Italian type, capable of eliminating the contending classes from the political arena.

Trotsky's Bonapartist model was intended to explain the *transitional*, intermediate situations through which a parliamentary regime passed over into fully-fledged fascism. He was well aware that Nazism itself was a more complex phenomenon rooted in the defeat of 1918 and the post-war chaos of German capitalism. Hitler's success lay in his ability to become the focus of 'anonymous historic forces', to express the exasperation of the pauperized petty bourgeoisie, of the upstarts from the old army, of the decaying middle strata in German society.

'At the start of his political career, Hitler stood out only because of his big temperament, a voice much louder than others, and an intellectual mediocrity much more self-assured. He did not bring into the movement any ready-made programme, if one disregards the insulted soldier's thirst for vengeance. Hitler began with grievances and complaints about the Versailles terms, the high cost of living, the lack of respect for a meritorious non-commissioned officer, and the plots of bankers and journalists of the Mosaic persuasion. There were in the country plenty of ruined and drowning people with scars and fresh bruises. They all wanted to thump with their fists on the table. This Hitler could do better than the others ... his harangues resounded, now like commands and now like prayers addressed to inexorable fate . . . Sentimental formlessness, absence of disciplined thought, ignorance along with gaudy erudition – all these minuses turned into pluses. They supplied him with the possibility of uniting all types of dissatisfaction in the beggar's bowl of National Socialism, and of leading the mass in the direction in which it pushed him . . . His political thoughts were the fruits of oratorical acoustics . . . That is how the "leader" took shape out of the raw material.'[37]

Hitler's triumph was the culmination of a cycle of shocks which had begun in 1918. The international and internal situation of German capitalism – reparations, inflation, bankruptcy and mass unemployment, had left it no more room for concessions. The Social Democrats did not permit the proletariat to bring the November revolution of 1918 to a successful conclusion and just as they saved the German middle classes so now 'fascism came in its turn to liberate the bourgeoisie from the Social Democracy'. The fascist leadership had shown itself superior to that of the proletariat – Hitler did not need 'political genius' – 'the strategy of his enemy compensated largely for anything his own strategy lacked'. The Nazis had even won over sections of the proletariat, not only a stratum of the labour aristocracy, but also a layer of the millions of unemployed who had previously swelled the Communist ranks. They had succeeded in penetrating the proletariat from above and below, drawing over many salaried employees, technical and administrative personnel, petty traders, hawkers and lumpenproletarians.[38]

Essentially a movement of counter-revolutionary despair, which agitated and whipped up the frustrations of the petty bourgeoisie to a white heat, everything in Nazism was 'as contradictory and chaotic as in a nightmare':

'Hitler's party calls itself socialist, yet it leads a terrorist struggle against all socialist organizations. It calls itself a workers' party, yet its ranks include all classes except the proletariat. It hurls its lightning bolts at the heads of the capitalists, yet it is supported by them. It bows before Germanic traditions, yet it aspires to Caesarism, a completely Latin institution.'[39]

The force of the movement lay not in its ideology but in its 'military cunning' and ability to exploit the weakness of its adversaries. Trotsky unrepentently maintained his Marxist conviction that in point of social consciousness 'the great bulk of the fascists consists of human dust'. Hitler's army of officials, clerks, shopkeepers, tradesmen and peasants belonged to the vacillating intermediate classes who were incapable of pursuing an independent, revolutionary policy. In terms of class consciousness and fighting capacity they were far inferior to the 'soldiers' of the proletarian army. Hence even Trotsky, in spite of his own analyses, found it difficult to believe that the great mass organizations of the German proletariat could capitulate without a struggle and concedé victory so tamely to the Nazis. He tended to dismiss in rather facile terms 'the immense poverty of National Socialist philosophy' just as he evaded more probing questions by describing Hitler's millions of followers as 'human rubbish'.[40] For Trotsky, Hitler's nationalism was 'the mythological shadow of the petty bourgeoisie itself, a pathetic delirium of a thousand-year Reich'.[41] The Nazi theory of race was a form of 'zoological materialism borrowed at second hand', 'a vapid and bombastic variety of chauvinism in alliance with phrenology'. It expressed the deluded fantasies of the pauperized petty bourgeoisie unearthed from the medieval graveyard.[42] Too much of a rationalist to take such mythological ideas seriously, Trotsky tended to lump them all together as manifestations of the endemic confusion in the Kleinbürger mentality. Racialism in practice resolved itself, according to Trotsky, into a form of economic liberalism, freed from the constraints of political liberty. Its only concrete expression lay in 'impotent though savage outbursts of anti-Semitism'.

'The Nazis abstract the usurious or banking capital from the modern economic system because it is the spirit of evil; and, as is well known, it is precisely in this sphere that the Jewish bourgeoisie occupies an important position. Bowing down before capitalism as a whole, the petty bourgeois declares war against the evil spirit of gain in the guise of the Polish Jew in a long-skirted caftan and usually without a cent in his pocket.'[43]

It is evident from this passage that Trotsky did not as yet foresee the tragic consequences of Nazism for Jewry. It was to take several years before Trotsky realized that with the Nazi triumph an entire era of Jewish emancipation in Europe had come to an end. In an interview with Jewish correspondents in Mexico City on January 18 1937 he admitted that his earlier optimism about 'assimilation' had not been justified by events.

'During my youth I rather leaned towards the prognosis that the Jews of different countries would be assimilated and that the Jewish question would thus disappear in a quasi-automatic fashion. The historical development of the last quarter of a century has not confirmed this perspective. Decaying capitalism has everywhere swung over to an exacerbated nationalism, one part of which is anti-Semitism. The Jewish question has loomed largest in the most highly developed capitalist country of Europe, in Germany.'[44]

Nearly two years later, Trotsky showed himself even more concerned by the menacing reality of Nazi and fascist anti-Semitism and the 'gigantic dimension of the evil burdening the Jewish people'. In a prophetic appeal to American Jews to face openly the need for revolutionary struggle, he wrote: 'It is possible to imagine without difficulty what awaits the Jews at the mere outbreak of the future world war. But even without war the next development of world reaction signifies with certainty the *physical extermination of the Jews*.'[45] This remarkable prediction of the approaching Holocaust makes it clear that Trotsky now fully grasped the enormity of the Nazi peril even if he mistakenly persisted in regarding racism and anti-Semitism as malignant convulsions of a purely *capitalist* death-agony. The transitional programme of the Fourth International in 1938 adopted Trotsky's call for an 'uncompromising disclosure of the roots of race prejudice and all forms  and shades of national arrogance and chauvinism, particularly anti-Semitism ...' In May 1940 the Manifesto of the Emergency Conference of the Fourth International evoked a horrifying picture of the 'monstrous intensification of chauvinism and especially of anti-Semitism.' Trotsky wrote:

'Today decaying capitalist society is striving to squeeze the

Jewish people from all pores; seventeen million individuals out of the two billion populating the globe, that is, less than one per cent, can no longer find a place on our planet! ... The struggle for "living room" is nothing but camouflage for imperialist expansion, that is, the policy of annexation and plunder. The racial justification for this expansion is a lie; National Socialism changes its racial sympathies and antipathies in accordance with strategic considerations. A somewhat more stable element in fascist propaganda is, perhaps, anti-Semitism, which Hitler has given a zoological form, discovering the true language of "race" and "blood" in the dog's bark and the pig's grunt ... Fascism is a chemically pure distillation of the culture of imperialism...'[46]

By the late 1930s the stabilization of the Nazi and fascist regimes along with the continued 'degeneration' of the USSR inevitably obliged Trotsky to reconsider some of his earlier prognoses. In certain respects his analysis of the dynamics of Nazism had indeed been vindicated. As early as 1933 he insisted that the historic mission of the fascist dictatorships was preparation for war. They could not be peacefully reformed or retired from service. The political orbit of the Hitler regime revolved upon the alternative 'war or revolution', and given its impotence in the field of economy, it would be 'forced to transfer its efforts to the field of foreign policy'. The essence of Trotsky's prophecy of November 2 1933 had been fulfilled with startling accuracy.

'The date of the new European catastrophe will be determined by the time necessary for the arming of Germany. It is not a question of months, but neither is it a question of decades. It will be but a few years before Europe is again plunged into a war, unless Hitler is forestalled in time by the inner forces of Germany.'[47]

On the other hand Trotsky's hopes for a radicalization of the German proletariat and a revolutionary overthrow of fascism from within had not materialized. Nor had his assessments of the political crises in France and Spain shown the same incisive quality as his analysis of the German situation. He had misinterpreted the riots of February 1934 in France as the prelude to future civil war and considerably overestimated the immediate

danger posed by French fascism. His indictment of the Socialist-
Communist alliance (the Popular Front) which he claimed was
'paving the way for fascism' was largely wide of the mark.[48]
France did not turn fascist in spite of Trotsky's misleading
analogies between the reformist policies pursued by its left-wing
leaders and the ultra-left strategy which had led to disaster in
Germany. Trotsky had to acknowledge as much and, even in
1940, following the French military catastrophe he rejected the
epithet 'fascist' for the 'despicable Pétain regime'. But precisely
because he qualified the Pétain government as a 'senile form of
Bonapartism of the epoch of imperialist decline', he convinced
himself that it could be easily overthrown by a revolutionary
mass uprising.[49]

The Spanish Civil War presented a more complex problem
which cannot be examined here in detail. Trotsky correctly
foresaw that Franco's victory would mean the unavoidable
acceleration of a new European war but held the Stalinist Comintern ultimately responsible for the defeat of the Spanish revolution. The policy of the Spanish Popular Front by 'setting itself
the task of rescuing the capitalist regime' had doomed itself to
defeat. It had strangled the socialist revolution 'in order to
demonstrate its trustworthiness and loyalty to London and
Paris'.[50] According to Trotsky, if 'the peasants had seized the
land and the workers the factories, Franco never would have
been able to wrest this victory from their hands!' The combined
actions of Socialists, Anarchists and Communists under the
Moscow-inspired banner of the 'People's Front' had demoralized
the masses of Spanish workers and peasants and shattered 'a
powerful and heroic revolution'. Trotsky evidently never considered whether the Spanish Republic might not have collapsed
even sooner without Russian assistance.

The Spanish tragedy reinforced Trotsky's view that the
'defence of democracy' was a hopeless method of combatting
fascism, which could only be defeated by a revolutionary vanguard party carrying out resolute Bolshevik policies. This whole
perspective on the Spanish events was shaped by his preoccupation in the late 1930s with the struggle against Stalinism
and the need for building 'a world party of revolution', the

Fourth International.[51] Only such a party pursuing the general strategy of 'permanent revolution' could engage in a real struggle with fascism, free of excessive prudence and the fatal compromises of the Popular Front. The defeats of the 1930s convinced Trotsky that fascism had triumphed not because of 'objective conditions' but as a result of 'the inability of the degenerated and completely rotten parties of the proletariat' to follow the example of the Bolshevik revolution.[52] Fascism was the revenge of history for the opportunism of both the Social Democratic and Communist Parties who had forgotten that Marxism was a set of directives for *revolutionary* action. The working class had been tragically late in fulfilling the tasks imposed upon it by the irreversible decay of capitalism.[53] Trotsky firmly placed the blame on the failures of the proletarian leadership. In 1940, he declared, that fascism had conquered power 'only in those countries where the conservative labour parties prevented the proletariat from utilizing the revolutionary situation and seizing power'.[54]

This had indeed been Trotsky's refrain throughout the 'thirties and formed the basis of his indictment of Soviet foreign policy. He clearly believed that the fate of every revolutionary movement had been largely determined by the betrayals of the Comintern and the Stalinist bureaucracy. There had been no less than three missed opportunities in Germany – in 1918–1919, 1923–24 and in 1929; one in China, one in France and one in Spain. In all these cases it was allegedly the Comintern and the Social Democrats who had 'criminally and viciously disrupted the conquest of power and thereby placed society in an impasse. Only under these conditions and in this situation did the stormy rise of fascism and its gaining of power prove possible.'[55] Much of this was quite removed from historical reality. The possibilities of Communist revolution in Germany had been fairly remote before 1933 and thereafter there was no real prospect of overthrowing Nazism from within. In Spain and France the revolutionary possibilities were even more problematic, just as they had been in China in 1927. This did not mean tht the progress of fascism could not have been checked (Trotsky's critique of Comintern strategy, especially in Germany was certainly acute) but simply that Stalin's international policies were not the decisive factor. The idea that Stalinism was the crucial reason for the defeat of the European revolution had become an *idée fixe* with Trotsky in his last years.

Equally doctrinaire was his return to Lenin's policy of revolutionary defeatism as developed during the First World War, which he now applied abstractly to a very different situation in 1939. Trotsky insisted that there could be no question of a 'united front' with the 'imperialist' democracies against Hitler and Mussolini. This would only 'provide support for the blackest reaction in Germany and Italy' and strengthen the yoke of Western imperialism over the colonial peoples.[56] Democracy, like fascism, was a tool of imperialism and to support its victory would be an unforgivable lapse into 'social patriotism'.[57] In face of the 'new partition of the globe' among the imperialist powers, the Social Democrats and the Communists were trying to dupe the masses into believing that the new slaughter would be a defensive war for 'the innocent, peace-loving democracies against the "fascist" aggressors'.[58] Trotsky, on the other hand, argued that the struggle against fascism demanded 'the expulsion of the agents of "democratic" imperialism from the ranks of the working class'. A life-and-death struggle by the proletariat in France, Britain, America and the USSR against their own domestic imperialism would rally the German and Italian workers as well as 'hundreds of millions of slaves of imperialism in the entire world'.[59] Only in this way, by transforming the imperialist war into a new revolutionary wave along the lines of 1917, could fascism be defeated. It was a wildly utopian vision which Trotsky bequeathed to the nascent Fourth International and one that was wholly beyond its realistic possibilities. Hitler's New Order did not survive but neither did the new world war fulfil Trotsky's expectations of world revolution and the 'inevitable' collapse of the capitalist system.

CHAPTER TWELVE

# THE FLAWED LEGACY

'... I cannot speak of the "indispensability" of my
work, even about the period from 1917 to 1921. But
now my work is "indispensable" in the full sense of
the word. There is no arrogance in this claim at all.
The collapse of the two Internationals has posed a
problem which none of the leaders of these Internationals is at all equipped to solve. The vicissitudes
of my personal fate have confronted me with this
problem and armed me with important experience in
dealing with it. There is no one except me to carry
out the mission of arming a new generation with the
revolutionary method over the heads of the leaders
of the Second and Third Internationals. And I am in
complete agreement with Lenin (or rather Turgenev)
that the worst vice is to be more than fifty-five years
old! I need at least five more years of uninterrupted
work to ensure the succession.'

Leon Trotsky, *Diary in Exile*

Leon Trotsky wrote down these revealing thoughts in the
private journal which he kept for a time during his exile in
France and Norway. Under the impact of the German catastrophe
and the blows of fate which had forced him to wander like an
outcast over the 'planet without a visa', Trotsky did not bend in
submission but set himself the titanic ambition of organizing a
new International. Objectively the task seemed hopeless enough
and Trotsky himself had hesitated for several years before events
convinced him of the utter bankruptcy of the Stalinist Comintern.
At least until 1933 he had believed that the Communist International could be returned to the true path of Marxism-Leninism

and that the Communist parties still represented the militant vanguard of the world proletariat. But the crushing defeat in Germany and the complete ostracization of the Left Opposition within the Communist movement left him little alternative except to attempt to build a new mass movement. Ironically, enough, the personalization of politics under Stalin had helped to forge the legend of heroic resistance and martyrdom which was Trotsky's main asset. By transforming him into the supreme heretic of international communism and the 'wandering Jew' of the socialist world, Stalin inadvertently increased Trotsky's moral authority. The more obsessed Stalin became with his powerless adversary, the more vehemently he denounced the lonely outcast as the author of every conceivable form of heresy, opposition, sabotage and betrayal – the more inevitably did he turn him into the embodiment of opposition to the Soviet regime.[1]

The struggle was, to be sure, grossly unequal. As Isaac Deutscher put it: 'there is in the whole of history hardly another case in which such immense resources of power and propaganda were employed against a single individual.'[2] On the other hand, Trotsky, freed from the pressure and constraints of power, found a new lease of life as a writer, journalist, historian and critic. At the same time he had a passionate need to root himself in the Communist movement which had rejected and excommunicated him, for outside of it there could be no salvation. The dissenter thus had to claim that his heresy was orthodox – that he was seeking to restore the betrayed meaning of Marx and Lenin – over the heads of the Third International. His personal action and fate were only meaningful if they could be integrated into the texture of historical events and the character of the epoch as a whole.

This dialectic of the individual and history was one that had always assumed a prominent place in Trotsky's writings. Already in April 1907 he had written: 'The whole of history is an enormous machine in the service of our ideals. It works with barbarous slowness, with insensitive cruelty, but it works. We are sure of it. But when its omnivorous mechanism swallows up our life's blood for fuel, we feel like calling out to it with all the strength we still possess: "Faster! Do it faster!" '[3] This was the voice of the young revolutionary, impatient for battle, yet aware that history could be a cruel goddess, an instrument both of hope and disillusion, of utopia and doom. The theme resounds through Trotsky's writings over the years – whether as victor or vanquished – he will look to history as a pitiless, inexorable force. Sometimes it embodies the voice of humanity struggling to emancipate itself from its chains, at other times it seems indifferent to the needs of the individual, riding over his aspirations like a merciless juggernaut. But always History moves onward, never allowing society to achieve a state of equilibrium – its dynamism governed by objective laws which alternately demand impassioned activism or the ability to wait and endure until the next wave surges forward. In the foreword to his autobiography Trotsky writes:

'Thus I know well enough, from my own experience, the historical ebb and flow. They are governed by their own laws. Mere impatience will not expedite their change. I have grown accustomed to viewing the historical perspective not from the standpoint of my personal fate. To understand the causal sequence of events and to find somewhere in the sequence one's own place – that is the first duty of a revolutionary. And at the same time it is the greatest personal satisfaction possible for a man who does not limit his tasks to the present day.'[4]

All through *My Life* this voice of philosophical fatalism can be found, rejecting the notion of *personal* tragedy and linking the destiny of the revolutionary to vaster forces that enable him to rise above his own life and that of contemporary reality. It is in this context that Trotsky approvingly quoted one of Rosa Luxemburg's letters from prison where she maintained 'that it is precisely the fighter who must try to be above things, or else he will get his nose stuck in all sorts of rubbish . . .'[5] More surprisingly, he also quotes the anarchist Proudhon, subscribing in particular to these words: 'I observe these changes in the life of the world as if I had received their explanation from above; what oppresses others, elevates me more and more, inspires and fortifies me; how can you want me then to accuse destiny, to complain about people and curse them? Destiny – I laugh at it;

and as for men, they are too ignorant, too enslaved for me to feel annoyed at them.'[6]

Trotsky quoted these lines as a kind of personal epitaph before the worst blows of fortune had struck him, engulfing his children and grandchildren, his followers and associates in the whirlwind of Stalinist terror and personal vengeance. Nevertheless, they help to explain the extraordinary fortitude, the note of defiant resignation but not defeat, with which he greeted such disasters. However cruel and implacable the dialectic of History might seem, Trotsky was convinced that its avenging sword would ultimately vindicate him and cast down his enemies. In 1940 the American critic Edmund Wilson perceptively observed that there was no other leading revolutionary 'for whom the Marxist conception of History, derived from the Hegelian Idea, plays so frankly teleological a role as it does in the work of Trotsky'.[7] In his solitude and exile, Wilson remarked, 'this History, an austere spirit, has seemed actually to stand behind his chair as he writes, encouraging, admonishing, approving, giving him the courage to confound his accusers, who have never seen History's face'.[8]

But if this Providential view of history fortified Trotsky against 'the slings and arrows of outrageous fortune', it also led him astray in his central preoccupation during the 1930s – the tasks of the coming epoch. His catastrophist vision of an irredeemably moribund capitalist system, first formulated in 1914, became fetishized into a dogma that helped to cripple still further the activity of the Fourth International. In 1914 he had proclaimed that the world war 'heralds the break-up of the nation-state; and at the same time, also the crack-up of the *capitalist form* of economy . . .'[9] This prophecy which he took with him to the grave, underlay his conviction that the coming epoch would be one of uninterrupted proletarian revolutions. Capitalism had exhausted its possibilities. There could be no restoration of its pre-war equilibrium and no expansion of its productive forces. The capitalist system had entered a period of general decline and crisis in which cyclical fluctuations would be unable to avert its doom and with it that of the nation-state.

The Great Depression and the malaise of the world economy momentarily seemed to offer some support to Trotsky's prognosis, but he provided no convincing empirical or theoretical arguments as to why this process was irreversible. The *a priori* dogmatism in his stance largely explains why he dismissed the American 'New Deal' measures in the 1930s as doomed from the start, and failed to foresee the possibilities of capitalist expansion in the United States. Though Trotsky espoused a *voluntaristic* Marxism when it came to the strategy and tactics of revolutionary leadership, he remained a determinist in his economic thinking. This led him into a mechanistic conception of the laws of capitalist development and a failure to perceive the relative autonomy of political action. In his view, the mere assertion that capitalism was not irrevocably doomed would lead to reformist and opportunist politics which would inevitably subvert the revolution.

Trotsky's *Transitional Programme*, written for the founding Congress of the Fourth International in 1938, is replete with examples of his mechanistic economic assumptions. Significantly entitled 'The Death Agony of Capitalism', Trotsky's analysis begins by asserting that 'the economic prerequisites for the proletarian revolution' have already reached their highest point of maturity under capitalism.

'Mankind's productive forces stagnate. Already new inventions and improvements fail to raise the level of material wealth. Cyclical slumps, under the conditions of the social crisis of the whole capitalist system inflict ever heavier deprivations and sufferings upon the masses. Growing unemployment, in its turn, deepens the financial crisis of the state and undermines the unstable monetary systems. Democratic as well as Fascist regimes stagger on from one bankruptcy to another ... The present crisis, far from having run its full course, has already succeeded in showing that "New Deal" politics, like Popular Front politics in France, open no new exit from the economic blind alley.'[10]

According to Trotsky, the objective conditions were already ripe for socialist revolution (indeed 'they have begun to get somewhat rotten') – only the 'subjective' factor, i.e. 'a historical crisis of the leadership of the proletariat', had prevented the fulfilment of the Marxian prophecies. In this analysis Trotsky managed to combine the *passive fatalism* of the Second International (which before 1914 had asserted in similarly mechanistic fashion the inevitable demise of capitalism) and the militant activism of the Leninist credo, divorced from its concrete sense of timing and tactics. But Trotsky's historicist conception failed to anticipate the success of Keynesian measures of state intervention just as it overlooked the social, ideological and political roots of bourgeois hegemony in the Western capitalist states.[11] It tied the validity of revolutionary Marxism to an *a priori* fatalist assumption that the world capitalist system was doomed as a result of its inherent laws of development. Hence the never-ending rash of statements about the imminent collapse of capitalism in a period when the working class was suffering one defeat after another and had reached its lowest ebb.

Trotsky's exaggerated optimism about the irresolvable crisis which would thrust the Fourth International forward as the avant-garde of world revolution stood in striking contrast to the isolated, powerless position of his small group. Indeed the Trotskyist politics of the Apocalypse might charitably be seen as a form of overcompensation for the real fragmentation and endemic failures of the movement. Precisely because the Fourth International was incapable of effectively intervening in the political conditions of the late 1930s, its expectations concerning the forthcoming crash were so glowingly coloured by messianic expectancy. Divorced from the mainstream of the working-class movement, incapable of breaking through the impregnable wall of Stalinist slander and hatred, the Trotskyist groups were condemned to inaction, sectarianism, squabbling and personal rivalries. Cut off from the possibility of mass action they became prisoners of their own internal dissensions and frittered away their energies in sterile scholastic disputes.

Trotsky did not appear deterred by the pitiful contrast between the tremendous goals which he set the Fourth International and the insignificance and ineffectiveness of his followers. He was convinced that events were confirming his prognosis and slogans – that the time was ripe for building a new revolutionary party on an international scale. In a message celebrating the Foundation of the Fourth International he described it as 'the World Party of Socialist Revolution' and the 'greatest lever of history'.[12] 'Separated from this lever', Trotsky wrote, 'every one of us is nothing. With this lever in hand, we are all.'[13] He took unconcealed pride in the persecutions to which the new International was subject in the USSR, Spain and other countries at the hands of Kremlin agents. It had taken ten years for the Moscow clique to transform the first workers' state into a sinister caricature but during the next decade 'the program of the Fourth International will become the guide of millions and these revolutionary millions will know how to storm earth and heaven'.[14]

It would not be difficult to multiply examples of other grossly exaggerated claims made by Trotsky in his last years. Again and again he insisted that because it followed a 'correct line' the Fourth International was a strong and immutable force which alone could provide the leadership that would save mankind from 'the catastrophes of European and world capitalism'. In a bitter polemic against disillusioned radical intellectuals like Victor Serge, Trotsky even resurrected Hegel's old dialectical formula to justify his missionary faith. 'All that is rational is real. Social Democracy and Stalinocracy even today represent stupendous fictions. But the Fourth International is an impregnable reality.'[15]

Trotsky had no doubt 'that the new world war will provoke with absolute inevitability the world revolution and the collapse of the capitalist system'.[16] The Fourth International was the 'revolutionary preparation of the vanguard' which was predestined to save the world from its mortal crisis. In more rational moments, however, Trotsky acknowledged that it was fighting *against* the stream, as a result of a long series of working-class defeats, the 'betrayals' of the Second and Third Internationals, and the extermination of the Left Opposition in the USSR.[17] The Trotskyist movement was 'a small boat in a tremendous current' and precisely because it swam against the stream, it was not connected to the masses. Its predominantly intellectual composition and its incapacity to organize workers, was a sore point with Trotsky but did not cause him to despair of the laws of history. His catastrophist vision of events persuaded him that out of the new world war, steeled revolutionary Marxist cadres

would emerge under the banner of his small group. The con-
flagration would become the political graveyard of the Second
and Third Internationals, enabling its successor to shake off the
apathy of the older generation and mobilize the youth in a
militant new vanguard.

Trotsky now gave tremendous significance to Lenin's theory
of the revolutionary Party without really grasping its meaning.
He reduced the 'historical crisis of mankind' to the 'crisis of the
revolutionary leadership' as if the colossal upheavals, dislocations
and traumas of the 1930s could be embraced by this one causal
factor. His 'idea' of the Party was not rooted in any concrete
organizational or social structure, let alone in the dynamics of a
particular national environment. Although Lenin's Bolsheviks
had also been very isolated in 1914 they at least operated from a
national base and in a far more favourable international situation.
The position facing the Fourth International was much bleaker.
The threat of fascism tended in particular to solidify support
around Stalinist Russia as a military and political counterweight.
Moreover the influence of the Stalinist parties who branded
Trotsky as a 'fascist agent' effectively prevented him from
reaching a Western working-class audience. The social composition of his movement (petty-bourgeois and intellectual), its
rootless, émigré character and numerical insignificance reinforced
its tendencies to chronic factionalism. From the beginning of its
history it was plagued by splits and extreme sectarianism. All
attempts to break out of this impasse seemed doomed. Trotsky
led the movement briefly into the mass Social Democratic parties
(the so-called 'French turn' which began the tactic of entryism –
in this case into the French Socialist Party) and then out again.
His efforts to join forces with left socialist and 'centrist' groups
aborted, partly because of his own intransigence. Expulsions of
dissidents and 'petty-bourgeois' members were no more successful
in recruiting workers – they merely provoked new splits. The
gap between Trotsky's enormous expectations and the pathetic
inadequacy of his forces seemed to be increasing daily. Instead
of creating a mass movement, the revolutionary 'Vanguard'
Party had assumed the role of a disembodied mouthpiece of
History.

Only the American section could boast more than a few hundred members at the founding Congress of the Fourth International. Thus the revolutionary 'leadership' to which Trotsky looked as the *deus ex machina* in the current world situation, was suspended in a void without any vital links to the masses. All it had left was the purity of its *Transitional Programme*, every one of whose prophecies was eventually falsified by history. As a result of the war, both world capitalism and Stalinism emerged greatly strengthened. The West experienced a sustained and spectacular boom, while the Red Army extended its control over all of Eastern Europe. Far from crumbling, the Socialist and Communist parties in Europe won a new lease of life, while the Fourth International continued to stagnate in puny, insignificant groups whose 'world revolutionary' perspectives were ever more remote from reality.

In the aftermath of World War II it was not world capitalism or the Stalinist system which was in crisis, but the Trotskyist movement itself which split yet again over the 'Russian question'. Under the leadership of Michel Pablo one section moved over towards Stalinism, on the assumption that in the coming Third World War the Stalinist Parties would have to radicalize themselves. The Pabloists concluded that the Trotskyist groups should dissolve themselves and *enter* the Communist parties as a clandestine Left Opposition. This 'revisionist' position provoked a new split and expulsions from the International which have continued down to the present. There are now at least four different organizations who claim to be the Fourth International, not to speak of those who are 'reconstructing' it. In countries like France, Britain and America there are numerous Trotskyist groups, each one claiming to be more *orthodox* than its rivals, in its adherence to the 1938 Programme.

This post-war degeneration of Trotskyism into a dogmatic sectarianism which even displays such familiar Stalinist traits as authoritarianism, witch-hunts and the leadership cult, cannot be laid directly at Trotsky's door. Nevertheless the seeds of this development were already apparent in Trotsky's own mistakes and in the weaknesses of the International which he founded. In a curious manner history has come full circle, for the modern

Trotskyist idea of the revolutionary Party is precisely that Leninist conception which Trotsky himself caricatured as early as 1904. The basis of his critique of Lenin had been the *substitutionist* character of Bolshevik Jacobinism which played the role of schoolmaster and guardian of the working class. Trotsky had accused Lenin of using the proletariat as an instrument of his own will-to-power and of divorcing the Party from the spontaneous movement of the masses. Lenin's alleged 'paranoia' derived, according to the young Trotsky, from this morbid suspicion of the masses. The contemporary versions of Trotskyism in their methods and tactics almost exactly embody the faults exposed in this early critique, turning it into a self-fulfilling prophecy. For all their ritual lip-service to the proletariat as the historic instrument of change, the Trotskyists have proved incapable of achieving any foothold in the working class. Instead they have sought substitutes in the Third World, the student revolt, Feminism, Black Power and other protest movements to compensate for their own lack of any mass base in the industrialized West.

Trotsky himself had always placed inordinate hopes on the Western working class whose revolutionary potential he vastly overestimated. But no German, French, American or British October emerged to save the Russian revolution from its own backwardness and bureaucratic reaction. Instead the revolution spread to China, Vietnam, Yugoslavia, Albania and other underdeveloped countries – under the leadership of Stalinized parties faithful to the Third International. These victories were not due to Stalin's polices anymore than was the defeat of revolution in the West, but they did reveal the inadequacy of Trotsky's schema of 'permanent revolution'. He had never believed in the possibility of peasant-based revolutions such as occurred in China, Vietnam or Cuba, anymore than he grasped the potential of guerilla warfare. In spite of his lucid criticism of Stalin's Chinese policies in 1927, Trotsky was unable to foresee the inner dynamics of the Chinese Revolution and its historic reorientation under Mao Tse Tung.

On the other hand, he deluded himself almost grotesquely concerning the imminence of revolution in Britain and especially

America, two countries for whose historical traditions he displayed little understanding. Trotsky's attempt to fit the United States into the framework of Marxian prophecies concerning the increasing pauperization of the middle classes and the inevitable degradation of the working classes, fell well wide of the mark.[18] In 1939 Trotsky was convinced that the American working class would 'in a few jumps catch up with Europe and outdistance it' in militant class-struggle. He saw a great future for Marxism in the USA, persuaded as he was that the evolution of American capitalism had borne out all of Marx's predictions. But his own prophecy that 'the best theoreticians of Marxism will appear on American soil' proved no more reliable than that of Marx.[19] Nor have his followers improved on Trotsky's unimpressive success-rate concerning prophecies about the imminent world revolution, though it is at least doubtful whether the 'old man' would have jumped as eagerly as his disciples on the Third World anti-colonial bandwagon in the 1960s. Mistaken predictions, however, never deterred Trotsky or his orthodox followers from branding every deviation from their own model of permanent revolution as 'revisionist' or unprincipled opportunism. In one sense, the Trotskyist is inevitably right, as Régis Debray has pointed out, for his highest destiny has been to be separated from destiny itself – i.e. the exercise of power.[20] Precisely because Trotskyism as a movement has never come to power it could afford to maintain its intransigent doctrinal purity and revolve for ever in its theoretical circle of pure forms.

In this ahistorical perspective every concrete embodiment of socialism must be rejected, for it can never measure up to the static and unchanging criteria of 'Trotskyism'. According to Trotskyist orthodoxy, the construction of an effective planned economy and of a communist society can, for example, only be accomplished on a *global* scale in which each national struggle forms a subordinate interlocking part. This dogma leads to the constant imposition of abstract principles on changing political situations without regard to their concrete specificity and the strategic needs that correspond to them. It leads to the repeated underestimation of national peculiarities in the name of the world revolution. Precisely because the Fourth International is a Trotskyist *world party*, the concept of a 'national' Trotskyism (as occurred in Ceylon) would be contradiction in terms and the ultimate Stalinist heresy. But by the very same token this makes it more difficult for Trotskyist parties to anchor themselves anywhere as a genuine mass movement.

The contradictions in contemporary Trotskyism are to a large degree the result of the flawed legacy bequeathed by its founder. The inflated claims which he made in his last years and his faulty *either-or* analysis of the world situation at the end of the 1930s, have been taken to absurd lengths by his disciples. They failed, like him, to grasp the changing dynamics of capitalist development and to adjust to the new post-war conditions. Like Trotsky himself they have been plagued by the problem of defining Stalinism and the East European Communist regimes imposed on the Russian model after 1945. Were they 'degenerated' or 'deformed' workers' states, or were they 'state capitalist' regimes? Were the world Communist Parties still potentially revolutionary, were they irredeemably subservient to Moscow or have they (more recently) abdicated the Leninist road in accepting a 'peaceful' democratic transition to socialism? Is the European working class a spent force or is it still the historic agent of revolutionary change?

The Trotskyists have failed to come up with any convincing answer to these questions. Instead the majority section in the Fourth International began in the 1960s to concentrate on the anti-colonial revolution. It adopted the strategy of moving 'from the periphery to the centre', in the wake of the Sino-Soviet split, the Algerian and the Cuban revolutions. Solidarity with the anti-imperialist struggle and with national liberation movements in the Third World, as well as with students, immigrants and oppressed minority groups in the advanced Western countries, seemed to provide a temporary substitute cause.

Trotskyism was even able to emerge as a driving force of the New Left movements in the 1960s and played an important political role that partly disguised its organizational weaknesses. The international student movement of 1968 and its aftermath gave Trotskyism the opportunity to increase its influence throughout the world and emerge after decades in the shadows, as a

self-conscious intellectual avant-garde.[21] Ernest Mandel, the
leading theoretician of the Fourth International, even claimed
that the students constituted the 'new, young revolutionary
vanguard' which the Trotskyists had been vainly seeking for
three decades.[22] According to Mandel, the heroic Vietnamese
struggle, the Cuban Revolution, the guerilla wars in Asia, Africa
and Latin America, Black Power and the student movement
were 'all basically one and the same struggle'.[23] As part of this
'authentic new world revolutionary ascent', Mandel sent greetings
to the 'vanguard of workers and students of Warsaw and Poland
in their fight against bureaucracy and for real soviet democracy'.[24]
At the same time he also reaffirmed Trotskyist support for the
Soviet Union and the 'socialist camp' in any confrontation with
imperialism or the bourgeoisie. One could scarcely ask for a
better illustration of political double-talk and ideological mystification. According to Mandel, the Polish vanguard were fighting
for 'a democracy based on workers, students and poor peasant
councils as Lenin taught us'. But it was Lenin (and Trotsky), not
imperialism, who destroyed this council democracy and founded
the modern Soviet Union (neither 'soviet' nor a genuine union)
which the Trotskyists still defend against the world bourgeoisie!
In these circumstances it is not surprising that some followers of
Trotsky have found it easier to appropriate the Third World as
an outlet for their own political illusions rather than confront
the realities of a non-revolutionary European proletariat that
has always disappointed their expectations.

   Nevertheless it would be a mistake to altogether write off the
Trotskyist movement. In spite of its rigidities and dogmatic
sectarianism, it has shown a political determination and tenacity
that has enabled it to survive decades of persecution and stagnation. Its stubborn commitment to world revolution, its critique
of bureaucratized socialism, its distinctive traditions of struggle
still have a certain appeal, especially in the student milieu. The
mystique of Trotskyism derives in large part from the charisma
of its founding figure, who claimed and did to a certain extent
embody the revolutionary Marxist tradition against Stalinism.
Trotsky's writings undeniably provide a unifying element in the
programme of the movement that bears his name. The distinctive

features of his legacy can be summed up as follows: the allegiance to Leninism (especially the theory of the Party) and to the Bolshevik tradition until 1924; the heritage of the Left Opposition in the USSR; the rejection of Popular Fronts and of peaceful co-existence in the international arena as a form of class collaboration; the defence of 'soviet' democracy within a system of proletarian dictatorship; the war on two fronts against Stalinism and social democracy; the call for workers' control in the factories and armed workers' militias organized in self-defence groups; the rejection of the nation-state and the striving for continental federations of workers' states leading eventually to a world republic of Soviets; the unconditional defence of the existing 'deformed' workers' states in the USSR, Eastern Europe and Asia against imperialism; the belief that in these states the bureaucracy can be overthrown by a purely *political* revolution whereas in the West a *social* revolution is necessary; the conviction that capitalism is in it final death-agony.[25] These programmatic points are fused together in Trotsky's theory of the permanent revolution which acts as a kind of intellectual testament and leit-motif underlying all Trotskyist conceptions.

This legacy is sufficiently rich and diverse to have enabled the Fourth International to maintain its existence as an independent Marxist school and an oppositional communist movement. Nevertheless the importance of the neo-Leninist tradition within modern Trotskyism gives it a curiously anachronistic character – for at bottom the demands of the present are always judged in terms of the model of October 1917. The Trotskyists still regard the building of Leninist parties as the essential pre-requisite for proletarian revolution, largely ignoring the specifically Russian and European context in which this party model emerged. They have taken Lenin's conceptualization of the relationship between Party and class to extraordinary lengths and become fixated in the view that the Party alone can provide the working class with political consciousness.[26] To a large extent they have inherited Trotsky's own misunderstanding of Lenin's theory of the Party and mechanically transplanted it to entirely different conditions, where it leads to a divorce from actual, existing class struggles. The exaggerated Trotskyist emphasis on the role of the revolutionary vanguard stands moreover, in contradiction to the young Trotsky's prescient warnings about the dangers of authoritarian elitism and the stifling of the creative self-activity of the masses.

Two separate traditions seem to be competing for the political soul of the Trotskyist movement, and to the extent that neo-Leninism wins the upper hand, this can only alienate potential support from within the anti-authoritarian New Left. In dogmatizing the subjective factors of 'consciousness' and 'leadership', the Trotskyists have moreover tended to separate them from their objective basis in the changing structures of capitalism and the social relationships which it generates. A similar failing is evident in the Trotskyist analysis of the Soviet regime which mechanically separates the base from the superstructure. The critique of the bureaucratic regime assumes that it exercises a 'parasitic' function on a healthy socio-economic base – that of a 'workers' state'. Thus the transformation of this system is viewed as a purely superstructural problem which would leave its basic social structure intact. What Trotsky in common with so many Bolsheviks (including Stalin) failed to see, was that nationalization and a planned economy did not necessarily transform the *social relations* of production, let alone create the basis for a more human society.

Trotsky's critique of the Soviet bureaucracy, while pioneering in many respects, remained fixed at the superstructural level and ignored the emergence of a new type of class society and mode of production at the economic base. Soviet workers are no less alienated and exploited in the production process than they were under capitalism. Indeed their situation has always been worse since they were deprived of elementary democratic rights that were safeguarded in the West. Trotsky's inability to grasp this elementary fact and his failure to distinguish between ownership and actual *control* of the means of production, led his followers to deny the existence of a new ruling class in the socialist countries. Although the Communist bureaucracy has been in power for six decades, it is still regarded by Trotskyists merely as a 'caste' which has provisionally usurped the 'proletarian' economic base! This theory is as remote from reality as Trotsky's assumption that Soviet 'Bonapartism' was a temporary aberration which would be rapidly swept away by the iron laws of history. It has led modern Trotskyism into the absurd position of arguing that the so-called 'workers' states' still exercise a revolutionary function in spite of being ruled by a counter-revolutionary caste.

Such doctrinal orthodoxy already prevented the Left Opposition in the 1930s from uniting around its banner the various Marxist groups that stood between Stalinism and Social Democracy. It has led to continuous splits and heresies within the Trotskyist movement itself. It remains a millstone around the neck of any organization which seeks to recruit support among the generation of the New Left. But to throw it overboard would mean to break with one of the cardinal pillars of the Trotskyist tradition.

Trotsky's legacy remains, then, deeply flawed, above all in the inheritance which he left to his followers. History has not dealt kindly with his major predictions, even though his writings provide so many valuable and penetrating insights into the fundamental political issues of our century. The industrial proletariat has not proved itself to be the messianic class of world history which Trotsky, along with Marx, Engels and Rosa Luxemburg, believed it to be. In many underdeveloped countries the struggle for national independence led to revolutionary movements of a type that Trotsky never envisaged, under the leadership of déclassé intellectuals and party bureaucrats espousing a Communist creed altogether remote from Trotsky's classical Marxism. Neither the bourgeoisie nor the proletariat have proved to be the decisive historical classes foreseen by the original Marxist paradigm. In their place the role of the state has loomed ever larger, a phenomenon that Trotsky glimpsed but could not really grasp. As a revolutionary politician, Trotsky was for a time more successful than as a prophet; yet even here his undeniable merits were long buried by a mountain of slander which sought to efface entirely his decisive role in the creation of Soviet Russia. To this day, Stalin's successors have been unable to come to grips with the man whom they brand as an arch-heretic and traitor to the cause he so ardently defended. Trotskyism remains a spectre that haunts the Soviet regime though its ideological and organizational base in the USSR was extirpated forty years ago.[27] The ghost of the murdered Trotsky would appear to be very much alive in the minds of a leadership that after sixty years of absolute power still fears to rehabilitate one of its founding-fathers.

In the West, Trotsky's reputation has survived the crude assaults of Stalinist orthodoxy and his place is probably secure in the pantheon of great revolutionary leaders. His works are readily available in numerous cheap editions and the creative flair visible in his writings ensures his enduring appeal for the radical intelligentsia. As the rights and wrongs of Trotsky's struggle with Stalin recede into the past one can expect a more balanced picture of his real achievements and failures to emerge. In this book I have tried to do justice to his undoubted qualities of heroism, energy and creative imagination without concealing the darker side of his personality – the fanaticism, the Marxist dogmatism and intolerance with which he sought to impose his messianic vision on the world. Trotsky's life and personal fate revealed a dialectical drama of intense passion which cannot be encompassed in any single formula. A master of literary style and a ruthless revolutionary leader, he combined in himself the highest qualities of the pen and the sword. He was a man of dramatic appeals, of enormous *élan vital*, capable of great audacity. At the same time his aloofness, aristocratic nonchalance, intellectual arrogance and independence of mind made him unsuited to the intricate manoeuvres of factional combat. The mass spellbinder, the strategist and theoretician of revolution, was an inept politician. He aroused admiration but not affection and, when his fall came, he was to be cursed as a symbol of perfidy and betrayal in a manner almost unprecedented in twentieth-century politics. But it was precisely in adversity that Trotsky's unflinching, indomitable powers of resistance, his restless, combative mind and imaginative vision flourished at their best. His destiny was to swim against the stream and he accepted the burdens of opposition with the same unyielding defiance and ardour that he displayed through a lifetime of revolutionary struggle.

# NOTES

## CHAPTER ONE

1  Leon Trotsky, *My Life*, Penguin Books, London 1975, p. 1.
2  Ibid., p. 18.
3  Ibid., p. 16.
4  Ibid., p. 39.
5  See Joseph Nevada, *Trotsky and the Jews*, Philadelphia 1972, p. 35. Also Joel Carmichael, *Trotsky: An Appreciation of His Life*, London 1975, p. 17, who points out the incongruity of this assertion.
6  *My Life*, op. cit., p. 18.
7  Ibid., p. 38.
8  Ibid., p. 39. Several years later, Trotsky records, his uncle married this very woman!
9  See Robert S. Wistrich, *Revolutionary Jews from Marx to Trotsky*, London–New York 1976, pp. 190–207, for further details.
10  *My Life*, op. cit., p. 87.
11  Ibid. Anna Bronstein, the mother of Trotsky, would 'when occasion required ... raise her eyes in prayer' at her husband's atheism. She was evidently more educated than David Bronstein, who was unable even to spell out words until he was an old man. Nevertheless, Trotsky, who preferred his father, considered him 'superior ... both in intellect and character', more tactful and a shrewd judge of people.
12  Ibid., p. 89.
13  Ibid., p. 90. Trotsky is very insistent that these restrictions did not affect his personal position because 'I was always at the top of the grade'.
14  Ibid., p. 89.
15  On Martov's Jewish background, see Israel Getzler, *Martov: A Political Biography*, Cambridge 1967, pp. 9–20, and Robert S. Wistrich, *Revolutionary Jews ...* op. cit., pp. 176–188.
16  *My Life*, op. cit., pp. 90–91.
17  Ibid., p. xli.
18  Ibid., p. 67. In spite of this, the early chapter in *My Life* on books and early conflicts, is disappointingly thin and gives little indication of what he read.
19  Ibid., p. 91.

20　Ibid., p. 92.

21　Ibid., p. 95.

22　Ibid., p. 100.

23　Ibid., p. 101. For an interesting psycho-analytic view of the young Trotsky which explores this search for personal and social integration, see Steven Englund and Larry S. Ceplair, 'Un essai de psycho-histoire: Portrait d'un Jeune Révolutionnaire, Léon Trotsky'. *Revue d'histoire moderne et contemporaine*, t. XXIV (1977), pp. 524–543.

24　*My Life*, p. 102: 'I swallowed books, fearful that my entire life would not be long enough to prepare me for action.' This note of impatience is as characteristic of Trotsky as his tense, even 'savage' striving for system.

25　Ibid., p. 108.

26　Ibid., p. 119.

27　See G. A. Ziv, *Kharakteristike po Lichnym Vospominanym*, New York 1921, who attributed Bronstein's conversion to his domineering character and egocentrism. 'He loved the workers and loved the comrades . . . because through them he loved his own self.'

28　Ibid. On Lassalle's Jewish background and political personality see Robert S. Wistrich, *Revolutionary Jews* . . . op. cit., pp. 46–58. Also Shlomo Na'aman, *Lassalle*, Hanover 1970. Lassalle's fiery conduct at his court trials, his proud language and authoritative manner made a great impression on Russian Jewish revolutionaries of Trotsky's generation. See P. B. Axelrod, *Perezhitoe i peredumannoe*, Berlin 1923, Vol I, pp. 73–74.

29　*My Life*, p. 123. This was one of Trotsky's favourite phrases. He was very impressed by the 'brilliant dilettantism' with which Labriola, a neo-Hegelian Marxist, had applied dialectics to the philosophy of history.

30　Ibid., p. 127.

31　Ibid., p. 129.

32　Ibid., p. 130. Dzerzhinsky was a Polish revolutionary of noble origins, who joined the Bolsheviks in 1917 and became the much-feared head of the Cheka.

33　The Nietzsche essay first appeared in four numbers of the *Eastern Review*, December 22, 24, 25 and 30, 1900. See *Sochineniya*, Vol XX, 'Kultura Starago mira', Moscow–Leningrad 1926. It has been published in French translation in *Cahiers Leon Trotsky*, I, January 1979, pp. 105–120, under the title 'A propos de la philosophie du surhomme'.

34　*Sochineniya*, Vol XX, ibid., pp. 74–79.

35　*My Life*, op. cit., p. 87.

## CHAPTER TWO

1　For the full text of Lenin's letter to Plekhanov proposing to co-opt Trotsky to the editorial board, see *My Life*, op. cit., pp. 158–9.

2　Ibid., p. 156.

3　For Trotsky's attitude to the Bund, see *Vtoroi s'ezd RSDRP Protokoly*, Moscow 1959, pp. 50–123. Also the article by Yehiel Harari, 'Le parcours de Trotsky',

*Les Nouveaux Cahiers*, no. 36, Printemps 1974, pp. 43–61. Trotsky's interventions on the Jewish issue provoked vehement protests at the Congress from the delegates of the Bund who held his remarks to be deliberately insulting and hypocritical.

4  For the background to this whole debate see Leopold H. Haimson, *The Russian Marxists and the Origins of Bolshevism*, Cambridge, Massachusetts 1955, pp. 166–181.

5  *Vtoroi ocherednoi s'ezd RSDRP, Protokoly*, Geneva 1903, pp. 238–239, 245–50. 'We constitute the conscious expression of an unconscious process.'

6  Ibid., pp. 248–50. Trotsky's main point was that the Lenin-Plekhanov formula was an ineffective weapon against opportunism.

7  Ibid., pp. 250–252 for Lenin's last appeal.

8  *My Life*, op. cit., pp. 166–167.

9  Ibid., p. 167.

10 N. Trotsky, *Vtoroi Syezd RSDRP (Otchet Sibirskoi Delegatsii)*, Geneva 1903, pp. 8–11.

11 Ibid., pp. 20–21. At the 1903 Congress, Martov had accused Lenin of introducing a 'state of siege within the party'.

12 Ibid., p. 29. Trotsky described the removal of the old *Iskra* board as the first step 'in our caricature Robespierrade'.

13 Ibid., pp. 29–30. In other words, Lenin's regime would collapse like that of Robespierre and open the way for opportunism.

14 *Nashi Politicheskye Zadachi*, Geneva 1904, pp. 47, 67, 74.

15 Ibid., p. 50. Trotsky called this organizational method *zamestitelstvo*, i.e. substitutionism.

16 Ibid., p. 54. For further discussion, see Isaac Deutscher, *The Prophet Armed. Trotsky: 1879–1921*, O.U.P. 1963, pp. 90–95.

17 *Nashi Politicheskye Zadachi*, op. cit., p. 93. Trotsky insisted that Lenin's ideal of the Jacobin Social Democrat was a contradiction in terms.

18 Ibid., p. 98. Trotsky saw in Lenin's mistrust of those around him a political danger as well as an unappealing character-trait.

19 Ibid., pp. 104–106. Trotsky's distrust of intellectuals first comes to the fore in these pages.

20 P. B. Akelsrod, 'Ob "edinenie rossisskoi sotsialdemokratii i eya zadachi', *Iskra*, December 15 1903.

21 Rosa Luxemburg, 'Organizatsionnye voprosy russkoi sotsialdemokratii', *Iskra*, July 1904.

22 V. I. Lenin, 'Shag vpered, dva shaga nazad', *Izbrannie Proizvedeniya*, 4th ed., Vol I, Moscow 1943, p. 403.

23 Isaac Deutscher, *The Prophet Armed* ... op. cit., p. 93 points out that Marxist polemics generally avoided personal mud-slinging. He attributes Trotsky's venomous tone to his inability to 'separate ideas from men'.

24 *Nashi Politicheskye Zadachi*, op. cit., p. 105. This implied that he did not believe in 1904 that Bolshevism could succeed in manipulating the Russian labour movement.

25  Leon Trotski, *Stalin. An Appraisal of the Man and His Influence*, London 1947, p. 112.
26  *My Life*, op. cit., pp. 166–170, 342–347. Leon Trotski, *Stalin*, ibid., pp. 112–113.
27  Leon Trotski, *Stalin*, ibid. '... that fatalistic optimism meant in practice not only repudiation of the factional struggle but of the very idea of a party ...'
28  *My Life*, op. cit., p. 168. Among those who upheld the *Iskra* banner, 'Lenin alone, and with finality, envisaged "tomorrow", with all its stern tasks, its cruel conflicts and countless victims.'
29  Boris Souvarine, *Stalin. A Critical History of Bolshevism*, London 1939, p. 132.
30  Ibid.
31  Ibid. See also *The Errors of Trotskyism*, London 1925, pp. 245–316 for an exhaustive though highly tendentious catalogue of pre-1917 Lenin-Trotsky mud-slinging, compiled by L. B. Kamenev.
32  *My Life*, op. cit., p. 168.
33  Ibid.
34  Ibid., p. 169.

## CHAPTER THREE

1   See Z. A. B. Zeman and W. B. Scharlau, *The Merchant of Revolution: The Life of Alexander Israel Helphand (Parvus) 1867–1924*, London 1965.
2   Leon Trotsky, *My Life*, op. cit., p. 172.
3   *Iskra*, January 1 1905. See also Isaac Deutscher, *The Prophet Armed*, op. cit., pp. 103–105.
4   Leon Trotski, 'Three Concepts of the Russian Revolution', in *Stalin*, op. cit., p. 430.
5   Ibid.
6   Ibid.
7   V. I. Lenin, 'Dve taktiki sotsialdemokratii v demokraticheskoi revolutsii', quoted in Jonathan Frankel, 'Lenin's Doctrinal Revolution of April 1917', *Journal of Contemporary History*, Vol 4, no. 2, 1969, p. 123.
8   I. Deutscher, ed., *The Age of Permanent Revolution: A Trotsky Anthology*, New York 1964, pp. 48–49.
9   Ibid., p. 50.
10  'Do g-go Yanvarya', *Nasha Revolyutsiya*, St Petersburg 1906, p. 22.
11  Deutscher, *The Prophet Armed*, op. cit., p. 119.
12  *My Life*, op. cit., p. 179.
13  Ibid.
14  *The Prophet Armed*, op. cit., p. 129.
15  Leon Trotsky, *1905*, Pelican Books, London 1973, p. 122. 'It was an organization which was authoritative and yet had no traditions; which could immediately involve a scattered mass of hundreds of thousands of people while having virtually no organizational machinery ... which was capable of initiative

and spontaneous self-control – and most important of all, which could be
brought out from underground within twenty-four hours.'

16  *My Life*, op. cit., pp. 182–3.
17  Ibid., p. 188.
18  Ibid., p. 187.
19  *1905*, op. cit., p. 123.
20  Ibid., p. 124.
21  Ibid., p. 266.
22  Ibid., pp. 266–7.
23  Ibid., p. 123.
24  Ibid., p. 201.
25  Ibid., p. 267.
26  Ibid.
27  Ibid., p. 268.
28  Ibid., pp. 269–70.
29  Ibid., p. 270.
30  Ibid., p. 409.
31  Ibid., p. 399.
32  Ibid., p. 400.
33  Ibid., p. 407.
34  Ibid., p. 411.
35  Ibid., p. 414.
36  See A. V. Lunacharsky, *Revolyutsionniye Siluety*, Moscow 1923 (English Translation, London 1967).
37  *My Life*, op. cit., p. 188.
38  *1905*, p. 279.
39  Ibid., pp. 280–1.
40  Ibid., p. 282.
41  Ibid., p. 283.
42  Ibid., p. 284.
43  Ibid., p. 73.

## CHAPTER FOUR

1  Isaac Deutscher, *The Prophet Armed*, op. cit., p. 150.
2  Karl Marx and Frederick Engels, 'Address of the Central Committee to the Communist League', London, March 1850, in: Marx/Engels, *Selected Works*, Vol I, Moscow 1962, p. 110.
3  Ibid., p. 117.
4  Franz Mehring, 'Die Revolution in Permanenz', *Die Neue Zeit*, XXIV (1905–1906), I, pp. 169–172.
5  *Nachalo*, November 25 1905.
6  V. I. Lenin, *Sochinenija*, Moscow 1954–1958, Vol IV, p. 213f.
7  For an extensive and illuminating discussion of the relation between back-

wardness and revolution, see Baruch Knei-Paz, *The Social and Political Thought of Leon Trotsky*, Oxford 1978.

8  Leon Trotsky, *The Permanent Revolution*, London 1962, pp. 6–10.
9  Ibid.
10  Leon Trotsky, 'Russia's Social Development and Tsarism' in: *1905*, op. cit., p. 26.
11  Ibid., p. 27.
12  'The Driving Forces of the Russian Revolution', ibid., pp. 56–57.
13  Ibid., p. 59.
14  Ibid., p. 61.
15  Ibid., p. 70.
16  Ibid., p. 72.
17  Ibid., pp. 72–73.
18  'Itogi i Perspektivy' in: *Nasha Revolyutsiya*, St Petersburg 1906, p. 255.
19  Ibid., pp. 255–6.
20  Leon Trotsky, *The Permanent Revolution*, op. cit., p. 247.
21  'Itogi i Perspektivy', op. cit., p. 285.
22  Leon Trotsky, 'The Party of the Proletariat and the Bourgeois Parties in the Revolution' in: *1905*, op. cit., p. 291.
23  Ibid., p. 293.
24  Ibid., p. 295.
25  Ibid., p. 297.
26  See his article 'Das Proletariat und die russische Revolution', *Die Neue Zeit*, XXVI, 2 (1907–08), pp. 782–791.
27  'Our Differences' in *1905*, op. cit., p. 319.
28  Ibid., p. 328.
29  Ibid., p. 331.
30  Ibid., p. 333.

## CHAPTER FIVE

1  Leon Trotsky, *My Life*, op. cit., pp. 227–8.
2  Isaac Deutscher, *The Prophet Armed*, op. cit., p. 197.
3  Ibid.
4  For Trotsky's highly unflattering view of the Russian intelligentsia, see 'Ob intelligentsii', in: *Literatura i Revolyutsiya*, Moscow 1923, pp. 255–269. The article was originally published in March 1912.
5  Ibid., p. 267.
6  Ibid., p. 268.
7  *My Life*, op. cit., p. 219.
8  Trotsky's correspondence with Karl Kautsky and the Austro-Marxist Rudolf Hilferding can be consulted in the archives of The International Institute of Social History in Amsterdam.
9  See Trotsky's article, 'Victor Adler', *Kievskaya Mysl*, July 13 1913, reproduced in Leon Trotsky, *Political Profiles*, London 1972, p. 13.

10  'Karl Kautsky', ibid., pp. 68–69.
11  *My Life*, op. cit., p. 221.
12  Ibid., p. 220.
13  Trotsky was however more magnanimous in this regard than Lenin. See his obituary for Karl Kautsky in: *Writings of Leon Trotsky (1938–39)*, New York 1974, pp. 98–99.
14  Leon Trotsky, 'Karl Liebknecht and Rosa Luxemburg', *Political Profiles*, op. cit., p. 138.
15  'Karl Liebknecht and Hugo Haase', ibid., pp. 107–110.
16  *My Life*, op. cit., p. 222.
17  'Karl Liebknecht', op. cit., p. 107.
18  *My Life*, op. cit., p. 222.
19  Ibid., p. 221.
20  Ibid.
21  'An Epoch Passes. Bebel, Jaurès and Vaillant', *Kievskaya Mysl*, January 1 1916, *Political Profiles*, op. cit., p. 77.
22  'Jaurès', *Kievskaya Mysl*, January 9 1909, ibid., p. 26.
23  Ibid., p. 27.
24  'Jean Jaurès', ibid., p. 39.
25  *My Life*, op. cit., pp. 144–145.
26  'Victor Adler', *Kievskaya Mysl*, July 13 1913, in: *Political Profiles*, op. cit., p. 11.
27  Ibid., p. 14.
28  Ibid., p. 17.
29  Ibid., p. 18.
30  'Fritz Adler', ibid., p. 61.
31  *My Life*, op. cit., p. 213.
32  Ibid., p. 215.
33  Ibid., p. 218.
34  Ibid., p. 216.

## CHAPTER SIX

1   *My Life*, op. cit., p. 241.
2   Leon Trotsky, 'War and the International' in: *The Age of Permanent Revolution*, op. cit., p. 76.
3   Ibid., p. 77.
4   Ibid., p. 74.
5   *Nashe Slovo*, April 12 1916 – quoted in *The Prophet Armed*, op. cit., p. 238.
6   Deutscher, op. cit., pp. 233–4.
7   *My Life*, op. cit., p. 342.
8   Ibid.
9   Ibid., p. 345.
10  Jonathan Frankel, 'Lenin's Doctrinal Revolution of April 1917', op. cit., pp. 125–6.
11  See L. Trotsky, *History of the Russian Revolution*, I, London 1932, pp. 329–330.

12 Leon Trotsky 'Speech ... Against the Coalition Government', in *The Age of Permanent Revolution*, op. cit., p. 97.
13 Ibid.
14 *The Prophet Armed*, op. cit., pp. 257–8.
15 L. Trotsky, *The History of the Russian Revolution*, London 1965, p. 14.
16 Ibid., p. 13.
17 Ibid., p. 15.
18 *My Life*, op. cit., pp. 306–7.
19 *The Prophet Armed*, op. cit., p. 287.
20 V. I. Lenin, *Sochineniya*, XXXVI, p. 1.
21 Ibid., pp. 47, 60, 114.
22 See Merle Fainsod, *How Russia is Ruled*, Cambridge, Mass., pp. 80–86.
23 Leon Trotsky, *History of the Russian Revolution*, op. cit., Vol I, pp. 285–292, 329–33.
24 Isaac Deutscher, *The Prophet Armed*, op. cit., pp. 304–311.
25 Ibid., p. 308.
26 Trotsky, *Sochineniya*, Vol iii, Bk. 2, pp. 51–53.
27 *My Life*, op. cit., p. 339.
28 Ibid.
29 Ibid., p. 341 the full text in Sukhanov, *Zapiski o revolutsii*, Berlin 1922–3, Vol 7, p. 203.
30 See Roger Pethybridge, *The Spread of the Russian Revolution. Essays on 1917*, London 1972.
31 *The History of the Russian Revolution*, Vol I, pp. 136–152.
32 Leon Trotsky, *1905*, op. cit., p. 121.
33 Maxim Gorky, *Untimely Thoughts: Essays on Revolution, Culture and the Bolsheviks*, 1971. See Melvin J. Lasky, *Utopia and Revolution*, London 1977, pp. 114–118.
34 See Rosa Luxemburg, *The Russian Revolution*, Ann Arbor, Michigan 1961, pp. 76–77.
35 Leon Trotsky, *The Stalin School of Falsification*, London 1974, pp. 85–98.
36 Ibid., p. 91.
37 Ibid., p. 93.
38 Ibid., p. 94.

## CHAPTER SEVEN

1 Leon Trotsky, *My Life*, op. cit., p. 351.
2 Ibid., p. 352.
3 Ibid., p. 354.
4 Ibid., p. 355.
5 On the background to this internationalist outlook, see Robert S. Wistrich, *Revolutionary Jews from Marx to Trotsky*, op. cit.
6 *My Life*, op. cit., p. 376.
7 See Peter Kenez, 'White Pogroms in the Ukraine 1919', *The Wiener Library Bulletin*, 1977, New Series Nos. 41/42, pp. 2–8.

8 See E. Tcherikover, *Antisemitizm un Pogromen in Ukraine 1917-18*, Berlin 1923, pp. 103-4. Also Joseph Nevada, *Trotsky and the Jews*, Philadelphia 1972, p. 156.

9 *The Trotsky Papers Vol I.* (1917-1919), edited by Jan. M. Meijer, The Hague 1964, pp. 361-3. See also Nevada, ibid., pp. 110-115 for Trotsky's general attitude to Jewish recruits in the Red Army.

10 See Paul Avrich, *Kronstadt 1921*, New York 1970, p. 146.

11 *Pravda o Kronshtadte*, Prague 1921, pp. 80-82, 91, 120.

12 See for example, *The History of the Russian Revolution*, I, p. 247 where Trotsky writes: 'It is not that aliens lead the revolution, but that the revolution makes use of the aliens.'

13 *My Life*, op. cit., p. 355.

14 Ibid., p. 383.

15 E. H. Carr, *The Bolshevik Revolution 1917-1923*, Vol 3, London 1971, p. 29.

16 *Sochineniya*, iii, ii, 206-9.

17 *The Prophet Armed*, op. cit., pp. 383ff.

18 Ibid., p. 395.

19 *Diary in Exile*, op. cit., 82-84. In spite of several sharp clashes, Trotsky observed that 'the instances when Lenin and I understood each other at a glance were a hundred times more numerous and our solidarity always guaranteed the passage of a question in the Politburo without disputes.'

20 *My Life*, op. cit., p. 455.

21 Ibid., p. 456.

22 *Kak Vooruzhalas' Revolutsiya*, ii, i (1924), pp. 59, 452.

23 Ibid., iii, ii (1925), pp. 242-258. At the XI Party Congress in March 1922 Trotsky asked his critics: 'How can the maxims of the military profession be determined with the help of the Marxist method? That would be the same thing as to create a theory of architecture or a veterinary textbook with the help of Marxism.'

24 Ibid., Vol i, p. 29.

25 *My Life*, op. cit., p. 429.

26 Ibid.

27 Ibid., p. 434.

28 *Kak Vooruzhalas' Revolyutsiya*, Vol i, p. 235.

29 *My Life*, op. cit., p. 427.

30 See *The Prophet Armed*, op. cit., pp. 442-445. Also *My Life*, ibid., pp. 440-452

31 Ibid., p. 452.

32 Victor Serge, *Memoirs of a Revolutionary 1901-1941*, O.U.P. 1967, pp. 140-1.

33 *Fourth International*, August 1943, p. 237.

34 *The First Five years of the Communist International*, Vol I, pp. 50-63.

35 Ibid., p. 63.

36 Ibid.

37 Jan Meijer, ed., *The Trotsky Papers, 1917-1922*, I, p. 623.

38 *Tretii Syezd Profsoyuzov*, April 6-13, 1920, Moscow 1921, pp. 88-89.

39 Ibid.

40 Ibid., p. 97.

41  *My Life*, op. cit., pp. 481–2.
42  J. V. Stalin, *Sochineniya*, Vol 6, p. 29.
43  *Desyaty Syezd RKP(b)*, Moscow 1921, pp. 350–1.
44  I. Howe, ed., *The Basic Writings of Trotsky*, London 1963, p. 142.
45  Ibid., p. 146.
46  Ibid., p. 158.
47  Leon Trotsky, *Their Morals and Ours*, New York 1974, p. 9.
48  *Sochenineniya*, Vol xcii, 6k.2, p. 518. See also Paul Avrich, *Kronstadt 1921*, op. cit.
49  L. D. Trotskii, *Kak Vooruzhalas' revolutsiia*, III, Pt. 1, pp. 203–4. Also 'Shumikha vokrug Kronshtadta', *Biulleten Oppozitsii*, May–June 1938, pp. 22–26, and 'Eschche ob usmirenii Kronshtadta', ibid., October 1938, p. 10.
50  Isaac Deutscher, op. cit., Vol 2, p. 28.

## CHAPTER EIGHT

1   *Kak Vooruzhalas' Revolyutsiya*, Moscow 1923–25, I, 60.
2   *Sochineniya*, XV, p. 298.
3   The best account of Trotsky's policies in this period is by Richard Day, *Leon Trotsky and the Politics of Economic Isolation*, C.U.P. 1973.
4   V. I. Lenin, *Selected Works*, Moscow 1937, IX, pp. 403, 406.
5   Day, op. cit., p. 127.
6   Ibid., p. 140.
7   *Izvestiya*, June 2 1925.
8   J. V. Stalin, *Sochineniya*, VI, p. 378.
9   Ibid., p. 377.
10  L. Trotsky, *The Third International After Lenin*, New York 1957, p. 40.
11  Leon Trotsky, *1905*, op. cit., p. 8.
12  See 'The Tasks of Soviet Reconstruction: 1921–1926', in: *The Age of Permanent Revolution*, p. 133 (the quote is taken from Leon Trotsky, *Whither Russia?*).
13  Ibid., p. 134.
14  Ibid.
15  *My Life*, op. cit., p. 501.
16  Ibid.
17  Ibid.
18  *Pravda*, 14.3.1923.
19  Ibid.
20  *Izvestia*, 21.8.1936.
21  See Victor Serge, *Memoirs of a Revolutionary*, op. cit., p. 234, who writes that Trotsky deliberately refused power 'out of respect for an unwritten law that forbade any recourse to military mutiny within a socialist regime.'
22  *My Life*, op. cit., p. 525.
23  Ibid., pp. 526–7.
24  Trotsky, *The New Course*, introduced by Max Schachtman, Ann Arbor Paperbacks, 1965, p. 13.

25 Ibid., p. 19.
26 Ibid., p. 45.
27 J. V. Stalin, *Sochineniya*, V, pp. 386ff.
28 *The New Course*, op. cit., p. 55.
29 See 'Theses on Revolution and Counterrevolution' in: *The Age of Permanent Revolution*, op. cit., pp. 142–3. These reflections were jotted down in Trotsky's diary on November 26 1926.
30 J. V. Stalin, *Sochineniya*, VI, pp. 27–45.
31 *Trinadsatyi s'ezd RKP(b)*, 23–31 maja 1924, g., Moscow 1924, pp. 166ff.
32 *My Life*, op. cit., p. 521.
33 *Pravda*, 24.1.1924.
34 *The Errors of Trotskyism*, London 1926, p. 123.
35 Ibid., pp. 187, 195.
36 Ibid., pp. 219–226.
37 Ibid., pp. 238–240.
38 Ibid., p. 235. See also J. V. Stalin, *Sochineniya*, VI, pp. 349–50.
39 Victor Serge, *The Life and Death of Leon Trotsky*, p. 3.
40 *Biulleten Oppozitsii* (Paris) no. 6, October 1929, pp. 14–20.
41 *My Life*, op. cit., p. 582.

## CHAPTER NINE

1 *My Life*, op. cit., p. 353.
2 Ibid., p. 605.
3 Ibid., p. xxxix.
4 Ibid., p. 604.
5 See: 'What is Historical Objectivity?' in: *Writings of Leon Trotsky (1932–33)*, New York 1972, pp. 193–187, for an interesting example of how Trotsky defined the problem of historical truth.
6 Ibid., p. 185.
7 Leon Trotsky, *The History of the Russian Revolution*, 3 vols, New York 1936, I, 136–152.
8 Ibid., p. 152.
9 Leon Trotsky, *1905*, op. cit., pp. 186–7.
10 Ibid., pp. 149–151.
11 Ibid., p. 151.
12 For Trotsky's detestation of Russian Black-Hundred anti-Semitism, see 'Pod znakom de'la Beilisa', *Sochineniya*, 4, op. cit., pp. 462–476.
13 *1905*, op. cit., p. 205.
14 Ibid., 370.
15 Ibid., 430.
16 'Leon Tolstoi' in: Leon Trotsky, *Littérature et Révolution*, Paris 1971, pp. 314–15.
17 Ibid., p. 317.
18 Ibid., p. 320.

224     TROTSKY: FATE OF A REVOLUTIONARY

19  Ibid., p. 332.
20  Ibid., p. 319.
21  Leon Trotsky, *Literature and Revolution*, Ann Arbor Paperback, 1960, p. 9.
22  Ibid., p. 19.
23  Ibid., p. 14.
24  Ibid., p. 218.
25  Ibid., p. 221.
26  See *Voprosy Kultury Pri Diktatura Proletariata* (1925), pp. 93–110.
27  *Literature and Revolution*, op. cit., p. 225.
28  Leon Trotsky, 'Speech on Party Policy in the Field of Imaginative Literature', May 9 1924, in: *Class and Art. Culture under the Dictatorship*, London 1974, p. 8.
29  Ibid., p. 9.
30  *Literature and Revolution*, op. cit., pp. 81–84.
31  Ibid., p. 109.
32  Ibid., p. 129.
33  Ibid., 143.
34  Ibid., p. 149.
35  Ibid., p. 150.
36  Ibid., p. 131.
37  Ibid., p. 132.
38  Ibid., pp. 255–6.
39  Ibid.
40  Leon Trotsky, *The Revolution Betrayed*, op. cit., pp. 184–5.
41  'Art and Politics', *Partisan Review*, August 1938.
42  'Pour un art révolutionnaire indépendant', July 25 1938, in: *Littérature et révolution*, op. cit., pp. 501–509.
43  Ibid.
44  *The Age of Permanent Revolution*, op. cit., p. 312.
45  Ibid., p. 301.

CHAPTER TEN

1  Leon Trotsky, *The Stalin School of Falsification*, London 1974, p. 113.
2  Ibid., p. 116.
3  Ibid., p. 123.
4  Ibid., p. 125.
5  Ibid.
6  Ibid., p. 136.
7  'Zaschita Sovetskoi respubliki i oppozitsiya', *Byulleten Oppozitsii* (October 1929), pp. 1–17.
8  See Siegfried Bahne, 'Trotsky on Stalin's Russia', *Survey*, April 1962, pp. 27–43.
9  Stephen F. Cohen, 'Bukharin-Kamenev meeting, 1928,' *Dissent*, Winter 1979, pp. 78–88.
10  Leon Trotski, *Stalin*, op. cit., p. 393.
11  Ibid., p. 383.

12   See Nicolas Krasso, 'Reply to Ernest Mandel', *New Left Review*, Nr. 48, March–April 1968, pp. 94–5.
13   'Sovetskoe khozyaistvo v Opastnosti!', *Byulleten Oppozitsii*, XXVI (1932), p. 6.
14   'The Danger of Thermidor' (January 11 1933) in: *Writings of Leon Trotsky (1932–33)*, New York 1972, p. 77.
15   'The Degeneration of Theory and the Theory of Degeneration. Problems of the Soviet Regime' (April 29 1933), ibid., pp. 215–225.
16   'The Class Nature of the Soviet State' (October 1 1933), ibid., p. 114.
17   Ibid., p. 118.
18   Leon Trotsky, *The Workers' State and the Question of Thermidor and Bonapartism*, London 1973, pp. 31–32.
19   Ibid., p. 38.
20   Ibid., p. 34.
21   Ibid., p. 36.
22   Ibid., p. 37.
23   Ibid., p. 44.
24   Ibid., p. 45.
25   See Alain Besançon, 'Soviet Present and Russian Past', *Encounter*, March 1978, pp. 80–89.
26   *The Case of Leon Trotsky*, New York 1937, p. 470.
27   Ibid., pp. 580–585.
28   Leon Trotsky, *The Revolution Betrayed*, New York 1937, p. 277.
29   Ibid., p. 278.
30   Ibid., p. 112.
31   Ibid., pp. 86–89.
32   Ibid., pp. 249–250.
33   Ibid., pp. 236–9.
34   Ibid., p. 244.
35   Ibid., p. 287.
36   Ibid., p. 288.
37   Ibid., pp. 289–90.
38   See Bruno Rizzi, *La Bureaucratisation du Monde*, Paris 1939.
39   'The USSR in War', in: *In Defence of Marxism*, New York 1942.
40   Ibid., p. 9.
41   See Max Schachtman, '1939: Whither Russia? Trotsky and his Critics', *Survey*, April 1962.

## CHAPTER ELEVEN

1   Isaac Deutscher, *The Prophet Outcast: Trotsky 1929–1940*, O.U.P. 1963, p. 129.
2   For the classical Marxist interpretations of fascism by August Thalheimer, Otto Bauer, Angelo Tasca, Arthur Rosenberg etc., see the texts in Wolfgang Abendroth, ed., *Faschismus und Kapitalismus. Theorien über die sozialen Ursprünge und die Funktion des Faschismus*, Frankfurt 1967.
3   On this general problem, see Tim Mason, 'The Primacy of Politics – Politics

and Economics in National Socialist Germany', S. H. Woolf, ed., *The Nature of Fascism*, New York 1968, pp. 165-195.

4 'What Next? Vital Questions for the German Proletariat', (January 27 1932) in Leon Trotsky, *The Struggle Against Fascism in Germany*, London 1975, p. 213.

5 V. I. Lenin, *Werke*, Berlin East, 1962, Bd. 33, p. 417.

6 Siegfried Bahne, 'Sozialfaschismus' in Deutschland. Zur Geschichte eines Politischen Begriffs', *International Review of Social History*, 1965, Vol 10, Pt. 2, pp. 216ff.

7 *Rasshirennyi Plenum Ispolnitel'nogo Komiteta Kommunisticheskogo Internationale* June 12–23 1923, 207, 211, 227. See also Ernest Nolte, ed., *Theorien über den Faschismus*, Köln 1970, p. 88.

8 'The Turn in the Communist International and the Situation in Germany' (September 26 1930) in Leon Trotsky, *The Struggle against Fascism*, op. cit., p. 15.

9 Leon Trotsky, *Where is Britain Going?*, London 1926, p. 119.

10 Ibid., p. 114.

11 Ibid.

12 Leon Trotsky, *Fascism, What is it and how to fight it*, New York 1972, p. 15.

13 L. Trotsky, *Europa and Amerika*, Berlin 1926, p. 17.

14 *The Militant*, January 16 1932.

15 Ibid.

16 Leon Trotsky, *Fascism*, op. cit., p. 7.

17 Leon Trotsky, *Stalin*, op. cit., p. 336.

18 Ibid., p. 413.

19 Ibid.

20 'How Long Can Hitler Stay?' (June 22 1933) in: *The Struggle against Fascism*, op. cit., p. 423.

21 *Protokoll des Vierten Kongresses der Kommunistischen Internationale* (1923), 920. See also G. Zinoviev, *Die Lehren der deutschen Ereignisse* (1924) and Theodore Draper, 'The Ghost of Social-Fascism' in: *Commentary*, February 1969, pp. 29–42.

22 J. V. Stalin 'On the International Situation' (September 20 1924) *Sochineniya*, Moscow 1950, Vol 6, p. 282.

23 'The Tragedy of the German Proletariat: The German Workers will Rise Again – Stalinism, Never!', *The Struggle Against Fascism*, op. cit., p. 381.

24 'The Turn in the Communist International', ibid., pp. 13–14.

25 Ibid.

26 'For a Workers' United Front Against Fascism' (December 8 1931), ibid., p. 109.

27 I. Deutscher, *The Prophet Armed*, 2, op. cit., p. 143.

28 'Offener Brief der KPD an die 'Werktätigen Wähler der NSDAP und die Mitglieder der Sturmabteilungen' *Die Rote Fahne*, November 1 1931. See also Hermann Weber, ed., *Der Deutsche Kommunismus. Dokumente*, Köln 1964, pp. 155–157.

29 'Thälmann and the "People's Revolution"' (April 14 1931): *The Struggle against Fascism*, op. cit., p. 34. Also 'Against National Communism' (Lessons

of the 'Red Referendum':, August 25 1931, ibid., p. 61.
30  'What Next?', ibid., p. 148.
31  'The German Catastrophe. The Responsibility of the Leadership' (May 28
    1933), ibid., p. 402.
32  'What Next?', op. cit., pp. 116–117, 123.
33  'The Only Road', ibid., p. 273.
34  Ibid., p. 281.
35  'German Bonapartism' (October 30 1932), ibid., p. 325.
36  'Before the Decision' (February 5 1933), ibid., p. 341.
37  'What is National Socialism?' (June 10 1933), ibid., pp. 408–9.
38  'What Next?', ibid., p. 217.
39  'The German Puzzle' (August 1932), ibid., p. 252.
40  'Before the Decision', ibid., p. 341.
41  'What is National Socialism?', ibid., pp. 410–411.
42  Ibid., p. 412.
43  Ibid.
44  Leon Trotsky, On the Jewish Question, New York 1973, p. 20.
45  Ibid., p. 29.
46  Ibid., pp. 30–31.
47  'What is National Socialism?', op. cit., p. 415.
48  Leon Trotsky, Diary in Exile, op. cit., p. 92.
49  'Bonapartism, Fascism, and War' (August 20 1940): The Struggle Against
    Fascism, op. cit., p. 468.
50  'Only Revolution Can End War' (March 18 1939) in: Writings of Leon Trotsky
    (1938–39), op. cit., pp. 234–5. Also Leon Trotsky, The Lessons of Spain, op. cit.,
    pp. 26–32.
51  See Pierre Brouc, 'Trotsky and the Spanish Revolution', Fourth International,
    April 1967, pp. 4–16.
52  'A Contribution to Centrist Literature' (November 15 1938), Writings of Leon
    Trotsky (1938–39), op. cit., p. 118.
53  'Bonapartism, Fascism, and War', op. cit., p. 467.
54  Ibid., p. 468.
55  Ibid.
56  'A Step Towards Social Patriotism. On the Position of the Fourth International
    Against War and Fascism' (March 7 1939), Writings, op. cit., pp. 207–213.
57  'Fight Imperialism to Fight Fascism', ibid., pp. 26–27.
58  'A Fresh Lesson' (October 10 1938), ibid., pp. 52ff.
59  'Phrases and Reality' (September 19 1938), ibid., p. 21.

## CHAPTER TWELVE

1  Isaac Deutscher, The Prophet Outcast, op. cit., p. 122.
2  Ibid., p. 126.
3  Leon Trotsky, 1905, op. cit., p. 365.
4  My Life, op. cit., p. xlii.

# SELECT BIBLIOGRAPHY

The primary and secondary sources I have listed below make no claim to being comprehensive. In any case Louis Sinclair's *Leon Trotsky: A Bibliography*, Stanford 1972, has made this task superfluous. Only those works are included which I found particularly helpful in the course of research on this book. Most of Trotsky's basic writings are now available in English (thanks largely to the Pathfinder Press in New York), and I have also listed works in Russian, French and German where relevant, as well as the most useful anthologies and secondary literature.

## WRITINGS OF TROTSKY IN ENGLISH

*The Case of Leon Trotsky*, New York 1937.
*The Revolution Betrayed*, New York 1937.
*Stalin*, London 1947 (re-issued: New York 1970).
*Trotsky's Dairy in Exile 1935*, Cambridge, Mass. 1958.
*Literature and Revolution*, University of Michigan 1960.
*Terrorism and Communism*, Ann Arbor 1961.
*History of the Russian Revolution*, 3 vols. Gollancz: 1965 (Russian original re-issued in 1 vol: New York 1976).
*The Trotsky Papers: 1917-1922*, 2 vols, edited by Jan M. Meijer, The Hague 1964, 1971.
*The New Course*, Ann Arbor 1965.
*Problems of the Chinese Revolution*, London 1969 (re-issued: Ann Arbor 1967).
*The Permanent Revolution* and *Results and Prospects*, New York 1969.
*Marxism in Our Time*, New York 1970.
*On Lenin: Notes towards a Biography*, London 1971.
*The Third International After Lenin*, New York 1971.
*Political Profiles*, London 1973.
*The First Five Years of the Communist International*, 2 vols, New York 1973.
*In Defense of Marxism*, New York 1973.
*The Class Nature of the Soviet State* London 1973.
*1905*, Penguin Books 1974.
*The Young Lenin*, Penguin Books 1974.
*Their Morals and Ours*, London 1974 (also: New York 1974).
*The Stalin School of Falsification*, London 1974 (issued: New York 1972).
*My Life*, Penguin Books 1975 (issued: New York 1970).

## WORKS IN RUSSIAN

*Sochineniya* Moscow/Leningrad 1924-1927.
*Vtoroi Syezd RSDRP: Otchet Sibirskoi Delegatsii,* Geneva 1903.
*Nashi Politicheskye Zadachi,* Geneva 1904.
*Do 9-go Yanvarya,* Geneva 1905.
*Itogi i Perspektivy,* Moscow 1919 (English trans: New York 1969).
*Pyat Let Kominterna,* Moscow 1924 (English trans: New York 1973).
*Kak Vooruzhalas Revolyutsiya,* 3 vols, Moscow 1923-1925.
*Zapad i Vostok,* Moscow 1924.
*K sotsializmu ili Kapitalizmu?,* Moscow-Leningrad 1926.

## ARTICLES AND BOOKS IN GERMAN

'Die Duma und die Revolution', *Die Neue Zeit,* XXV, 2 (1906-07), pp. 377-385.
'Uber den Marxismus in Russland', ibid., XXVI, I (1907-08), pp. 7-10.
'Das Proletariat und die Russische Revolution', ibid., XXVI, 2, (1907-08), pp. 782-791.
'Die Entwicklungstendenzen der russischen Sozialdemokratie', ibid., XXVIII, 2 (1909-10), pp. 860-871.
'Die russische Sozialdemokratie', *Der Kampf,* II (1908), Heft I, pp. 25-33.
*Der Krieg und die Internationale,* Berlin 1919.
*Die russische Revolution* 1905, Berlin 1923.
*Europa und Amerika,* Berlin 1926.

## ANTHOLOGIES

*The Age of Permanent Revolution,* edited by Isaac Deutscher, New York 1964.
*The Basic Writings of Trotsky,* edited by Irving Howe, London 1964.
*The Essential Trotsky,* London 1963.
*Écrits, 1928-1940,* 3 vols, Paris 1955-1959.
*Leon Trotsky on the Jewish Question,* New York 1970.
*Littérature et révolution,* Paris 1971.
*Le Mouvement Communiste en France, 1919-1939,* edited by Pierre Broué, Paris 1967.
*Politique de Trotsky.* edited by Jean Baechler, Paris 1968.
*On Britain,* New York 1973.
*On France.* New York 1968.
*Problems of Everyday Life,* New York 1973.
*The Spanish Revolution (1931-39).* New York 1972.
        *Struggle against Fascism in Germany,* London 1975 (issued in New York 1970).
            *... of Leon Trotsky (1929-40),* 12 vols, Pathfinder Press, New York 1971-74.

**SECONDARY LITERATURE**

Ascher, Abraham. *Pavel Axelrod and the Development of Menshevism*, Oxford 1973 (issued: Cambridge, Mass. 1972).

Avenas, Denise. *Économie et politique dans la pensée de Trotsky*, Paris 1970.

Avrich, Paul. *Kronstadt 1921*, Princeton 1970.

Balabanoff, Angelica, *My Life as a Rebel*, London 1938 (re-issued: New York 1968).

Barsch, Günter. *Trotzkismus als eigentlicher Sowjetkommunismus?*, Berlin/Bonn Godesberg 1977.

Baschanow, Boris. *Ich war Stalins Sekretär*, Berlin/Wien 1977.

Berkman, Alexander. *The Kronstadt Rebellion*, Berlin 1923.

———. *The Bolshevik Myth*, London 1925.

Brahm, Heinz. *Trotzkijs Kampf um die Nachfolge Lenins*, Cologne 1964.

Brossat, Alain, *Aux origines do la révolution permanente: la pensée politique du jeune Trotsky*, Paris 1974.

Carmichael, Joel. *Trotsky: An Appreciation of his Life*, London 1975.

Carr, E. H. *The Bolshevik Revolution*, 3 vols, Harmonsworth 1966.

———. *The Interregnum, 1923-1924*, London 1960.

———. *Socialism in One Country, 1924-1926*, 3 vols, London 1958-64.

Chamberlain, W. H. *The Russian Revolution*, 2 vols, New York 1965.

Ciliga, Anton. *The Kronstadt Revolt*, London 1942.

Cohen, Stephen F. *Bukharin and the Bolshevik Revolution: A Political Biography 1888-1938*, London 1974 (issued: New York 1973).

Daniels, Robert V. *The Conscience of the Revolution: Communist Opposition in Soviet Russia*, Cambridge, Mass. 1960.

Day, Richard B. *Leon Trotsky and the Politics of Economic Isolation*. Cambridge 1973.

Deutscher, Isaac. *The Prophet Armed: Trotsky 1879-1921*, London 1954 (re-issued: New York 1980).

———. *The Prophet Unarmed: Trotsky 1921-1929*, London 1959 (also New York 1959).

———. *The Propher Outcast: Trotsky 1929-1940*, London 1963 (re-issued New York 1980).

Eastman, Max. *Leon Trotsky: The Portrait of a Youth*, New York 1925.

Erlich, Alexander. *The Soviet Industrialization Debate, 1924-1928*, Cambridge, Mass. 1960.

Fainsod, Merle. *How Russia is Ruled*, Cambridge, Mass. 1958.

Fischer, Ruth. *Stalin and German Communism*, Harvard 1948.

Frank, Pierre. *La Quatriéme Internationale*, Paris 1969 (English trans: New York 1979).

Gaucher, Roland. *L'Opposition en U.R.S.S. 1917-1967*, Paris 1967.

Getzler, Israel. *Martov*, Melbourne 1967.

Gombin, Richard. *Le Projet Révolutionnaire*, Paris 1969.

Haimson, Leopold. *The Russian Marxists and the Origins of Bolshevism*, Cambridge, Mass. 1955.

Howe, Irving. *Trotsky*, London 1978.

Knei-Paz, Baruch. *The Social and Political Thoughts of Leon Trotsky*, O.U.P. 1978.

Kochan, Lionel. *Russia in Revolution*, London 1970.

Lunacharsky, A. V. *Revolutionary Silhouettes*, London 1967.

Luxemburg, Rosa. *The Russian Revolution*, Ann Arbor 1961.

Marie, J. J. *Le Trotskysme*, Paris 1977.

Mavrakis, Kostas. *Du Trotskyisme,* Paris 1973 (English trans: Boston 1976).

Meyer, Alfred G. *Leninism,* Cambridge, Mass. 1957.

Molyneux, John. *Marxism and the Party,* London 1978.

Morizet, André. *Chez Lénine et Trotski,* Paris 1922.

Nedava, Joseph. *Trotsky and the Jews,* Philadelphia 1972.

Nettl, J. P. *Rosa Luxemburg,* 2 vols, London 1966.

Nove, Alec. *Was Stalin Really Necessary?,* London 1964.

Pethybridge, Roger. *Witnesses to the Russian Revolution,* London 1964 (re-issued: New York 1968).

Plamenatz, John. *German Marxism and Russian Communism,* London 1954 (re-issued: Westport, Conn. 1975).

Reed, John. *Ten Days that Shook the World,* London 1961 (re-issued: New York 1967).

Schapiro, Leonard. *The Origins of the Communist Autocracy,* London 1955.

——. *The Communist Party of the Soviet Union,* London 1960.

Serge, Victor. *Memoirs of a Revolutionary,* O.U.P. 1967.

——. *Vie et Mort de Trotski,* Paris 1951.

Souvarine, Boris. *Stalin,* London 1939 (re-issued: New York 1972).

Stalin, J. V. *Sochineniya,* Moscow 1946-1953 (re-issued: Stanford, Calif. 1967).

Sukhanov, N. *Zapiski o Revolutsii,* vols i-vii, Moscow 1922.

Tucker, Robert C. *The Soviet Political Mind,* London 1972 (re-issued: New York 1972).

——. *Stalin as Revolutionary 1879-1929,* London 1974 (issued: New York 1973).

Ulam, Adam B. *The Bolsheviks,* New York 1968.

Wilson, Edmund. *To the Finland Station,* London 1962 (re-issued: New York 1972).

Wistrich, Robert S. *Revolutionary Jews from Marx to Trotsky,* London 1976 (also: New York 1976).

——. *The Left Against Zion,* London 1979.

Wolfe, Bertram, D. *Three Who Made a Revolution,* London 1964 (also: New York 1964).

Wolfenstein, E. V. *The Revolutionary Personality: Lenin, Trotsky, Gandhi,* Princeton 1967.

Zeman, Z. A. B. and Scharlau, W. B. *The Merchant of Revolution: The Life of Alexander Israel Helphand (Parvus), 1867-1924,* London 1965.

Ziv, G. A. *Trotski: Kharakteristika po Lichnym Vospominaniam,* New York 1921.

# INDEX